IMPACT INVESTING AND SOCIAL ENTERPRISES

Global Progress and Challenges

Editors
Alan S. Gutterman and
Robert L. Brown

AMERICAN**BAR**ASSOCIATION
International Law Section

Cover design by Nick Panos/ABA Design

Printed in the United States of America.

26 25 24 23 22   5 4 3 2 1

A catalog record for this book is available from the Library of Congress.

Contents

PART I

PART II

EUROPE

Part I

1

Introduction

Alan S. Gutterman[1] and Robert L. Brown[2]

Impact investing is aimed directly at creating a positive environmental or social impact by identifying and solving a particular environmental or social problem. Impact investing is an advanced stage of sustainable investing that began with the socially responsible investment movement that emerged in the 1970s and that was marked by the use of negative or exclusionary screening processes designed to avoid specific assets due to consideration of specific environmental, social, and governance (ESG) criteria, including moral values (e.g., tobacco or gambling), standards and norms (e.g., human rights), ethical convictions (e.g., animal testing), or legal requirements (e.g., controversial armaments such as cluster bombs or land mines, excluded in order to comply with international conventions). The next stage was based on "best-in-class" (positive) screening, which contrasts significantly with negative screening and calls for investment and lending decisions to be made based on demonstrated high ESG performance of sectors, companies or projects and adherence to minimum standards of business practice based on international norms relating to climate protection, human rights, working conditions, and action plans against corruption.

As time went by, investors began to use positive screening in a more focused manner by concentrating their activities on specific high-profile sustainability-related themes such as clean tech, infrastructure, affordable

1. Of Counsel, Harvey Esquire, Los Angeles and Silicon Valley, California; President, Global Law Business, LLC.
2. Senior Counsel, Lynch Cox Gilman & Goodman, Louisville, Kentucky.

housing, energy-efficient real estate, or sustainable forestry.[3] The term "impact investing" was coined by the Rockefeller Foundation in 2007, and today the most commonly used definition is the one proposed by the Global Impact Investing Network (GIIN) (https://thegiin.org/impact-investing/): "Investing made with the intention to generate positive, measurable social and environmental impact alongside a financial return." A similar formulation was adopted by the G8's Social Impact Investment Taskforce: "The defining characteristic of impact investment is that the goal of generating financial returns is unequivocally pursued within the context of setting impact objectives and measuring their achievement." The Taskforce also declared: "The world is on the brink of a revolution in how we solve society's toughest problems. The force capable of driving this revolution is 'social impact investing,' which harnesses entrepreneurship, innovation and capital to power social improvement."[4]

Impact investing has occurred in both emerging and developed markets and the goals of impact investors in committing their capital and ancillary resources range from below market to market rate returns. Impact investing has occurred in a broad range of sectors, including sustainable agriculture, renewable energy, conservation, and microfinance. Governments and private enterprises have turned to impact investing tools to address challenges that have arisen relating to the delivery of basic services such as housing, healthcare, and education.

GIIN has identified the following core characteristics of impact investing:

- **Intentionality.** Impact investors invest with the intent to have a positive social or environmental impact through their investments.

3. A. Krauss, P. Kruger & J. Meyer, *Sustainable Finance in Switzerland: Where Do We Stand?* 18–19 (Zurich: Sustainable Finance Institute, Sept. 2016), https://www.sfi.ch/en/publications/sustainable-finance-in-switzerland-where-do-we-stand; *Environmental, Social and Governance Issues in Investing: A Guide for Investment Professionals* (CFA Institute, 2015), https://www.cfainstitute.org/-/media/documents/article/position-paper/esg-issues-in-investing-a-guide-for-investment-professionals.ashx; and *Changing Dynamics of Sustainable Finance: The Regulatory Push in the Direction of Sustainable Growth* (Sia Partners, Feb. 25, 2020), https://www.sia-partners.com/en/news-and-publications/from-our-experts/changing-dynamics-sustainable-finance-regulatory-push.

4. *Impact Investment: The Invisible Heart of Markets* 18 (Social Impact Investment Taskforce, 2014). The Taskforce was convened in 2013 to bring together governmental and sectoral experts from the G7 countries, the European Commission, and Australia to discuss and report on recommendations for "catalyzing a global market in impact investment."

- **Expectation of financial returns.** Impact investments are not grants that do not need to be repaid: investors expect a financial return on their capital or, at minimum, a return of their capital.
- **Range of return expectations and asset classes.** Impact investments target financial returns that range from below market to risk-adjusted market rate (two-thirds of the capital for impact investment seeks risk-adjusted market rates), and can be made across asset classes, including but not limited to cash equivalents, fixed income, venture capital, and private equity.
- **Impact measurement.** A hallmark of impact investing is the commitment of the investor to measure and report the social and environmental performance and progress of underlying investments, ensuring transparency and accountability while informing the practice of impact investing and building the field.

A wide range of individual and institutional investors have already entered the impact investment marketplace, including fund managers, development finance institutions, diversified financial institutions/banks, private foundations, pension funds and insurance companies, private funds, hybrid funds, ethical banks, microfinance institutions, social stock exchanges, crowdfunding, government institutions, family offices, individual investors, NGOs, and religious institutions. Continued growing enthusiasm can be expected, given that feedback from investors indicated that portfolio performance has generally met or exceeded their expectations for both social and environmental impact and financial return.

The GIIN has noted that since impact investing is a relatively new term, used to describe investments made across many asset classes, sectors, and regions, it has been challenging to develop a rigorous methodology for estimating the total size of the market. The GIIN has been working to strengthen its database and methodology. Its 2020 Annual Impact Investor Survey included an estimate that more than 1,720 organizations were managing $715 billion in impact investing assets under management (AUM) as of the end of 2019.[5] Established companies have been compelled to respond to calls by institutional investors to incorporate responsible ESG initiatives into their business models as a condition to continued support in public capital markets. Other companies seeking to demonstrate to impact investors their commitment to environmental and social responsibility have opted for emerging forms of legal entities,

5. According to GIIN's 2019 Annual Impact Investment Survey the size of impact AUM grew by a 17 percent compound annual growth rate from 2015 to 2019, https://thegiin.org/impact-investing/need-to-know/#how-big-is-the-impact-investing-market.

so-called social enterprises, which explicitly incorporate sustainability and multi-stakeholder interests into their governance and reporting frameworks.

Susan Mac Cormac et al. noted several important trends in the impact investment sector as it entered the 2020s. First, foundations are allocating larger portions of their endowments to impact investing and shifting their investment strategies to include greater emphasis on making program-related impact investments. In some cases, nonprofits are establishing their own wholly owned investment funds to invest only in projects that further the nonprofit's tax-exempt purpose. Second, investment managers overseeing the assets for wealthy individuals and families, so-called family offices, are no longer relying strictly on the use of private foundations, which are restricted in the way that assets can be invested due to tax considerations, and are instead creating impact-first fund structures (or investing in impact-first fund structures managed by others). Third, there is growing interest in the use of "hybrid funds," which are funded by both for-profit and nonprofit investors and are often structured as an integrated combination of for-profit and nonprofit entities. Fourth, managers of for-profit funds are accommodating the interests of their investors in impact investing by establishing affiliated entities, referred to as "side cars," which focus on impact-related investment opportunities. Finally, traditional private equity investors are demonstrating more interest in impact investing.[6]

Ideas for the path forward for the continued development of the impact investing market and ecosystem have been collected in the GIIN's "Roadmap for the Future of Impact Investing: Reshaping Financing Markets," which was produced by roughly 350 stakeholders engaged by GIIN in order to suggest both a vision for more inclusive and sustainable financial markets and to articulate a plan for the future progress of impact investing. The Roadmap details the following six categories of action to drive progress toward the vision:[7]

---

6. S. Mac Cormac, J. Finfrock & B. Fox, *Impact Investing*, *in* The Lawyer's Corporate Social Responsibility Deskbook 233–34 (A. Gutterman et al. eds., 2019).

7. *Roadmap for the Future of Impact Investing: Reshaping Financial Markets* (Global Impact Investing Network, Mar. 20, 2018), https://thegiin.org/research/publication/giin-roadmap (as modified from additional descriptions appearing in *Highlights from Roadmap for the Future of Impact Investing: Reshaping Financial Markets* (Global Impact Investment Network, 2020)).

- Strengthen the identity of impact investing by establishing clear principles and standards for impact investing and sharing best practices for impact measurement, management, and reporting
- Change the paradigm that governs investment behavior and expectations about the responsibility of finance in society via asset owner leadership, alignment of incentives with impact, and updated fundamental investment theory
- Design tools and services that support the incorporation of impact into the routine analysis, allocation, and deal-making activities of investors (e.g., develop ratings for impact and build analysis and allocation tools that incorporate risk, return, and impact)
- Develop products suited to the needs and preferences of the full spectrum of investors, from retail to institutional and of various types of investees, commit capital to emerging fund managers, and advance blended-finance vehicles
- Increase supply of trained investment professionals and pipeline of investment-ready enterprises focused on impact through targeted professional education (both graduate education and professional training and certification) for both finance professionals and business managers
- Introduce policies and regulation that both remove barriers and incentivize impact investments, including clarify fiduciary duty, establish tax incentives for impact investments, and create an environment conductive to impact investing

The path forward for impact investing is also closely tied to the evolution of thought on the "purpose" of businesses and design and use of new forms of social enterprises. As the 2010s ended, an influential movement supported by a diverse range of stakeholders was calling for a critical reassessment of the social contract between the corporation and society and changes in the way that business is conducted. For example, after acknowledging that "[t]he corporation . . . uses capital, labor, land, materials, and nature in varying proportions to produce a dazzling array of things that clothe, feed, house, entertain, and finally bury us" and affirming his belief that the corporation is an extraordinary institution with the potential to create remarkable benefits, Colin Mayer went on to caution as follows:

> At the same time, [the corporation] is the source of inequality, deprivation, and environmental degradation, and the problems are getting worse. They are getting worse because the corporation is getting bigger to a point where in some cases it is larger

> than nation states. And as nations find themselves unable to service their debt obligations, they turn to corporations to supply the goods and services that they provided in the past. But is the corporation capable of bearing the responsibilities that are being placed on its shoulders? The evidence is not encouraging.[8]

In a report on its research on the "Future of the Corporation," the British Academy argued that it was time to reformulate our understanding of the purpose of the corporation, discarding the notion that corporations are to be formed and operated solely for profit in favor of the principle that corporations should focus their attention and resources on pursuing public purposes that contribute to public interests and societal goals. Under such a model, profits would not be prohibited; however, they would be a product of a corporation's purpose, but not the purpose of the corporation. According to the report, the new purpose of the modern corporation should be to profitably solve problems for people and planet, while avoiding profiting from the creation of problems for people and planet.[9] Other influential voices have been coming forward with similar thoughts. For example, in his "2019 Letter to CEOs" Larry Fink, the CEO and chair of Blackrock, the largest investment management firm in the world, wrote that "every business needs a purpose. [. . .] Purpose is not the sole pursuit of profits but the animating force for achieving them."[10] The Business Roundtable issued a statement on the purpose of the corporation that recognized the vital role that businesses play in the broader economy by creating jobs, fostering innovation, and providing essential goods and services, and it affirmed businesses' fundamental commitments to all of their stakeholders including creation of *long-term* value for shareholders.[11] A group of sustainability and purpose advisors called on businesses to align their core identities and actions with a "sustainable purpose," described as a purpose that "is a meaningful, enduring reason for an organization to exist that provides solutions to global

---

8. C. Mayer, Prosperity: Better Business Makes the Greater Good (Oxford University Press, 2019) (as reproduced in *Prosperity, Colin Meyer—On The Purpose of Business* (Jan. 14, 2019), https://www.thendobetter.com/investing/2019/1/14/prosperity-colin-mayer-on-the-purpose-of-business).

9. Reforming Business for the 21st Century (The British Academy, 2019).

10. Larry Fink, *Larry Fink's 2019 Letter to CEOs*, https://www.blackrock.com/corporate/investor-relations/larry-fink-ceo-letter (last visited Apr. 20, 2022).

11. *Statement on the Purpose of a Corporation* (Business Roundtable, 2019), https://opportunity.businessroundtable.org/ourcommitment/.

challenges, or benefits society, in a way that sustains the social and environmental systems we rely upon."[12]

Stakeholder primary, or "stakeholderism" as it is sometimes called, is still not universally accepted and support for Friedman's principles remains, particularly among his disciples at the University of Chicago, who have argued that providing managers with too much latitude to advance the interests of non-shareholder stakeholders may actually make things worse for them. An article in *The Economist* in September 2020 outlined some of the challenges, beginning with the difficulties in balancing the competing interests of stakeholders: a shareholder who is also an employee may prefer higher wages even if that depresses profits and money spent on reducing pollution will not be available to fund skills training for workers.[13] Managers will never be able to reach a consensus on the contentious political and social issues that were involved when Hobby Lobby denied contraceptive insurance to its employees on religious grounds or when Nike supported Colin Kaepernick's protest against police brutality. The article also referenced critics of the sincerity of the managers that have publicly called for a shift in corporate purpose, noting that many of the companies that signed on to the Business Roundtable statement on corporate purpose "had failed to 'walk the talk'" and in fact had spent more on lobbying and had a higher incidence of environmental and labor compliance violations than their peers from 2016 to 2020.[14]

In a chapter on "Alternative Business Entities" prepared for a publication of the ABA Business Law Section in 2019 on Corporate Social Responsibility, Mac Cormac and her colleagues introduced the topic with a reminder that businesses operating under the ordinary corporation form have attempted to use a variety of legal and contractual tools to preserve their focus on a social mission including charter provisions, constituency statutes, the "business judgment rule," and voting rights and shareholder agreements.[15] For example, ordinary corporations are permitted

12. https://www.sustainablepurpose.com/.

13. *The Perils of Stakeholderism*, THE ECONOMIST, Sept. 19, 2020, at 65.

14. The signatories of the Business Roundtable statement were also criticized in another article for failing to back their words with actions and change their legal forms to benefit corporations (described later), which means that in practice they "continue to have obligations only to shareholders, despite their high-minded rhetoric." F. Alexander, *Real Change in Real Time: Benefit Corporations See New Interest, in* STAKEHOLDER CAPITALISM: THE FIX THAT OUR ECONOMY NEEDS TO BUILD SHARED AND DURABLE PROSPERITY FOR ALL 9 (B Lab).

15. The discussion in this paragraph is adapted from S. Mac Cormac, J. Finrock & B. Fox, *Alternative Business Entities, in* THE LAWYER'S CORPORATE SOCIAL

to include mission-related provisions in their corporate charters; however, they noted that where these provisions conflict with the traditional fiduciary duties of directors and officers, all things being equal, fiduciary duties will prevail.[16] More than 30 states (but neither Delaware nor California) have adopted constituency statutes that permit or require directors to pay regard to the interests of all corporate stakeholders in their decision making, but according to Mac Cormac et al. these statutes have limited legal enforceability and, like mission-related charter provisions, cannot override traditional corporate fiduciary duties.[17] As for the "business judgment rule," Mac Cormac et al. pointed out that in spite of all that has been written about shareholder primacy, fiduciary duties do *not* mandate that all management decisions be made for the purpose of maximizing the *immediate* value of the corporation's shares[18] and argued that "the business judgement rule provides Delaware corporate directors and officers with significant latitude to pursue mission-aligned activities that are in the best interests of the shareholders and the corporation, e.g., activities that improve both the corporation's brand and its long-term profitability."[19] Finally, they explained that ordinary corporations are generally free to include special voting provisions in their charter documents, including requirements that a supermajority of voting shares, or certain classes of shares, approve specified fundamental decisions (e.g.,

---

RESPONSIBILITY DESKBOOK: PRACTICAL GUIDANCE FOR CORPORATE COUNSEL AND LAW FIRMS 249, 249–51 (A. Gutterman et al. eds., American Bar Association Business Law Section, 2019).

16. See S. Mac Cormac, Morrison & Foerster LLP, *Preserving and Enhancing Impact: Corporate Forms*, presentation at Impact.tech, Oct. 2016, slides 6–7, https://www.slideshare.net/Impactdottech/preserving-and-enhancing-impact-corporate-forms.

17. *See* Which Legal Structure Is Right for My Social Enterprise: A Guide to Establishing a Social Enterprise in the United States 40, (Thomson Reuters Foundation and Morrison & Foerster LLP, Apr. 2012), http://www.trust.org/contentAsset/raw-data/171b5a61-eb36-43d9-8049-7cebe575491f/file.

18. *See* M. TODD HENDERSON, EVERYTHING OLD IS NEW AGAIN: LESSONS FROM DODGE V. FORD MOTOR COMPANY 27 (Univ. of Chi.: John M. Olin Law & Economics Working Paper No. 373 (2007)).

19. *See* S. Mac Cormac & H. Haney, *New Corporate Forms: One Viable Solution to Advancing Environmental Sustainability*, 24 J. APPLIED CORP. FIN. 49, 50 (2012); *see also* Shlensky v. Wrigley, 237 N.E.2d 776 (Ill. App. 1968). However, Mac Cormac et al. conceded that the effectiveness of this strategy to preserve social mission "may be compromised if the sale of the corporation appears imminent and inevitable," predicting that under such circumstances "the Revlon doctrine may require that the directors maximize shareholder value by selling to a bidder willing to forgo mission but pay the highest price or face shareholder activism." *See* Revlon, Inc. v. MacAndrews & Forbes Holdings, Inc., 506 A.2d 173 (Del. 1986).

decisions relating to the conduct of the corporation's stated social mission), and that shareholders of such corporations are also free to enter into voting agreements among themselves that include similar requirements, as well as other provisions designed to protect shareholders in the event of proposed deviations from the corporation's social mission (e.g., "tag-along," "drag-along," and change-of-control approval rights).[20]

While the strategies just described are interesting and creative, there is growing momentum, particularly among sustainable entrepreneurs and impact investors, to clearly free directors of historical constraints and thus promote more aggressive and entrepreneurial sustainability efforts. Mac Cormac et al. noted that "increasingly, founders, employees and consumers alike are pushing companies to promote their social or environmental efforts, to embrace a social enterprise entity, to secure a 'B Corp' certification, and/or to establish a relationship with a non-profit, all of which can bolster the credibility of companies."[21] In response, politicians in a majority of the states and the District of Columbia have endorsed and formalized the constituency theory by adopting statutes that permit formation of "benefit corporations," a new form of for-profit corporation that explicitly expands the fiduciary duties of directors beyond maximizing shareholder value, which is still one of the primary goals of a corporation, to include consideration of whether the corporation's activities have an overall positive impact on society, their workers, the communities in which they operate, and the environment.

While the rate of adoption of benefit corporation status has been slow, particularly among public companies (only a handful of U.S. public companies had embraced benefit corporation status as of 2020), the recognition of benefit corporations has contributed to sharpened focus on the separate interests of non-shareholder stakeholders and created a host of new issues and challenges for directors of all types of corporations, such as how to measure and compare nonfinancial performance aspects of corporate activities, how to hold corporations accountable to stakeholders who do not have the rights to vote held by shareholders, and how to structure incentive packages for executives and managers tied to complex multi-stakeholder goals and commitments.

* * *

The first part of this publication focuses on key issues in impact investing, including legal structure, measurement and reporting, forming an impact investment fund, and doing the deal. In the second part we shift to

20. *See* S. Mac Cormac, *supra* note 16, at slide 5.
21. Mac Cormac, Finrock & Fox, *supra* note 15, at 249, 251.

regional and country coverage using the comparative approach and drawing on the expertise of local experts across multiple jurisdictions who discuss trends in those regions and countries relating to impact investing, social enterprises, and related issues in their impact investing ecosystems, both progress and challenges. A good deal of the early momentum in impact investing has occurred outside of the United States, and there is much to learn from the experiences of other countries.

2

Structuring Social Enterprises in the United States

Alan S. Gutterman[1]

Benefit Corporations

A White Paper issued in 2013 by the Corporate Laws Committee (Committee) of the Business Law Section of the American Bar Association (ABA White Paper) reported that since 2010 a number of U.S. jurisdictions had adopted provisions "allowing corporations to opt in to a legal structure that expressly expands the purpose of the corporation beyond advancing the pecuniary interests of its shareholders" and "allow or require directors to consider environmental, societal, or other impacts of corporate activity, even at the expense of shareholder value."[2] Corporations adopting these provisions are generally known as "benefit corporations" and the ABA White Paper explained that benefit corporations could be thought of as opting out of the "property" model of corporation law exemplified by the Michigan Supreme Court's 1919 decision in *Dodge v. Ford Motor Co.*,[3] which established the proposition that solvent corporations are vehicles with the sole purpose of maximizing shareholder wealth. The property model has had its challengers, notably the "entity model," which viewed the corporation as a vehicle that can simultaneously serve the interests of multiple constituencies and thus was

1. Of Counsel, Harvey Esquire, Los Angeles and Silicon Valley, California; President, Global Law Business, LLC.

2. Corporate Laws Committee of the ABA Business Law Section, *Benefit Corporation White Paper*, 68 Bus. Law. 1083 (Aug. 2013).

3. 204 Mich. 459, 170 N.W. 668 (1919).

"tinged with a public purpose," but since the 1980s commentators and judges have generally confirmed the ascendency of the property model.[4]

The ABA White Paper noted that the first benefit corporation statutes were typically based on, or heavily influenced by, the Model Benefit Corporation Legislation (MBCL) drafted for B Lab Company (B Lab), a Pennsylvania nonprofit corporation that has been described as "the driving force behind the adoption of benefit corporation legislation across the country."[5] The drafters of the MBCL,[6] sometimes referred to herein as the "B Lab model," emphasized their intent to authorize the organization of a form of business corporation that offers entrepreneurs and investors the option to build, and invest in, a business that operates with a corporate purpose broader than maximizing shareholder value and that consciously undertakes a responsibility to maximize the benefits of its operations for all stakeholders, not just shareholders. Rather than relying on governmental oversight to enforce that purpose and responsibility, the MBCL relies on innovative provisions relating to transparency and accountability.

Although the specific language in the statutes of the various jurisdictions might differ, these provisions typically (1) required that a benefit corporation consider general public welfare before acting, (2) permitted that more specific interests be considered as well, and (3) required that the corporation's compliance be measured against a standard imposed by an independent third party.[7]

---

4. Corporate Laws Committee, *supra* note 2, at 1084 (citing W. Allen, *Our Schizophrenic Conception of the Business Corporation*, 14 CARDOZO L. REV. 261, 264–65 (1992)). The ABA White Paper noted that the entity model has survived in those states (but notably not in Delaware) that adopted "other constituencies" statutes that permitted, but did not require, directors to consider the interests of corporate "stakeholders" other than just the shareholders. These statutes, sometimes referred to as "flexible benefit corporations", could presumably be interpreted expansively to permit directors to consider "people" and "planet" along with "profits." *Id.* at 1086–87. No such provision was included in the Model Business Corporation Act (MBCA) as of 2013; however, one of the purposes of the ABA White Paper was to describe and discuss provisions the Committee believed would be appropriate for states following the MBCA to adopt if they determined to include benefit corporation provisions in their statute.

5. *Id.*

6. The discussion of the MBCL herein is based on the April 17, 2017, version of the MBCL unless the context specifically indicates otherwise.

7. Corporate Laws Committee, *supra* note 2, at 1083, 1087. *See also* W. Clark, Jr. & E. Babson, *How Benefit Corporations Are Redefining the Purpose of Business Corporations*, 38 WM. MITCHELL L. REV. 817 (2012).

Loewenstein noted that the drafting process for the MBCL did not have the benefit of a vetting process that other model legislation usually receives, including the input from a diverse group of advisers and consultants that is gathered by the American Law Institute during the course of its efforts to draft widely accepted model laws, and argued that the lack of broad input may have led to various problems that states like Delaware and California attempted to address when developing their nonconforming benefit corporation statutes.[8]

Maryland was the first state to adopt legislation recognizing a "benefit corporation," which the statute described as a "corporation formed to create a material positive impact on society; consider how decisions affect employees, community and the environment; and publicly report their social and environmental performance using established third-party standards."[9] In Maryland, a benefit corporation must create a "general public benefit," which was defined as a material, positive impact on society and the environment, as measured by a third-party standard, through activities that promote a combination of specific public benefits, including providing individuals or communities with beneficial products or services; promoting economic opportunity for individuals or communities beyond the creation of jobs in the normal course of business; preserving the environment; improving human health; promoting the arts, sciences, or advancement of knowledge; and/or increasing the flow of capital to entities with a public benefit purpose.

While it is conceivable that a traditional for-profit corporation could pursue many of the "public benefit" activities mentioned earlier, the actions of the directors would be hamstrung by the *Ford* decision and other cases that have clearly and continuously proclaimed that the directors' duty of good faith to the corporation requires that they carry on the business of the corporation so as to maximize the profits of the stockholders. The statutes creating benefit corporations, however, allow directors to consider the interests of stakeholders other than the stockholders.

---

8. Mark Loewenstein, Benefit Corporation Law 2–3 (Sept. 16, 2016), SSRN: https://ssrn.com/abstract=2840003 or http://dx.doi.org/10.2139/ssrn.2840003. Loewenstein is not the only critic of the MBCL (the additional suggestions in this paragraph are based on S. Mac Cormac, *When and How to "B"—Responsible B Corp Conversion*, Morrison & Foerster LLP (Sept. 6, 2017) (Much of the state legislation that follows the B Lab "model" code is poorly drafted, with provisions that conflict with the rest of the applicable corporations codes and potentially result in increased risk and liability.).

9. D. Sampselle, Sustainable Organization Design Principles, OTMT 608.13, 12–13 (see Maryland Corporations and Associations Article §§ 5-6C-01 through -08).

For example, while the Maryland statute did not create a separate duty of the director to the beneficiaries of the public benefit purposes of the corporation, it did mandate that directors must consider the effects of any action or decision not to act not only on the stockholders but also on the employees and workforce of the benefit corporation and the subsidiaries and suppliers of the corporation; the interests of customers as beneficiaries of the general or specific public benefit purposes of the benefit corporation; community and societal considerations, including those of any community in which offices or facilities of the corporation or the subsidiaries or suppliers of the benefit corporation are located, and the local and global environment.

When Delaware, the recognized leader in statutory and case law innovations in the area of corporate law, passed its statute in 2013 amending the Delaware General Corporation Law (DGCL) to recognize "public benefit corporations" (PBCs), the governor made the following observations:[10]

> Delaware public benefit corporations will function like and enjoy all the same benefits as traditional Delaware corporations and they will have three unique features that make them potential game changers. These three features concern corporate purpose, accountability, and transparency.
>
> Corporate Purpose: Delaware public benefit corporations will have a corporate purpose "to operate in a responsible and sustainable manner." In addition, to provide directors, stockholders, and ultimately the courts, some direction, they are also required to identify in their certificate of incorporation a specific public benefit purpose the corporation is obligated to pursue. The overarching language helps ensure that a public benefit corporation serves the best long-term interests of society while it creates value for its stockholders. The requirement to identify a specific public benefit purpose gives managers, directors, stockholders,

10. J. Markell, *A New Kind of Corporation to Harness the Power of Private Enterprise for Public Benefit*, HUFFINGTON POST (July 22, 2013), http://www.huffingtonpost.com/gov-jack-markell/public-benefit-corporation_b_3635752.html. It has been reported that since Delaware adopted PBCs in 2013, thousands of social ventures, as well as more traditional companies, have incorporated as PBCs, and that 295 venture-backed PBCs raised a combined $2.5 billion from 2013 to 2019. For a comprehensive guide to Delaware's public benefit corporation statute, see F. ALEXANDER, THE PUBLIC BENEFIT CORPORATION GUIDEBOOK: UNDERSTANDING AND OPTIMIZING DELAWARE'S BENEFIT CORPORATION GOVERNANCE MODEL (Morris Nichols Arscht & Tunnell, 2016).

and the courts, important guidance to ensure accountability, while preserving flexibility for business leaders and their investors to choose the specific public benefit purpose they feel will drive the greatest total value creation.

Accountability: Unlike in traditional corporations, whose directors have the sole fiduciary duty to maximize stockholder value, directors of public benefit corporations are required to meet a tri-partite balancing requirement consistent with its public benefit purpose. Directors are required to balance "the pecuniary interest of stockholders, the best interests of those materially affected by the corporation's conduct, and the identified specific public benefit purpose."

Transparency: Delaware public benefit corporations are required to report on their overall social and environmental performance, giving stockholders important information that, particularly when reported against a third party standard, can mitigate risk and reduce transaction costs. Given the trend in public equity markets toward integrated ESG (Environmental, Social and Governance) reporting and the growing private equity market for direct impact investing, this increased transparency can help investors to aggregate capital more easily as they are able to communicate more effectively the impact, and not just the return, of their investments.

California is another state that has promoted the creation of benefit corporations. For many years that state has recognized consumer cooperative corporations, small business corporations and business, and industrial corporations. Recently, however, the choices have been expanded to include two additional corporate entities: benefit corporations and social purpose corporations. In California, a "benefit corporation" may be formed for the purpose of creating general public benefit, defined as a material positive impact on society and the environment, taken as a whole, as assessed against a third-party standard that satisfies certain requirements.[11] A benefit corporation may also identify one or more specific public benefits as an additional purpose of the corporation, including, without limitation, providing low-income or underserved individuals or communities with beneficial products or services, promoting economic opportunity for individuals or communities beyond the creation of

11. See California General Corporation Law (CGCL) § 14600, generally cited as Cal. Corp. Code §§ 14600 *et seq.*

jobs in the ordinary course of business, preserving the environment, and improving human health.

Directors of California benefit corporations are required to consider the impacts of any action or proposed action upon specified considerations, including, among others, the shareholders and employees of the corporation, customers of the corporation who are beneficiaries of the general or specific public benefit purposes, and the environment. In addition, directors of benefit corporations are allowed to consider the impacts of those actions on, among other things, the resources, intent, and conduct of any person seeking to acquire control of the benefit corporation. California benefit corporations must prepare an annual benefit report that includes, among other things, a statement indicating whether, in the board's opinion, the benefit corporation failed to pursue its general public benefit and any specific public benefit; a description of the ways in which the benefit corporation pursued those benefits; the extent to which those benefits were created; and the process and rationale for selecting the third-party standard used to prepare the benefit reports.

The ABA White Paper reported that many of the states that have adopted benefit corporation legislation have included a new form of legal action, typically styled as a "benefit enforcement proceeding," which may be initiated as a claim for the "(1) failure of a benefit corporation to pursue or create general public benefit or a specific public benefit purpose set forth in its articles; or (2) violation of any obligation, duty or standard of conduct"[12] under the statute. According to the ABA White Paper, one of the "obligations" specifically enforceable in many versions of these benefit enforcement proceedings is the obligation to prepare and circulate the annual benefit report. The ABA White Paper observed that there were variations among the benefit corporation states regarding who may sue and be sued in a benefit enforcement proceeding (i.e., who the proper plaintiffs and defendants may be). For example, the MBCL provides that a benefit enforcement proceeding may be in the form of a direct claim commenced or maintained by the benefit corporation itself, or it may be commenced or maintained derivatively by a shareholder, a director, or the holders of 5 percent or more of the equity interests of a 50 percent-or-greater stockholder of the benefit corporation; however, many of the states adopting benefit corporation legislation have not provided that all directors or a 5 percent owner of a parent entity may pursue derivative benefit enforcement proceedings. The ABA White Paper noted that many, but not all, of the states adopting benefit corporation legislation

12. Corporate Laws Committee, *supra* note 2.

have provided that the corporation cannot be liable for monetary damages for failure to pursue or create a public benefit.

Flexible and Social Purpose Corporations

As noted earlier, the ABA White Paper pointed out several states had recognized the entity model of the corporation by adopting "other constituencies" statutes that permitted, but did not require, directors to consider the interests of corporate "stakeholders" other than just the shareholders, an opening that presumably permitted directors to consider "people" and "planet" along with "profits."[13] The corporations that could be formed under these statutes were referred to as "flexible benefit corporations" or "social purpose corporations." There are several significant differences between flexible benefit corporations and benefit corporations. For instance, directors of flexible benefit corporations may, but need not, take the interests of other constituencies into consideration when deciding, plus flexible benefit corporations are not required to measure performance against a third-party standard (but must report on their performance).[14]

The formation and operations of California social purpose corporations is governed by the California Social Purpose Corporations Act (SPCA),[15] which provides that a social purpose corporation may be formed for special purposes, in addition to any other lawful purpose, including, but are not limited to, charitable and public purpose activities that could be carried out by a nonprofit public benefit corporation.[16] The SPCA requires management and directors to specify objectives for measuring the impact of the social purpose corporation's efforts relating to its special purpose, and to include an analysis of those efforts in annual reports, together with specified financial statements, to shareholders and requires that specified information be made publicly available.[17]

Formation and Organization of Benefit Corporations

Once the decision has been made to select a benefit corporation as the entity for the proposed business, attention turns to the actual formation

13. Corporate Laws Committee, *supra* note 2, at 1086–87.
14. *Id.* at 1089.
15. *See* CAL. CORP. CODE §§ 2500 *et seq.*
16. CAL. CORP. CODE § 2602(b)(2).
17. *Id.* §§ 3500 *et seq.*

and organization of the corporation.[18] Each of the states that recognizes benefit corporations has its own specific requirements, and the laws of the state in which the corporation will be incorporated should be carefully reviewed. The MBCL has been the model for the provisions adopted by most states with respect to formation and governance of benefit corporations, including the requirements for drafting, filing, and amending the articles of incorporation. In most cases, the most efficient thing for the promoters of a new benefit corporation is to incorporate in the state where most of the operational activities associated with the corporation will be performed, assuming that state authorizes the formation of benefit corporations. This generally provides the corporation with more than enough flexibility and certainty with respect to governance issues since most corporation law statutes are being continuously updated to reflect new developments that are being integrated into the MBCL. It is possible, however, for the entity to be formed and operated under the laws of another state (e.g., Delaware) when it is believed that the benefit corporation laws of that state relating to governance issues may provide advantages not available under the laws of the state where initial operational activities will occur.[19]

Two of the biggest tasks for forming and organizing a new benefit corporation are drafting its articles of incorporation and bylaws, often referred to together as the "charter documents." However, preparing and filing the articles of incorporation is just the first step in getting a new

18. While the discussion in this chapter assumes that the benefit corporation is being newly formed, it is also possible for an existing "traditional" corporation to convert to a benefit corporation while continuing to engage in the activities that were in place before the conversion. For example, in Delaware, conversion is permitted if approval is obtained from both the board and at least two-thirds of the outstanding stock of the corporation entitled to vote thereon to effectuate the conversion. With some exceptions that apply only to public companies and other corporations with large numbers of shareholders, opponents of the conversion among the shareholder group are entitled to statutory appraisal rights.

19. In general, as discussed earlier, state statutes, although varying from case to case, address three major areas: corporate purpose (i.e., creating a material positive impact on society and the environment); accountability (i.e., expanded fiduciary duties of directors that extend beyond shareholders to include consideration of nonfinancial interests); and transparency (i.e., an obligation to report on its overall social and environmental performance as assessed against a comprehensive, credible, independent, and transparent third-party standard). The statutes in MBCL states (i.e., states with a benefit corporation statute modeled after the MBCL) are relatively similar; however, statutes adopted in influential states such as California and Delaware have departed from the MBCL in many ways.

corporation "up and running." Acceptance of the articles for filing by the secretary of state of the state of incorporation completes the "formation" stage and at that point the corporation is legally in existence; however, if the founders want to begin using the corporation to conduct business it will need to be "organized," a process that includes the organizational meeting of the directors; preparation of shareholders' agreements, and the initial issuance of shares; qualification of the new corporation as a foreign corporation in other jurisdictions; the initial meeting of shareholders; and the creation and organization of the minute book.

Formation of a benefit corporation should begin with a meeting between counsel experienced in representing benefit corporations and the founders of the proposed corporation. At that meeting, counsel should gather all the information normally collected prior to formation of any corporation. In addition, the following issues must be carefully considered before moving forward with formation of a benefit corporation:

- What are the goals of the party or parties who will be responsible for the organizing activities?
- Are the proposed purposes those that could or should be conducted by a benefit organization (as opposed to a traditional general business corporation, nonprofit corporation, limited liability company, partnership, or sole proprietorship)?
- Do the founders have realistic plans for obtaining start-up funding, as well as continuing revenues?
- Do the founders understand the time-consuming steps that will be involved in the formation and organization of the new corporation?
- Do the founders understand the special corporate governance and reporting requirements that are imposed on benefit corporations?

Several important and challenging additional issues and activities must be considered by the founders and initial directors of a benefit corporation as a result of the unique multi-stakeholder focus of such a corporation.[20] For example, even before the time that the benefit corporation is formed and organized, the prospective directors and officers of a benefit corporation must understand that they will be called upon to balance the interests of multiple stakeholders, not just the owners/shareholders, of the

20. For comprehensive discussion of additional steps to be taken to launch a new business, see A. Kroeker, *Starting a New Business*, *in* EMERGING COMPANIES GUIDE: A RESOURCE FOR PROFESSIONALS AND ENTREPRENEURS 5 (A. Gutterman & R. Brown eds., 3d ed. 2020).

corporation. This means that the directors will need to consider not only the traditional pecuniary interests of the shareholders but also the best interests of those materially affected by the corporation's conduct (e.g., employees, creditors, customers, and suppliers) and the action necessary to achieve the specific public benefits that have been identified in the corporation's articles of incorporation.[21] Specifically, each director, and the board as a whole, must consider the effects of any action or inaction taken as a director on:[22]

- The shareholders of the corporation;
- The employees and work force of the corporation, its subsidiaries and its suppliers;
- The corporation's customers as beneficiaries of the corporation's general public benefit or specific public benefit purposes;
- Community and societal factors, including the communities in which the offices or facilities of the corporation, its subsidiaries, and its suppliers are located;
- The local and global environment;
- The short-term and long-term interests of the corporation; and
- The effect of remaining independent (i.e., not acquired) on the corporation's ability to serve these interests, and the ability of the corporation to accomplish its general and specific public benefit purposes.

While statutory permission to consider the interests of stakeholders other than shareholders is a significant advantage for directors and officers seeking to pursue socially responsible outcomes from the activities of the corporation, it also means that those persons need to develop a non-traditional business plan that incorporates not only financial viability, and a competitive return on investment for shareholders, but also strategies

21. DGCL § 365(a). The suggested language to be included in the certificate of incorporation for a Delaware public benefit corporation is as follows: "The Corporation shall be a public benefit corporation as contemplated by subchapter XV of the Delaware General Corporation Law (the 'DGCL'), or any successor provisions, that it is intended to operate in a responsible and sustainable manner and to produce a public benefit or benefits, and is to be managed in a manner that balances the stockholders pecuniary interests, the best interests of those materially affected by the corporation's conduct and the public benefit or benefits identified in this certificate of incorporation. If the DGCL is amended to alter or further define the management and operation of public benefit corporations, then the corporation shall be managed and operated in accordance with the DGCL, as so amended."

22. MBCL § 301(a).

relating to pursuit and achievement of the stated public benefits. Among other things, the directors need to understand the principles and practices of stakeholder engagement and be able to oversee the development of appropriate day-to-day operational practices for a sustainable business.

The directors must also begin preparations for complying with the transparency requirements imposed in various ways on benefit corporations. According to the ABA White Paper, benefit corporations typically must submit a "benefit report" either within 120 days following the end of its fiscal year or at the same time that it delivers any other annual report (e.g., a Form 10-K) to its stockholders. The purpose of the report is to provide a discussion and assessment of the corporation's efforts to pursue and create general public benefit and any specific public benefits included in the company's listed purposes, including any circumstances hindering the corporation's ability to create these public benefits. The report must also include a statement on whether the company complied with its obligations as a benefit corporation during that period. Many benefit corporation statutes require that a benefit corporation's adherence to its public benefit goals, as disclosed in the annual benefit report, must be measured against a comprehensive "third-party standard" that assesses the effects of the business on employees, customers as beneficiaries of the general and any specific public benefit, community and society, and the local and global environment. Statutes modeled after the MBCL may also require that a benefit corporation designate a "benefit director" who must opine as to the success of the corporation in acting in accordance with its general public purpose and specific public purposes.

Governance and Management

Articulating a purpose, that is, a meaningful and enduring reason to exist that aligns with long-term financial performance, is an essential foundation for creating a social enterprise and provides a clear context for daily decision making and unifies and motivates relevant stakeholders.[23] However, satisfying multiple stakeholders involves a difficult balancing process, and a corporation's purpose needs to continuously be revisited and reexamined as circumstances change. Throughout the life cycle of the corporation, governance mechanisms and procedures need to be in place to ensure that the corporation, through the day-to-day actions of

23. Chartered Management Institute, *The What, the Why and the How of Purpose—A Guide for Leaders* (2018), https://www.managers.org.uk/~/media/Files/Reports/Guide-for-Leaders-White-Paper.pdf.

its managers and employees, remains faithful to its purpose and accepts accountability and an obligation to report transparently on its progress. Development and implementation of these mechanisms and procedures will require a diverse range of skills and innovative approaches to dealing with traditional topics such as corporate governance, investors' relations, raising capital, organizational culture, compensation and incentives, and measuring and reporting on performance.[24]

In order to be successful, social enterprises must implement strong governance and management systems and clear, predictable, and transparent processes that allow them to identify early on potential risks arising from operations and respond strategically to minimize or manage negative impacts, and optimize potential positive benefits.[25] There are a number of elements for an effective governance and management system, beginning with the board of directors or other governing board of the enterprise and then extending throughout the organization to include the chief executive officer (CEO) and other senior executives and everyone who works for or with the organization. The leaders of social enterprises will need to adopt and implement policies and procedures and a complete management system and invest time and resources to engage with multiple stakeholders, including supportive and engaged owners willing to provide capital for the business provided that the company remains focused on its stated purpose, and measure and report on the organization's financial, environmental, and social performance.[26]

Reporting and Communications

Reporting and stakeholder communications need to be an integral part of a social enterprise's activities and commitments: enterprises need to be prepared to be transparent and open with their stakeholders regarding their corporate social responsibility (CSR) and sustainability successes and failures, and this means accepting risks of criticism from groups that feel that the enterprise has not "done enough." Reporting can

---

24. D. Grayson, *On Purpose*, Business Fights Poverty (Jan. 24, 2019), https://businessfightspoverty.org/articles/on-purpose/ (citing D. Grayson, C. Coulter & M. Lee, All In: The Future of Business Leadership (London: Routledge 2018)).

25. Africa Oil Kenya B.V., *Corporate Social Responsibility Processes and Practices Manual: Operating Guidelines* (July 2015).

26. Notable companies that have adopted mission-aligned governance include Patagonia, Kickstarter, and Laureate Education in the United States; Natura in Brazil; and Pasticceria Filippi in Italy; it is useful to study the governance documents available on the websites of these companies and in public filings.

be facilitated through use of one of the frameworks for sustainability reporting that have emerged, such as the Global Reporting Initiative,[27] and companies should consider verifying their reporting through the use of external auditors in order to increase the credibility of the report and assure readers that the information is accurate. In addition, reports should be reviewed to ensure that they comply with relevant statutory requirements. The final version of the report should be printed for distribution to stakeholders and also made available for viewing and downloading on the company's website along with the company's CSR and sustainability principles and policies as outlined earlier in the chapter.[28]

Communications regarding CSR and sustainability activities and the results of those activities should be conducted using a wide range of channels such as the company's website and newsletters to the company's customers. Companies should also collaborate with value chain partners and other stakeholders on communications planning and execution, and should participate in events related to sustainability as a means for gathering information and raising awareness of the company's involvement. While much of the communication activity relates to disseminating the results of the CSR and sustainability initiatives and programs, dialogue with stakeholders should begin early in the process so that stakeholders can provide inputs into the company's decisions regarding CSR and sustainability commitments and areas of focus.

Performance Measurement and Evaluation

For all the good intentions and motives associated with acting in a socially responsible manner, businesses and their stakeholders need to have ways to measure and evaluate the effectiveness and impact of CSR and sustainability initiatives. Companies should measure performance against fulfilment of their purposes, and their profits should be measured against achievement of both purposes and financial performance and net of the various types of costs associated with achieving them.[29] Companies

---

27. Global Reporting Initiative, *Setting the Agenda for the Future*, https://www.globalreporting.org/.

28. For further discussion of reporting and disclosure, see M. Littenberg, *Reporting and Disclosure*, *in* The Lawyer's Corporate Social Responsibility Deskbook: Practical Guidance for Corporate Counsel and Law Firms 45 (A. Gutterman et al., eds., 2019); and A. Gutterman, Sustainability Reporting and Communications (New York: Business Expert Press, 2020).

29. The British Academy called for profit and loss statements to recognize expenditures on workers, societies, and natural assets made by companies to deliver their

should restate their profits to make provisions for the costs of remedying failures to fulfill their purposes and avoiding negative impacts on their workers, societies, and natural assets both within and outside the firm. Measurement techniques should extend beyond the traditional emphasis on financial and material assets to include the investments that companies make in their workers, societies, and natural assets both within and outside the firm.

Measurement is essential for tracking progress against the company's CSR and sustainability goals and objectives; however, how to go about doing that is by no means easy and ideas in this area are rapidly evolving. Initial efforts recognized the concept of a "double bottom line," which involves looking at both financial indicators, like earnings, and social responsibility indicators, such as community involvement. Companies have relied on so-called balanced scorecard methods that recognize four perspectives for measuring performance: people and knowledge, internal business, customers, and financial.[30] Companies have also been doing "social audits," which are systematic evaluations and reports of how well a firm is meeting its ethics and social responsibility objectives.[31] A social audit report typically summarizes corporate activities under headings such as charitable contributions, support of local community groups and activities, employment of protected groups, political contributions, pollution control and cleanup, health and safety measures, and efforts to improve the quality of work life for employees. Companies should sign up to a standardized set of metrics that assess the extent to which they adhere to common minimum standards of conduct in relation to people and planet; determine the metrics that are most relevant to their specific purposes; and adopt key performance indicators to evaluate and reward employees against them.[32]

Another way that organizations can measure and demonstrate their commitment to social and environmental responsibility is through

---

corporate purposes as investments and for allowing companies to expense them over their relevant lives in an analogous fashion to physical assets. THE BRITISH ACADEMY FUTURE OF THE CORPORATION, PRINCIPLES FOR PURPOSEFUL BUSINESS: HOW TO DELIVER THE FRAMEWORK FOR THE FUTURE OF THE CORPORATION 26 (2019).

30. The traditional approach to the "balanced scorecard" is generally attributed to Kaplan and Norton. *See* R. KAPLAN & D. NORTON, THE BALANCED SCORECARD: TRANSLATING STRATEGY INTO ACTION (Cambridge, MA: Harvard Business School Press, 1996).

31. M. KELLY, J. MCGOWEN & C. WILLIAMS, BUSN 66 (Independence, KY: South-Western Publishing Company, 2014).

32. THE BRITISH ACADEMY FUTURE OF THE CORPORATION, *supra* note 29, at 25.

participation in ratings agencies and ratings systems that have been created in order to give external stakeholders a means by which they can assess the social and environmental impact of the organization's activities. In order to participate in these systems, some of which actually offer opportunities for certification, organizations must be prepared to adjust their internal structures in order to comply with the requirements of the system and ensure that the information necessary for measurement can be collected, analyzed, and properly reported. While there are similarities among the most popular systems, there is still no universal standard, and many of the systems operate without extensive efforts to verify or audit the information provided by organizations. Organizations should expect that they will be required to submit to site visits and renew their certifications on a regular basis.[33]

Perhaps the most well-known certification program is overseen by B Lab, which is the certifying body for certification as a Certified B Corp that provides access to the Certified B Corp logo, which is often seen as a "Good Housekeeping Seal of Approval" for sustainable businesses. B Lab has explained that certified B corporations are purpose-driven and create benefits for all stakeholders, not just shareholders. B Lab also offers a portfolio of services to, and a vibrant community of practice among, Certified B Corps. The certification process reflects B Lab's understanding that organization under the MBCL or other benefit corporation statute does not guarantee that a corporation's day-to-day operations meet the expectations of consumers or investors interested in developing relationships with sustainable businesses.

Certified B Corps and benefit corporations share the same characteristics with respect to accountability and transparency (i.e., directors are required to consider the impact of the company's activities on all stakeholders, and a report of overall social and performance assessed against a third-party standard must be prepared and publicly published). As for performance, benefit corporations "self-report" while Certified B Corps must achieve a minimum verified score on a "B Impact Assessment." Benefit corporation status depends on the law of the particular state in which the corporation is organized; however, Certified B Corp status is available to every business regardless of corporate structure, state, or country of incorporation. While benefit corporations must pay state filings, Certified B Corps must pay annual certification fees to B

33. Thomson Reuters Foundation and Morrison & Foerster, Which Legal Structure Is Right for My Social Enterprise? A Guide to Establishing a Social Enterprise in the United States 111–12 (Sept. 2016).

Lab based on the amount of revenues from the company's activities. During the early years of Certified B Corps, there was no requirement that a company also be a benefit corporation in order to be certified; however, benefit corporation status is now required for obtaining and maintaining Certified B Corp certification, although it is not necessary that the corporation be organized under a statute based on the MBCL (i.e., Delaware benefit corporation status, for example, would be satisfactory).

The steps that must be completed for validating a company's social and environmental performance are referred to as the "assessment process" and begin with a "B Impact Assessment" that assesses the overall impact of the company on its stakeholders, considering various factors such as number of employees and sector and location of the company's primary operations. The questions in the B Impact Assessment have been created and revised by the Standards Advisory Council, a group of independent experts in business and academia, and cover financial performance; suppliers; the impact of the business on all its stakeholders; best practices regarding mission, measurement, and governance; and the company's "impact business model."

Companies that complete the B Impact Assessment will receive a B Impact Report that contains an overall score based on performance in the key impact areas of governance, workers, community, environment, and consumers and will then move on to an assessment review and submission of supporting documentation. At this point, the focus will be on the operations of the company and demonstration of practice relating to the company's social and environmental impact. Additional steps in the assessment process include completion of a disclosure questionnaire, which allows companies to confidentially disclose to B Lab any sensitive practices, fines, and sanctions related to the company and its partners, and background checks by B Lab staff, which include a review of public records, news sources, and search engines for company names, brands, executives/founders, and other relevant topics.[34]

---

34. The B Impact Assessment process itself has been touted as a useful tool that companies can use to create action plans for addressing the impact of fundamental social issues in their businesses, such as "systemic racism." *See How Companies Can Move from Words to Action to Address Systemic Racism, in* STAKEHOLDER CAPITALISM: THE FIX THAT OUR ECONOMY NEEDS TO BUILD SHARED AND DURABLE PROSPERITY FOR ALL 26 (Berwyn, PA: B Lab).

Alternative Business Structures for Social Enterprise

While benefit corporations have attracted a significant amount of attention, there have been other attempts to create and popularize alternative business structures for social enterprises.[35] For example, traditional for-profit corporations are not foreclosed from pursuing a social mission under statutes that allow such corporations to be incorporated for "any lawful business or purpose" and can attempt to use creative internal governance regulations and contracts among shareholders to keep the corporation focused on its mission.[36] Social enterprises may also use limited liability companies (LLCs) and nonprofit corporations to pursue their social missions, and innovative hybrid (tandem) structures have been created to combine the best features of for-profit and nonprofit entities.[37] Lessons can also be learned from steps taken by jurisdictions outside of the United States (as discussed in Part Two of this book) with respect to recognition of social enterprises in their legal systems, particularly since a number of these jurisdictions have been pioneers in creating laws and policies to support business sustainability and corporate social responsibility.

35. One definition of the term "social enterprise" is "an organization that pursues objectives of general interest, community interest or social benefit through the performance of an entrepreneurial activity involving the use of business logics and methods." B. Reiser, *Theorizing Forms for Social Enterprise*, 62 Emory L.J. 681 (2013) (as cited in A. Fici, Recognition and Legal Forms of Social Enterprise in Europe: A Critical Analysis from a Comparative Law Perspective, Euricse Working Papers No. 82|15 3 (2015)).

36. DGCL § 101(b).

37. A good summary of the corporate forms of social enterprises available in the United States to promote impact can be found at https://www.mofo.com/special-content/impact-investing/social-enterprise.html.

3

Measurement and Reporting

Alan S. Gutterman[1] and Robert L. Brown[2]

Impact investing requires an intention to generate social and environmental impact alongside a financial return. Impact investors, therefore, must have a means for identifying and measuring "impact" and reporting on the results of their efforts to the ultimate owners of the assets being invested.

One of the challenges with the evolution of impact investing has been developing reliable and consistent measures and ratings of performance (i.e., environmental and/or social impact) for individual projects and the overall progress of enterprises with respect to environmental, social, and governance (ESG) criteria. A number of ESG ratings schemes have emerged, and companies have opportunities to seek and obtain certification of their sustainability credentials by external assessors.

As time has gone by there has been more interest in quantifying the relative environmental and social impacts of projects and companies in order to facilitate comparisons, and there is also greater scrutiny of the ESG ratings schemes themselves. However, many have pointed to the difficulties of gauging social impact as opposed to environmental matters. For example, while reductions in pollution can be measured, the relative value of supporting and enabling ongoing education of young people in a developing country cannot be distilled down into a number, and each investor will need to assess such a project by reference to their own ethical lens and personal value system.[3]

---

1. Of Counsel, Harvey Esquire, Los Angeles and Silicon Valley, California; President, Global Law Business, LLC.

2. Senior Counsel, Lynch Cox Gilman & Goodman, Louisville, Kentucky.

3. K.K., *The Economist Explains: What Is Sustainable Finance?*, THE ECONOMIST (Apr. 17, 2018), https://www.economist.com/the-economist-explains/2018/04/17/what-is-sustainable-finance.

According to So and Capanyola, the measurement methods used by impact investors can be grouped into four main categories:[4]

- **Expected return methods**, which weigh the anticipated benefits of an investment against its costs (e.g., the social return on investment (SROI) method, which is discussed below and focuses on calculating an investment's present social impact value compared to the value of the inputs).
- **Theory of change methods**, which outline the intended process for achieving social impact using a logic model that maps linkages between input, activities, output, outcomes, and impact and also takes into consideration impact risks (i.e., the factors that could jeopardize achievement of the expected impact).
- **Mission alignment methods**, which measure the execution of strategy against the project's mission and end goals over time using scorecards or social value criteria to monitor and manage key performance metrics relating to operational performance, organizational effectiveness, finances, and social value.
- **Experimental and quasi-experimental methods**, which include "after-the-fact" evaluations using randomized control trials or other counterfactual approaches to determine the impact of an intervention compared to the situation if the intervention had not taken place.

Ivy So and Alina Capanyola observed that impact investors use impact measurements for different purposes during different parts of the investment cycle, which they broke out into the following phases: (1) estimating impact while conducting due diligence to assess the potential social return before committing to an investment; (2) planning impact by choosing the metrics and data collection methods that the investor will use to monitor a program's effects; (3) monitoring impact after the investment has been made and throughout the life of the investment through measuring and analysis of data to track the intervention's efforts; and (4) evaluating impact by measuring an investment's social consequences after the program concludes to assess portfolio performance and next steps for the investor, including reinvestment.[5]

4. Ivy So & Alina Capanyola, *How Impact Investors Actually Measure Impact*, Stan. Soc. Innovation Rev. (May 16, 2016), https://ssir.org/articles/entry/how_impact_investors_actually_measure_impact.
5. *Id.*

Impact Measurement and Management

Impact measurement and management (IMM) has been described as the process by which impact investors can understand the effects of their investments on people and the planet (i.e., measurement) and then determine the appropriate actions to take to adapt the processes that are being used and improve their outcomes (i.e., management). IMM is an evolving field, still significantly young in relation to the theories and frameworks that have been developed for measuring financing performance. IMM includes a number of different tools, including monitoring and evaluation, ratings, key performance indicators, and disclosures, with research continuing toward development of best practices. IMM can and should be used by impact investors for several important purposes, including understanding whether the short-term changes and long-term effects from an investment are playing out as anticipated, identifying methods and opportunities for improving the impact performance of an investment, and building a knowledge base that can be used for making better decisions about future investments.[6]

Impact investors can choose from among various principles, frameworks, and standards when developing strategies for measuring and managing the impact of their investments. Principles include rules and best practices to ensure the overall integrity of processes and behaviors and examples include the International Finance Corporation (IFC) Operating Principles for Impact Management, the Principles for Responsible Investment, and the Impact Management Principles of the European Venture Philanthropy Association. Principles are not specific measurement techniques; their purpose is to communicate the intentions of the investor with respect to engaging in IMM.[7] For example, the IFC Operating Principles for Impact Management were launched at the World Bank Group/IMF spring meetings in 2019 and include the following steps through each of the typical stages of investment (i.e., strategic intent, origination and structuring, portfolio management, and impact at exit):[8]

1. Define strategic impact objective(s) consistent with the investment strategy
2. Manage strategic impact and financial returns at portfolio level
3. Establish the investor's contribution to the achievement of impact

---

6. S. Godeke & P. Briaud, Impact Investing Handbook: An Implementation Guide for Practitioners 122 (Rockefeller Philanthropy Advisors, 2020).

7. *Id.* at 126.

8. https://www.impactprinciples.org/9-principles.

4. Assess expected impact of each investment, based on systematic approach
5. Assess, address, monitor, and manage the potential risks of negative effects of each investment
6. Monitor the progress of each investment in achieving impact against expectations and respond appropriately
7. Conduct exits, considering the effect on sustained impact
8. Review, document, and improve decisions and processes based on the achievement of impact and lessons learned
9. Publicly disclose alignment with the Principles and provide independent verification of the extent of alignment

Frameworks are used to implement the intentions of the impact investor expressed in the principles just referred to and include specific methodologies for organizing IMM, such as the United Nation's Sustainable Development Goals (SDGs), the G8 Impact Measurement Working Group Report, and Acumen, through its Lean Data Project.[9]

Social Return on Investment

A commonly used tool for impact evaluation is Social Return on Investment (SROI), which has been described as a systematic way of incorporating social, environmental, economic, and other values into decision-making processes that creates a holistic perspective on whether a development project or social business or enterprise is beneficial and profitable.[10] As is the case with traditional cost-benefit analysis, SROI includes a ratio, referred to as a SROI ratio; however, the SROI ratio is not used as a means for comparing various projects but rather as an aid in developing the narrative for a particular project. Advocates of the SROI approach have stressed that stakeholder perspectives are essential and the goal of the SROI process, which involves extensive consultation with stakeholders (particularly the key beneficiaries of the project), is to assess the value of the project from the stakeholders' perspectives.

The steps of the SROI process include defining:

9. Godeke & Briaud, *supra* note 6, at 126.

10. The discussion of SROI in this paragraph is adapted from Menno Salverda, *Social Return on Investment*, BetterEvaluation, http://betterevaluation.org/approach/SROI (last visited May 5, 2022).

- Scope and boundaries (objectives and scope) of project and analysis (i.e., issues to be addressed and the objectives in addressing them);
- Identification and selection of key stakeholders, particularly those who will be most impacted by the project;
- Engagement of stakeholders to identify their perceptions of important outcomes and to develop a business plan for based on mapping the relationships among the organization's resources and outcomes for each stakeholder;
- Identification of "what goes in" (i.e., inputs for each outcome) and "what comes out" (i.e., results) for each intended outcome;
- Development of indicators for measuring inputs, activities, and outcomes, with a particular emphasis on outcomes; and
- Quantifying impact of the organization's efforts, translating the articulated benefits and costs into a monetary value and calculating the SROI ratio by comparing the investments (inputs) on the one hand and the financial, social, and environmental returns (outcomes and impact of an intervention) on the other.

The SROI should be placed in context with narratives that provide context for the numbers and explain what cannot be captured in the SROI ratio alone. The entire process should be continuously verified, and the end product should be an SROI report that communicates the results to all stakeholders, explains the steps that were taken, and serves as a foundation for future steps, including adjustments to the business plan.

External Reviews

While impact investors can select their own tools for measuring the impact of their investments and require their investees to implement performance measurement and assessment systems, planning for external reviews of impact performance by independent expert organizations is a reasonable and prudent check on the actions and decisions of the enterprise managers. In its Green Bond Principles (GBP) and Social Bond Principles (SBP), the International Capital Market Association suggested four different types of independent external reviews that issuers could use to assess and demonstrate the alignment of their Green/Social Bonds or bond program to the core components that are included in both the GBP and SBP:[11]

11. *Green Bond Principles: Voluntary Process Guidelines for Issuing Green Bonds* (Paris: Int'l Cap. Mkt. Ass'n, June 2018) and *Social Bond Principles: Voluntary*

- **Second party opinion.** An institution with environmental expertise, which is independent from the issuer and its advisor for its Green/Social Bond framework, can issue a second-party opinion following an assessment of the issuer's overarching objectives, strategy, policy, and/or processes relating to environmental and/or social sustainability, and an evaluation of the environmental and/or social features of the type of projects intended for the use of proceeds.
- **Verification.** Issuers can obtain independent verification of their Green/Social Bonds against a designated set of criteria typically related to business processes and/or environmental/social criteria. The GBP/SBP noted various types of verification, including evaluation of the environmentally sustainable features of underlying assets and assurance, and attestation regarding an issuer's internal tracking method. The attestation could cover use of proceeds, allocation of funds from Green/Social Bond proceeds, statement of environmental/social impact, and alignment of reporting with the GBP/SBP.
- **Certification.** Issuers can have their Green/Social Bond or associated Green/Social Bond framework or use of proceeds certified against a recognized external green or social standard or label that defines specific criteria and then requires testing for alignment with such criteria by qualified, accredited third parties.
- **Green/Social Bond scoring/rating.** Issuers can have their Green/Social Bond, associated Green/Social Bond framework, or a key feature thereof such as use of proceeds evaluated or assessed by qualified third parties, such as specialized research providers or rating agencies, according to an established scoring/rating methodology that focuses on, among other things, environmental/social performance data or the process relative to the GBP/SBP.[12]

One important and widely used tool for independent impact certification and rating is the Global Impact Investing Ratings System (GIIRS), which has been described as a comprehensive, comparable, and transparent system for assessing the social and environmental impact of companies and funds with a ratings and analytics approach analogous to

Process Guidelines for Issuing Social Bonds (Paris: Int'l Cap. Mkt. Ass'n, June 2020).

12. The GBP/SBP noted that Green/Social Bond Scoring/Rating is different from credit ratings but pointed out that credit ratings also reflect material environmental/social risks.

Morningstar Investment rankings.[13] Another valuable aspect of GIIRS is its collection of aggregated impact data and ratings information in a product called GIIRS Ratings & Analytics that organizations can use when assessing and reporting social and environmental impact. GIIRS, which is powered by B Analytics (https://b-analytics.net/), provides a composite score by assessing performance in several impact categories, including workers, customers, communities, and the environment, each of which are weighted in advance based on geography, sector, and size. The ratings process begins with completion of an online GIIRS Assessment, which is based on the B Impact Assessment used to certify "B corporations," and continues with an assessment review by GIIRS staff that includes interviews and a desk review of selected documents provided by the enterprise at the request of GIIRS.

Reporting

In order to know whether or not an enterprise is achieving its goals relating to impact performance it is necessary to have in place procedures for reporting and otherwise communicating information regarding impact performance to the enterprise's stakeholders. While certain corporate sustainability disclosures have now become minimum legal requirements in some jurisdictions, in general such disclosures are still a voluntary matter and directors have some leeway as to the scope of the disclosure made by their companies and how they are presented to investors and other stakeholders. Some companies continue to limit their disclosures to those specifically required by regulators; however, most companies have realized that they need to pay attention to the issues raised by institutional investors and other key stakeholders and make sure that they are covered in the disclosure program. At the other extreme, there are companies that have embraced sustainability as integral to their brands and have elected to demonstrate their commitment by preparing and disseminating additional disclosures that illustrate how they have woven sustainability into their long-term strategies and day-to-day operational activities.[14]

In order to ensure the quality of sustainability reporting and facilitate the efficient creation of comparable reports, it is necessary to have robust reporting standards that can be applied in a global economy in which the

13. *GIIRS and SROI: What Is the Relationship?* Social Value UK (Feb. 8, 2013), https://socialvalueuk.org/resource/iris-and-sroi/.

14. For further discussion of Sustainability Reporting, *see* A. Gutterman, Sustainability Reporting and Communications (Business Expert Press, 2020).

operational activities and reporting responsibilities of companies transcend national borders. International organizations, such as the United Nations (UN); regional organizations, such as the European Union (EU); and stock exchanges and independent organizations, such as the Global Reporting Initiative (GRI), have all been involved in the development and implementation of key international initiatives on sustainability reporting. Many of these initiatives take the form of national policies and instruments that incorporate elements of international or corporate social responsibility reporting frameworks. For example, The GRI Standards are referenced in government or market instruments in dozens of countries around the world, such as the preamble of the EU Directive on disclosure of nonfinancial and diversity information, and are frequently one of several normative or management standards referred to in reporting instruments, usually accompanied by references to the UN Global Compact,[15] Organisation for Economic Co-operation and Development (OECD) Guidelines for Multinational Enterprises,[16] and the International Organization for Standardization (ISO) 26000 Guidance Standard on Social Responsibility.[17]

Mandatory reporting of ESG remains the exception rather than the rule in most jurisdictions, although the EU has adopted a directive on nonfinancial reporting that requires larger companies to report on ESG issues.[18] The Swiss Finance Institute (SFI) highlighted several of the challenges relating to measurement, quantification, and reporting of ESG issues, including the inherent difficulty in quantifying and aggregating complex, often qualitative, environmental and social issues, causes, costs, and impacts, and the lack of universal legal obligations to report using a comprehensive, unified, and standardized reporting framework.[19] On the

15. https://www.unglobalcompact.org/.

16. https://www.oecd.org/corporate/mne/.

17. *Carrots & Sticks: Global Trends in Sustainability Reporting Regulation and Policy* 23 (KPMG Int'l, the Global Research Initiative (GRI), the United Nations Environment Programme (UNEP) & the Centre for Corporate Governance in Africa, 2016), www.carrotsandsticks.net.

18. A. Krauss, P. Kruger & J. Meyer, *Sustainable Finance in Switzerland: Where Do We Stand?* 17 (Zurich: Swiss Finance Institute, Sept. 2016). The SFI also noted that the stock exchanges in Johannesburg and London required disclosures on carbon emissions and other ESG issues and that countries such as France had adopted disclosure requirements for institutional investors. *Id.*

19. *Id.* (citing T. Rowley & S. Berman, *A Brand New Brand of Social Performance*, 38 Bus. & Soc'y 109 (2000); and *Policy Briefing: Financial Stability and Environmental Stability* (Cambridge Institute for Sustainability Leadership and United Nations Environment Programme, Sept. 2015) (noting that environmental

second point, the SFI noted that while a directive had been approved by the EC (European Community) for implementation throughout the EU, each country would have its own country-specific laws that may differ substantially from one another and thus result in reporting that is less standardized than traditional financial reporting. The SFI pointed out that several voluntary sustainability reporting frameworks had been developed, including the GRI and the Sustainability Accounting Standards Board for companies and the UN Principles of Responsible Investing for investors; however, the SFI criticized the quality of the available nonfinancial information (research has found that ESG measurements from different data providers are often inconsistent) and argued that attempts to produce credit rating-like ESG measurements were flawed because such measurements were not necessarily public information and changes in methods or ratings were typically not announced publicly.[20]

In a report issued on July 6, 2020, the U.S. Government Accountability Office evaluated the state of public company disclosures related to ESG issues and found, among other things, that it can be expected that investors will continue to pressure public companies to provide more detailed disclosure about their ESG initiatives and results of those initiatives to enable investors to track and eventually compare performance, and that investors were concerned with "gaps and inconsistencies in companies' disclosures that limit their usefulness" and comparability.[21] For example, there was no consistency among the companies regarding the metrics they used to report on the same topics, and companies often changed the metrics they used to report on a topic from year-to-year, making it difficult to make comparisons over time and across companies.

issues are difficult to quantify due to their interconnectedness and the uncertainty relating to when, how often, and how strongly environmental risks materialize)).

20. *Id.* at 18.

21. *Public Companies: Disclosure of Environmental, Social and Governance Factors and Options to Enhance Them* (U.S. Government Accountability Office, GAO-20-530, July 2020). It was reported that the U.S. Government Accountability Office (GAO) analyzed the disclosures of 32 large and midsize public companies on 33 topics related to climate change, resource management, human rights, personnel management, workforce diversity, occupational health and safety, board accountability, and data security; and interviewed 14 large and midsize institutional investors (seven private-sector asset management firms and seven public pension funds), 18 public companies, 13 market observers (including nongovernmental ESG standard-setting organizations, academics, and other groups), and stock exchange and industry association representatives. H. Gregory, H. Palmer & L. Wood, *Emerging Trends in ESG Disclosures Highlighted in U.S. GAO Report* (Aug. 1, 2020).

In addition, companies often failed to fully disclose the results of their activities relating to management of ESG-related risks or opportunities.

Another problem for investors is easily finding all ESG-related disclosures of a company in one place, since most companies distribute such information in a variety of different ways, including annual reports, proxy statements, multi-issue sustainability reports, single-issue reports, dynamic web pages, investor presentations, earnings calls, and shareholder bulletins. The report also found that investors have identified and affirmed linkages between positive ESG activity and financial value and, as such, have increasingly incorporated ESG performance into their voting decisions at annual meetings of the public companies in which they have invested. While regulators such as the Securities and Exchange Commission are cognizant and attentive to changes in expected ESG disclosures, for the time being leadership will continue to come from nongovernmental standard setters and framework developers such as the GRI and SASB.[22]

22. *Id.*

4

Forming an Impact Investment Fund

Ellen Kaye Fleishhacker, with assistance from Claire Eaton and William LeBas[1]

Introduction

Impact funds are pooled investment vehicles that make investments with the intention of both promoting a measurable social or environmental impact and seeking financial returns.[2] While that description is—perhaps somewhat unhelpfully—vague as a starting point, it illustrates some of the complexity and variety that sponsors and investors face when characterizing, marketing, operating, and investing in Impact Funds. For example:

- There is a range of financial return outcomes that Impact Funds seek—from "return first" models that prioritize economic returns while still focusing on impact as a way to drive those returns, to "return plus impact" models that seek to balance returns and impacts, to "impact first" models that prioritize impact over returns.
- Likewise, the role of environmental, social, and governance (ESG) factors in Impact Funds is different than in other forms of investing. Specifically, Impact Funds intend to effect a social or environmental impact, whereas other forms of "ESG investing" use ESG factors as one determinant in whether to make a particular financial investment.
- To achieve a social or environmental impact, Impact Funds may invest broadly or by focusing on one of many possible themes

1. Arnold & Porter Kaye Scholer LLP. This chapter is intended to be a general summary of the law and does not constitute legal advice. The reader should consult with counsel to determine applicable legal requirements in a specific fact situation.

2. For purposes of this discussion, we will refer to such impact funds as "Impact Funds," "Funds," or the "Fund."

(e.g., social themes, such as affordable housing, community health, and financial inclusion, and environmental themes, such as clean water, renewable energy, and sustainable transportation).

- Further, there is a wide variety of Impact Fund sponsors—from tax-exempt organizations and their for-profit affiliates, to specialized Impact Fund sponsors, to well-established private equity and hedge fund sponsors.
- Finally, there are many types of Impact Fund investors—ranging from sovereign entities to major institutional investors to family offices to individuals—and many possible Impact Fund structures to meet their tax and regulatory needs.

This chapter provides a broad overview of the types of issues and considerations that matter to Impact Fund sponsors (particularly those based in the United States), investors, and their legal counsel. To that end, this chapter focuses on (1) different models of incorporating ESG and impact into investment funds, (2) how Impact Funds define and measure impact, and (3) special considerations in forming Impact Funds, including regarding structuring, tax, and regulatory considerations, as well as documentation and disclosures.

This chapter focuses primarily on closed-end private Impact Funds that pursue a single, targeted thematic "impact" strategy, while also offering examples of how such funds differ from closed-end Impact Funds that pursue a broader impact mandate. Although undeniably a significant part of the Impact Fund ecosystem, this chapter provides only some high-level observations regarding other types of investment products focusing on impact, including publicly traded funds and registered investment companies, private open-end funds that pursue liquid and semi-liquid investment opportunities, and private open-end and closed-end funds that pursue credit strategies, including lending funds and special situations or distressed credit funds.

Different Models of Incorporating ESG and Impact into Investment Funds

The following is a brief description of the range of ways that different investment funds may seek to fulfill ESG and impact goals.

Negative Screens

Although not a focus of this chapter, it is helpful to understand how mutual funds, exchange-traded funds (ETFs), and hedge funds may screen for

ESG and/or impact investments. These investors, when they have opted to consider ESG factors, have historically used "negative" screening to filter out companies that generally do not promote ESG or impact objectives. The market sometimes refers to this method as "Responsible Impact Investing." Negative screening typically involves the use of a broad, categorical approach that excludes investments based on their sector or other obvious/general attributes (e.g., screening out all companies that derive more than a certain percentage of their profits from controversial lines of business, such as the sale of firearms). Such broad-based negative screening methods are often necessary because passive investors generally will not have the ability to dictate governance or other corporate changes or explicitly require from companies the types of measurements and tailored reporting necessary for impact investing.

In addition, negative screening historically has been a key feature of requests by certain investors in non-ESG or non-Impact Funds. This is particularly true for investors who have internal policies prohibiting investments in certain classes of investments. For example, some institutional investors have imposed restrictions on their direct or indirect investment in companies operating in certain industries. These types of investor-specific restrictions have a long history in private equity fund side letter negotiations, and market trends seem to indicate that the number and breadth of these "excused" investments will continue to grow. Sponsors of both open- and closed-end funds have long used this negative screen approach as a way to mitigate not only reputational risk and meet investor stewardship expectations but also to avoid investments that carry undue investment risk (e.g., liability and litigation associated with high-risk industries). Avoiding negative coverage in the media remains a key focus for sponsors (and their publicity and investor relations teams).

Positive Screens

Another approach is to screen using positive filters, meaning to focus investment only in favor of companies engaged in certain, desirable practices or industries. The market sometimes refers to this method as "sustainable impact investing." This method of screening typically requires more analysis than negative screening, as positive screening requires the investor to look at such metrics as a company's labor practices, diversity, environmental record, or other attributes. Recently, the number of ETFs that focus on specific ESG initiatives or corporate measures has grown significantly, including ETFs investing in companies with gender diversity on boards or companies that promote alternative energy. As Main Street and institutional investors continue to invest with their conscience, this trend is certain to continue. Most Impact Funds, while making use of both negative and positive screens as part of their diligence processes, do more than rely on these screens.

Controlling Influence

As opposed to passive investments in publicly traded instruments, because Impact Funds often make "control" investments that involve varying degrees of economic control and/or board representation for operating companies, these sponsors often have the ability to negotiate how they will manage the company in order to pursue impact outcomes. These control positions also can help the Fund dictate what types of reporting the company will engage in at the portfolio company-level and what types of reporting (and when) it will report up to the sponsor and Fund in the course of the investment. Because portfolio-level measurement is so crucial to many elements of operating an Impact Fund, sponsors must assess whether they will have these incidents of controlled ownership when designing the screening, monitoring, and reporting elements of their Funds. If they will not have controlling leverage (e.g., because they are a minority venture capital investor), then they will need to keep that in mind when explaining how they will be able to influence impact, or collect relevant data, at the portfolio company-level. For example, affordable housing funds often need to have access to certain types of information regarding renters on an aggregate apartment unit basis. If an affordable housing Impact Fund invests in passive interests in real estate properties, then it will need to ensure that the manager of the assets will be prepared to provide the types of information the Fund needs to meet its reporting obligations.

Thematic Investment

Impact Funds that invest in properties that are used for affordable housing are an example of "thematic" impact investment. Sometimes these funds may invest in private equity-style real estate investments or sometimes in real estate opportunities financed with low-income housing tax credits and other government subsidies. In any case, the impact thesis is to invest in properties that the sponsor will refurbish and manage to preserve or create affordable housing and also hopefully to generate yield and economic returns. There are many other types of thematic Impact Funds outside of the affordable housing example we are using throughout this chapter, including funds focused on societally pressing issues, such as access to education, green/solar technology development, emerging medical technologies, and therapies. The list goes on and is as varied as creativity, economics, and societal issues in need of improvement permits. Certain investors in these thematic Funds also may have non-financial objectives (either altruistic or non-return-based incentives) that permit managers to target opportunities that do not generally meet the risk/return profile for other private equity, infrastructure, and real estate opportunities. As an example, and continuing with the theme of affordable housing, certain financial institution investors may find such Funds attractive because they generate Community Reinvestment Act credits, which many banking institutions seek for their own regulatory reasons. As opposed to multi-sector funds, thematic Impact Funds generally are also stand-alone strategies for a sponsor—and perhaps their only strategy—rather than part of an impact focus that the sponsor layers on a larger investment program or opportunity set.

Defining and Measuring Impact

One of the first decisions sponsors have in raising—and often step one in conceiving of—an Impact Fund is how they will define and measure "impact." The sponsor's definition of impact will drive nearly every other decision in the formation, marketing, fundraising, and investment activity of the Fund. For some Impact Fund sponsors, this decision may be obvious: for example, managers that invest in affordable housing may define impact based on the number of affordable units that the Fund supports, develops, and preserves. Often, for these types of investments, there may also be specific governmental measurements that help to determine "affordability," including averaging tenant income. By contrast, for managers pursuing less targeted thematic investment mandates (e.g., global health), the process for defining and measuring the Impact Fund's "impact" will be more challenging, and will depend on the sponsor's investment strengths and possibly investor input.

While the "alternatives" investment industry, including private equity, has largely circled around a number of key measures and standards to help define and evaluate "impact," neither managers nor investors have yet found a universally accepted single concept of what constitutes a valid way to define impact. In fact, managers that pursue esoteric or niche investment strategies will need to be creative about what impact might mean for their asset type due to limited market precedent. Therefore, managers must often evaluate the various measures of impact available in the market and identify which of them may (or may not) be most appropriate given a Fund's potential investor interest and expectations and the nature of the particular investment focus.

The following are some of the more common frameworks for measuring impact. Nongovernment organizations (such as the United Nations) or nonprofit and/or self-regulatory organizations, like the Global Impact Investing Network (GIIN) and the Sustainability Accounting Standards Board promulgate many of the standards set forth in the following sections, and many of these organizations established their focus primarily in response to the initial growth of ESG as a key feature of alternative assets investing.

Importantly for U.S. managers, the U.S. Securities and Exchange Commission (SEC) has remained largely silent on how managers should define "impact" where used as an investment strategy. However, as this chapter discusses later in more detail, the SEC's silence on defining and measuring impact has not stopped it from scrutinizing the practices, policies, and standards that Impact Fund managers establish for themselves.

GIIN Framework

GIIN has provided a useful—if general—lexicon for speaking about "impact." GIIN defines "impact" to mean "investments made into companies, organizations, and funds with the intention to generate measurable social and environmental impact alongside a financial return."[3] Elaborating on this definition, GIIN breaks down impact into four core elements:

- Intentionality. In an impact investment, investors intend to make a positive social or environmental impact through investing.
- Use of evidence and impact data in investment design. Impact investing should use evidence and data where available to drive intelligent investment design.
- Managing impact performance. Impact investment sponsors should actively manage their investments in light of the investment focus and have feedback loops in place to share how an investment is performing in light of such criteria.
- Contribution to the growth of the industry. The impact investment industry should use shared terminology, conventions, and indicators to promote learning and enhance the understanding of impact investing.

The GIIN framework provides a high-level starting point for managers to think about how they will design and operate their impact

3. *See* GIIN, *What You Need to Know about Impact Investing*, https://thegiin.org/impact-investing/need-to-know/#what-is-impact-investing (last visited Feb. 26, 2021).

programs. However, the framework is importantly agnostic regarding whether investors should prioritize or subordinate investment returns to impact objectives and how they should identify particular sectors or outcomes for impact investment. As such, GIIN offers a flexible and heuristic approach for Impact Fund sponsors to apply to their own investment strategies and focus, and to set their own methods for developing data and managing impact performance.

Sustainability Accounting Standards Board (SASB)

In addition to the GIIN framework, and although primarily developed in response to identifying and encouraging investors to meet certain ESG objectives, the Sustainability Accounting Standards Board (SASB) has promulgated its own set of standards (SASB Standards) to measure the impact of investments across industries. SASB published the current SASB Standards in a "Conceptual Framework" in 2017, which it updated and re-released for public comment in August 2020 (comments closed on December 31, 2020).

The current SASB Standards focus on five major tenets of sustainability: (1) environmental; (2) social capital; (3) human capital; (4) business model and innovation; and (5) leadership and governance. These key tenets drive industry-specific objectives for promoting ESG goals. Currently, the SASB Standards identify ESG issues most relevant to financial performance in 77 distinct industries. As just one example, the SASB Standards provide ways to measure workforce and supply-chain issues in the apparel, accessories, and footwear industries. SASB continually expands these industry-specific measurements and ESG focuses for existing and new industries.

In its 2017 Conceptual Framework, SASB also introduced the idea of "sustainability accounting" as a way to address these areas of sustainability in a business's finances (i.e., similar to the way in which audits of company financials incorporate U.S. generally accepted accounting principles). SASB has advocated for the adoption of specific and measurable ESG accounting standards as a way for investors to compare potential investments across managers and asset classes and as a way for companies to determine and demonstrate whether they are achieving stated or intended sustainability goals.[4]

4. Sustainability Accounting Standards Board, *SASB Conceptual Framework* (February 2017), https://www.sasb.org/wp-content/uploads/2020/02/SASB_Conceptual-Framework_WATERMARK.pdf.

The SASB approach to identifying specific ESG issues that are germane to specific target industries, and its broader focus on applying accounting rigor to measuring ESG objectives, have been very influential in the ESG space. Consequently, and because of the overlapping nature of ESG and impact concerns and methods for measurement, the SASB Standards and sustainability accounting methods are also large drivers of investor expectations and manager processes in the Impact Fund ecosystem.

UN Principles for Responsible Investing and Sustainable Development Goals

The United Nations Principles for Responsible Investing (Principles) are key ESG principles developed by the United Nations (UN). Currently, the Principles have over 3,000 signatories, which include investment managers and asset owners with over $100 trillion in assets under management.[5]

Signatories adhering to the Principles incorporate ESG analysis, policies and procedures and disclosures into their investment and reporting practices. Participants also produce an annual report that details how they have incorporated the Principles and other responsible investment practices into their investment activities. While the Principles focus broadly on ESG in the asset management industry—as opposed to specifically defining "impact"—they have influenced sponsors of Impact Funds (and for investors in such Funds) as they seek to develop detailed, transparent, and comprehensive impact investing frameworks.

In January 2015, the UN also established the Sustainable Development Goals (SDGs), which are a collection of 17 sustainability goals developed to address public, humanitarian, and social needs. The SDGs promote investment in positive public outcomes, such as financing of clean energy, clean water, food access, healthcare services/access, employment access, environmental protection, social housing, social justice, low-income and poverty protection, educational access, public safety, affordable transportation, and public works investment. In the same way that GIIN and SASB have been influential in establishing particular ways to approach measuring impact and ESG, the SDGs have provided investment managers with specific "ways to do good" that may align with specific investment sectors they are targeting, for example, access to education, water availability and conservation, and affordable housing, to name a few.

5. UN Principles for Responsible Investment, *About the PRI*, https://www.unpri.org/pri/about-the-pri (last visited Feb. 26, 2021).

Other Standards and Investor-Driven Requests

For-profit organizations, industry trade groups, nonprofits, and other organizations have promulgated a plethora of other standards and metrics that can help managers to develop their definition of impact. These include the Global Reporting Initiative (GRI) standards, Impact Reporting and Investment Standards (IRIS), guidelines developed by the American Investment Council (a private equity industry trade group), the B Impact Assessment and B Analytics performance standards (developed by the B Lab, a nonprofit that certifies companies meeting its standards as "B corporations"), standards set by corporate bodies (for example, the 2019 Business Roundtable CEO statement), and available "screening" measures for public companies developed by major institutional investors.

How Do Investor Discussions Shape the Definition and Measurement of Impact?

Both in the public markets and alternatives space, larger institutional investors have been a driving force in bringing ESG and impact to the forefront. In alternatives, European institutional investors were among the first to adopt ESG policies and deployment of capital into Impact Funds. In addition, U.S. pension funds have made ESG integration and impact investing part of their strategic plan. The growth in appetite for Impact Funds from other types of smaller institutional investors, such as funds of funds (which may invest on behalf of pensions and other institutions) and family offices, has added to the number of "cooks in the kitchen" that managers must liaise with as part of the fundraising process. There is no reason to believe this number of interested parties will decrease.

Increasingly, investors are looking for information—and are not shy to provide feedback—during the formation and capital raising stages (pre-marketing and marketing), the due diligence process and side letter negotiation process and in requesting (and often dictating) the level of reporting that the Impact Fund provides (either to individual investors or at the Fund-level). To that end, some "typical" side letter provisions related to impact might include:

- Requirements that the manager use certain ESG or impact criteria as a metric for the Fund's investment decisions;
- Penalties for the manager or investor rights in the event that the Fund "breaches" its impact commitment;
- Availability of excuse or exclusion provisions for certain types of investments, and specific terms relating to how the investor may exercise such rights;

- Requirements that the manager itself and its vendors meet certain ESG metrics (such as regarding racial and gender diversity and environmental sustainability); and
- Requirements for specialized impact reporting, including the potential for customized reporting for an investor who requires more than the manager's standard reporting (and specifying whether the manager, Fund or investor pays for this).

Balancing investor requests with the manager's investment focus and operational capabilities and constraints is always part of the dance of fundraising. But what is relatively unique in the Impact Fund market—at least to date—is the way in which these investor concerns are shaping the types of Funds that a sponsor brings to market. For thematic Impact Funds, this is evident in the specific types of funds that managers are raising. For larger, sector-agnostic Impact Funds, this is evident in the significant expense, planning and footprint that managers have invested in building out larger programs to support their Impact Funds.

Third-Party Advisors

There are a number of consulting firms, accounting firms, and other advisors (sometimes including the non-profit and self-regulatory organizations listed previously) that can assist investment firms in determining what types of impact focus and processes may make sense for their business, particularly if they are looking to "add" an impact-targeted product as a subset of their current Fund or investment offerings. These third parties can also be crucial in helping managers develop the internal infrastructure to actualize procedures for the Impact Fund within the manager's organization. For example, investors frequently ask about the use of third parties in the due diligence process for Impact Funds, and the use of third-party resources for Impact Funds is evident in the increasing number of explicit references to ESG consultants and service providers in fund expenses both for impact-focused and more general ESG products. Managers can build credibility with investors when raising first-time Impact Funds by showing that a third party has reviewed (i.e., vetted) the proposed impact evaluation processes. When economically feasible, bringing in these types of third-party consultants early (and opening lines of communication between them and fund formation counsel) also can help to ensure that the manager is designing the Fund optimally to define, invest in, and measure impact.

Forming an Impact Fund

As these conversations occur and as the manager and its personnel continue to refine the Fund's impact thesis (or theses), fund counsel will often be a crucial part of converting these investor requests and manager undertakings into the Fund's operating and marketing documents. Part of the formation and drafting process will depend on the types of fundamental issues that come up in any new fundraising (Impact Fund or not), including the types of industries, regions, and assets the Fund is focusing on and nuances that the investment strategy may drive. Ultimately, for the Fund to be successful—both economically and in terms of meeting its impact objectives—the manager will need to find the right opportunities at the right price and where it can make and implement the right management decisions.

The fundraising and formation process is often iterative as the manager begins to develop its thesis internally and approach key anchor investors to test market interest. Accordingly, and almost always for first-time funds, fund counsel will first prepare a term sheet or summary of terms that sets out the key structure and economic terms for the proposed Fund. Often, this process of putting pen to paper helps managers, in consultation with their Fund counsel, begin to make concrete decisions about the Fund's structure, terms, investment focus, and impact thesis. Some sponsors will use refined drafts of the term sheet as a basis for marketing the Impact Fund or, in certain cases, will include high-level proposed terms in a marketing deck to begin testing the waters and to gain market input. Even at these early premarketing stages, internal or external counsel should be involved to ensure that the sponsor is presenting marketing materials appropriately, that such materials include proper legal disclaimers, and that the outreach process is complying with applicable law and regulations.

Structuring the Fund

A key decision for the manager, in consultation with counsel, will be to determine how it will organize and structure the Fund. In many ways, the considerations that go into structuring are the same for an impact and non-impact Fund: will the Fund use a partnership or limited liability company structure; will the Fund have a separate manager or general partner and will that entity be the same as the investment manager; and will the Fund use a carried interest partner if the Fund will be able to earn performance-based compensation? The answers to these questions will be contingent on both the types of investments the Fund will make and upon the types of investors that the Fund is targeting. For example, will the Fund need the flexibility to raise parallel, alternative, or feeder funds, including the ability to form alternative investment vehicles to make investments? Will the Fund be raising money outside the United States and, if so, will it form a parallel fund (and where)? Again, many of these decisions are not unique to Impact Funds, and their sponsors still predominantly use the same structures as they use for their other closed-end vehicles, namely Delaware partnerships and the sponsor's preferred non-U.S. jurisdiction for any offshore entities.

Where the sponsor entity is a charitable organization or nonprofit, there is an increasing variety of "topside" or above-the-Fund structuring that may occur, depending on who will control the general partner or the manager. Sometimes, the nonprofit will establish for-profit entities that will serve in the general partner and investment manager functions, and the nonprofit entity will use the for-profit entities to further one aspect of the nonprofit's larger mission. In other cases, additional structuring of entities and management functions may be necessary to split economics between an outsourced management team that is looking to receive management and performance-based compensation from the nonprofit that is sponsoring the Fund but seeking to avoid jeopardizing its nonprofit status.

Certain Tax Considerations

As is the case in any private fund structuring, tax considerations are essential. A full discussion of the tax structures used by Impact Funds is beyond the scope of this chapter, but a sponsor's tax counsel and accountants should be involved from the initial planning stages to make sure that the sponsor is using the optimal structure. This structure should consider the tax implications of the Fund's proposed investment strategy (the types of assets and jurisdictions in which the Fund will invest), and the projected tax needs of the Fund's investor base. Giving sufficient forethought to investor needs will help to ensure that the Fund is market-ready and that the sponsor will not need to make significant mid-marketing changes in order to accommodate key investors (although changes of this nature, which may require consent of existing investors, are sometimes unanticipated and unavoidable).

In particular, because charities or other nonprofit organizations are often significant investors in Impact Funds (and particularly in certain thematic Funds), sponsors will need to understand the concerns that these investors might have from a tax perspective. For example, private foundation investors may have issues with investments that may jeopardize their private foundation status and investments that do not comply with their "program-related investments" requirements. Non-taxable investors may be concerned about Funds that generate unrelated business taxable income (UBTI), which may trigger tax-filing obligations. In addition, if the Fund will raise money from non-U.S. investors, sponsors may need to provide structuring solutions—including parallel funds or feeder entities—to meet the needs of those non-U.S. investors.

Certain Regulatory Considerations

A detailed description of all of the regulatory considerations for Impact Funds is outside the scope of this chapter. However, we do note some of the recent U.S. regulatory scrutiny given to ESG, and what it may mean for Impact Fund managers.

SEC Guidance Regarding and Interest in ESG

Importantly for Impact Fund sponsors, in a 2019 Interpretive Release, the SEC made it clear that an advisor "may shape [its advisory] relationship by agreement, provided that there is full and fair disclosure and informed consent."[6] This interpretive statement was widely taken to mean that sponsors can meet their fiduciary obligations to a fund client by considering other objectives as part of the fiduciary relationship—aside from economic returns—if full and fair disclosure of these common outcomes is contained in the fund's governing documents.[7]

While this fundamental emphasis on disclosure and process characterizes much of the U.S. regulatory scheme in the private funds space generally, it can be particularly challenging for managers raising Impact Funds because the market is relatively new and market practice varies widely on issues (such as measuring and reporting impact) that are a key regulatory focus. Further, given the fluid nature of how Impact Funds may sometimes define "impact," building credible documentation and rationales for decisions may require a significant amount of internal process.

---

6. U.S. Sec. & Exch. Comm'n, *Commission Interpretation Regarding Standard of Conduct for Investment Advisers* 9 (June 5, 2019), https://www.sec.gov/rules/interp/2019/ia-5248.pdf.

7. Relevant for employee-directors who sit on portfolio company boards, there have also been helpful corporate developments in Delaware fiduciary law that give directors a greater ability to consider certain non-economic factors as part of the business judgment rule.

This can be harder than it sounds, because, at the agency level, the SEC has not specifically told market participants how they should define and measure impact and ESG (and some SEC commissioners have signaled that they do not believe that regulatory bodies should seek to define ESG and impact).[8] Further, despite the SEC's public disagreement about the agency's role in defining impact (and likely the wide difference of perspectives among SEC staff itself), it is notable that the SEC's Division of Examinations (formerly, the Office of Compliance Inspections and Examinations) has indicated it intends to continue focusing on ESG issues through its exams of registered investment advisers.[9] In addition, on April 9, 2021, the staff of the Division of Examinations issued a risk alert[10] that highlighted their observations from recent exams of registered investment advisers, registered investment companies, and private funds offering ESG products. In the risk alert they (1) encouraged sponsors promoting ESG investing to evaluate whether their ESG-related disclosures are accurate and consistent with internal firm practices; (2) noted that sponsors should ensure that their approaches to ESG investing are both implemented consistently and appropriately addressed in the firm's policies and procedures; and (3) noted that sponsors should also maintain records relating to important stages of the ESG investing process.[11]

Perhaps the SEC's focus on impact (and ESG more broadly) should not be surprising given that Impact Funds—even more than other private funds—have unique disclosure, process, and measuring issues. In this way, the SEC's focus on impact is to make sure that managers are not abusing investor trust under the veneer of "greenwashing" (i.e., overstating ESG efforts and impact), for which the SEC places the burden of proof on the sponsor.

Meeting this "burden of proof" in practice will require that managers be able to demonstrate—and, importantly, document—that they

---

8. *See* Harvard Law School Forum on Corporate Governance, *Remarks by Commissioner Peirce on the Role of Asset Management in ESG Investing* (Sept. 18, 2020), https://corpgov.law.harvard.edu/2020/09/18/remarks-by-commissioner-peirce-on-the-role-of-asset-management-in-esg-investing/.

9. *See* U.S. Sec. & Exch. Comm'n, *2020 Examination Priorities*, https://cdn.wide-area.com/acuris/files/private-equity-law-report/documents/OCIE%202020%20National%20Examination%20Program%20Priorities.pdf and U.S. Sec. & Exch. Comm'n, *2021 Examination Priorities*, https://www.sec.gov/files/2021-exam-priorities.pdf.

10. U.S. Sec. & Exch. Comm'n, *The Division of Examinations' Review of ESG Investing* (Apr. 9, 2021), https://www.sec.gov/files/esg-risk-alert.pdf.

11. *Id.* at 7.

are abiding by relevant impact- and non-impact related elements of their impact process as stated in the Fund's documents. For example: if a manager says it will evaluate certain criteria for Fund investments, it should maintain internal checklists and/or high-level investment committee meeting minutes to document that such evaluations have occurred; if a manager has promised that it will provide impact-specific reporting on an annual basis, it will need to develop and deliver that reporting on the stated timeline in the promised format.

While these examples of what the SEC may focus on in an examination are straightforward, there are many other instances where it may be unclear whether a statement in marketing or disclosure creates a concrete obligation to take a specific course of action. For example, in the preceding scenario, if the manager has said it "may consider" certain impact-related criteria by its investment committee, it may be ambiguous whether that has created an obligation to do so or merely a description of what might occur. In many cases, this ambiguity may be disadvantageous, both because regulators may interpret such statements as a concrete undertaking (where not intended) and because investors may feel the manager has been misleading (if viewed similarly and the manager does not engage in such analysis). Clarity in design and documentation—while sometimes easier said than done—can help to alleviate these ambiguities that may turn into regulatory problems.

Regulatory Examinations

Regulatory scrutiny primarily arises in the context of an exam (although in certain instances it could arise as a result of specific Fund investor complaints). For example, in March 2021, the SEC's Division of Examinations stated that it would "focus on" ESG products that registered investment advisers offer to investors.[12] Before that, in January 2020, the SEC's Division of Examinations announced that it had a "particular interest" in the accuracy and adequacy of disclosures provided by advisers offering clients new types of emerging investment strategies, such as strategies focused on sustainable and responsible investing, that incorporate ESG criteria.[13] In addition, in 2019 it was widely reported that the SEC staff had focused a sweep examination on the use of ESG criteria in certain advisers' investment processes. To that end, Impact Fund sponsors should

12. U.S. Sec. & Exch. Comm'n, *2021 Examination Priorities, Office of Compliance Inspections and Examinations*, at 28.

13. U.S. Sec. & Exch. Comm'n, *2020 Examination Priorities, Office of Compliance Inspections and Examinations*, at 15.

expect that the Division of Examinations staff might ask for the following types of information (among other types) in future examinations:

- Processes for developing the definition of terms relating to ESG or impact (e.g., the use of any internal definitions, the use of third-party definitions);
- Written policies and procedures (e.g., related to determining whether an investment qualifies as an appropriate impact or ESG investment, and documentation supporting such decisions and recommendations);
- The manager's internal compliance programs (e.g., impact audits, annual reviews, and reports on impact compliance from third parties);
- Information on the systems or data the manager uses to evaluate or "score" ESG investments (e.g., are they proprietary or external measurements and how the manager uses the "scores" to make investment decisions); and
- Performance information related to impact investments (e.g., how financially profitable they are and how much "impact" they had).

Other U.S. Regulatory and Legal Considerations

In the United States, there are a host of other ESG-related regulatory and legal requirements that may apply to a Fund depending on the nature of its investors. These include specific requirements that may apply to banking investors, government and state pension fund investors, charities and tax-exempt investors, and other institutions. For example, Funds that seek investors that are subject to the U.S. Department of Labor's (DOL's) regulation under the Employee Retirement Income Security Act of 1974, as amended (ERISA), which may include corporate pension funds and other retirement and institutional investors, should be aware of both (1) the DOL's "ESG Investing Rule," which states how and when ERISA fiduciaries may consider selecting plan investments to take into account non-pecuniary considerations, and (2) the "Proxy Voting Rule," which requires plan fiduciaries to put the economic interests of plan participants and beneficiaries first and to ensure that voting decisions support those interests. These complex rules, taken together, and unless changes occur after the date of this writing, would require that Impact Fund sponsors seeking to attract investment by persons subject to ERISA market and operate their Funds with these rules in mind.

To that end, in October 2021, the DOL released proposed regulations[14] pursuant to which plan fiduciaries, in certain circumstances, might be able to consider ESG factors when making investment decisions without violating their duties of loyalty and prudence. Specifically, the preamble notes that a purpose of the proposed regulations is to reduce uncertainty that may deter plan fiduciaries from taking steps in "improving investment portfolio resilience against the potential financial risks and impacts associated with climate change and other ESG factors."[15] The comment period for the proposed regulations ended on December 13, 2021, and as of the date of this writing, the DOL is reviewing the comments and will make any changes before issuing the final rule.

Non-U.S. Regulatory Considerations

While critical to understand for managers sponsoring non-U.S. vehicles and raising investor money from outside the United States, a thorough discussion of the non-U.S., and particularly the European Union (EU), regulatory approach to ESG and impact is outside the scope of this chapter (and which this book addresses in more detail in the country chapters in Part II). As a general matter, we note that regulation of Impact Funds and ESG investing in the EU has a longer history and is comparatively more robust and prescriptive than the SEC's approach to regulation in the United States. For example, as of March 2021, alternative investment fund managers (AIFMs) marketing in the EU need to comply with the EU Sustainable Finance Disclosure Directive (SFDR). Unlike the SEC's broad "fair and balanced" approach to Impact Fund disclosure, the SFDR is highly prescriptive. The SFDR requirements vary based on the size of the alternative investment fund (AIF), but the SFDR will require all AIFs to include at least some disclosure of how they consider and incorporate ESG factors if they market investments in the EU. The SFDR requirements apply to a broad range of investment managers, including all AIFMs (including U.S. sub-advisers). The SFDR also requires money managers to make policy decisions about how they will integrate

---

14. *Prudence and Loyalty in Selecting Plan Investments and Exercising Shareholder Rights, A Proposed Rule by the Employee Benefits Security Administration*, https://www.federalregister.gov/documents/2021/10/14/2021-22263/prudence-and-loyalty-in-selecting-plan-investments-and-exercising-shareholder-rights; *see also* U.S. Dep't of Labor, *US Department of Labor Proposes Rule to Remove Barriers to Considering Environmental, Social, Governance Factors in Plan Management*, 86 FR 57272, https://www.dol.gov/newsroom/releases/ebsa/ebsa20211013.

15. *Prudence and Loyalty in Selecting Plan Investments*, *supra* note 14, at 57275.

sustainability into their business, and the regulation will require that they make certain sustainability risk and other disclosures both when marketing to potential and current investors and on their public-facing websites. The SFDR is just one example for sponsors operating and raising investor capital from abroad of the need to devote considerable resources to understanding how the foreign regulatory scheme will apply to their Funds at the outset.

Key Terms and Documenting the Limited Partnership Agreement of Impact Fund

Many of the terms of an Impact Fund, and the process for drafting the Fund's governing documents, will be the same as for any other closed-end fund. Managers with existing fund structures may base the governing documents on the same template or precedent they have used for prior funds, with modifications for the actual terms and nature of the Impact Fund. For sponsors raising first-time funds, they will often work with their counsel to develop appropriate governing documents from precedent that fund counsel has developed internally. Terms that the parties often negotiate in private fund offerings and that may take on special importance in an Impact Fund include the following.

Key Economic Provisions

- **Management fees.** Impact Funds often need to have higher management fees—and may have higher "start-up" expenses—than other funds pursuing other investment strategies. This is often a product of the additional expenses that may result from needing to maintain unique internal infrastructure to support the Fund.
- **Performance hurdles.** If the general partner (GP) or its affiliates will earn performance-based compensation, due to the often lower-return targets for some Impact Fund assets, the GP may seek to have a lower performance hurdle than in other funds in order for it to receive performance allocations.
- **Fund expenses and organization expenses.** Managers should carefully review the list of Fund expenses to ensure they have flexibility to appropriately allocate expenses that may be unique to the Impact Fund's strategy; also, due to the additional "start-up" costs that may be associated with an Impact Fund, the manager may also seek to either avoid—or have a higher than usual expense cap for the Fund. Expenses should also allow for necessary service providers, such as impact measurement consultants, special impact auditors, and so on.

Governance and Key Person

- **Committee structure.** Most funds (impact or otherwise) have an Investment Committee (which is often situated in the investment manager) that will make key decisions for the Fund. In certain circumstances, Impact Funds may also create advisory boards or may consult with industry advisers/operating consultants for their expertise with respect to specific impact investments. Fund documents should spell out how the parties will divide relevant investment decision-making.
- **GP devotion of time and removal.** While devotion of time and key person issues are a focus of many fundraises, they may take on additional focus if there are key investment or operational personnel crucial to the impact program.
- **Investment strategy and limitations.** The investment strategy for the Fund will need to be well-defined, and the manager should be prepared to incorporate specific impact requirements in the partnership agreement. Investors may also request specific investment limitations given the impact-focused nature of the Fund, and may also require that the partnership agreement contain terms aimed at protecting the investors' non-profit or other status (e.g., provisions about program-related investments, UBTI or Community Reinvestment Act (CRA) credits).
- **Conflicts and divergent interest.** The Fund will need mechanics to deal with conflicts of interest and situations where the manager must seek limited partner or advisory committee consent, both for conflicts purposes and for instances where limited partner consent is necessary to address deviations from the Fund's impact focus. For example, Impact Funds may have mechanisms to consult with the advisory committee in instances where the manager does not expect to be able to achieve an investment's impact objectives as originally contemplated in the offering documents. In addition, conflicts may arise where the manager measures the Fund's impact without third-party oversight, because it will have incentive to maximize reported impact outcomes.
- **Investment allocations and co-investments.** For managers with other funds or with Impact Funds they may invest alongside—or consider investments similar to—their other funds, they must consider how they will address investment allocations (and how they will document allocation decisions). This will also be true if the manager will offer co-investments to investors or third parties, including when co-investment may be appropriate and on what terms.

Other Considerations

- **Investment period and term.** Managers will need to determine whether typical fund durations and investment periods are appropriate based on the Fund's investment focus. Some assets may need longer holding periods to meet outcomes.
- **Closing timelines.** Managers will need to consider how long they will need to market (and how extension mechanics will work).
- GP commitment. GP commitments are always a point of investor discussion, but may be a particular focal point, especially for first-time Impact Funds.
- **Other ESG factors.** Apart from the Fund's investment program, Impact Fund investors may seek to impose requirements that the Fund and the manager adhere to ESG requirements in their own operations, for example, hiring a certain percentage of minority-owned vendors, acquiring carbon credits to offset business travel, and so on.

Offering Documents and Disclosures of the Impact Fund

In addition to the partnership agreement, the vast majority of closed-end Impact Funds have a private placement memorandum (a "PPM," sometimes called an offering memorandum or confidential investment memorandum). Unlike the partnership agreement, which is a contract, the PPM serves multiple functions: it summarizes the key terms, it provides the narrative (or "why") for the Fund's investment strategy and approach to impact, and it is a disclosure document that provides the investor with key information about conflicts, tax disclosures, and other regulatory information related to the Fund.

As the PPM is essentially the prospectus for the private offering of interest in the Fund, antifraud rules under the U.S. Securities Act of 1933, as amended (the "Securities Act"), will apply; if the advisor is registered as an investment advisor with the SEC under the Advisers Act, then requirements of the marketing rules promulgated thereunder will also apply (and the Advisers Act generally has certain antifraud rules that apply to advisers not required to be registered or relying on exemptions from registration).[16] Managers affiliated with, or that sell Fund interests

16. Significant additional regulatory considerations arise in the context of a private offering of Fund interests under the Securities Act and under the U.S. Investment Company Act of 1940, as amended (the "Company Act)". The rules regarding private offerings and "investment company" exemptions under the Securities Act and

through, SEC-registered broker-dealers (including placement agents) will also need to evaluate Fund marketing materials under Financial Industry Regulatory Authority, Inc. (FINRA) rules.

Describing the Impact Strategy

Because impact definitions can be amorphous, it will be important for the PPM to describe the Fund's impact strategy in detail, often while also leaving room for further development of that strategy. This description should also be clear about how the Impact Fund intends to balance impact outcomes with potential financial returns. Managers should be careful to avoid using hyperbole or overpromising regarding the Fund's potential impact.

Past Impact Performance

It will also be important for the Impact Fund manager to be thoughtful and careful about how it reports the "impact" of prior funds, including with explanatory notes regarding how it has measured impact, how the current fund's impact thesis may deviate from that of a prior fund, and how past impact results are not necessarily indicative of future results. A manager should be mindful of anti-fraud and marketing rule requirements where reporting the past performance of specific investments, and it should not "cherry-pick" by discussing prior investments with positive impacts while omitting less successful investments.

Description of Impact Measurement

The PPM should also describe what types of measures the manager used to develop the Fund's investment thesis and objectives, and provide details on how the Fund plans to measure and provide reporting on both financial and impact-related performance. Many PPMs for Impact Funds have painstakingly developed template reporting and measurement information to help give assurance to prospective investors that the manager has the right systems in place to reach impact outcomes. Sponsors may also provide more detail on how "far down" the ownership ladder they expect the Fund's impact objectives to reach, for example, how they will implement impact initiatives at portfolio companies, in company supply chains and vendor relations and in the communities in which portfolio companies may operate. Whether the Fund will make controlled

Company Act, respectively, are complex and are key reasons why it is crucial to engage with experienced legal counsel before any marketing or distribution of materials to prospective Fund investors occurs.

investments may dictate how much influence the sponsor may have and how much reporting it may require from portfolio companies; the PPM should be clear whether the investment strategy will not exercise control over certain investments.

Other Disclaimers and Disclosures

Sponsors will also need to include appropriate disclaimers (including related to performance), be fair-and-balanced in their presentation of how the investment program will work, highlight potential performance and operational pitfalls, and include disclosures of associated risks (the sponsor typically develops these with counsel). Some examples of potentially important disclaimers and disclosures include:

- An explanation of how the manager intends to address divergences between the Fund's impact objectives and its financial objectives during the life of the Fund.
- For Impact Funds that prioritize impact outcomes over economic returns, sponsors should disclose the financial risks, including potential loss of investment in the Fund or lower than anticipated returns or the costs of remedying negative developments at portfolio companies as part of the strategy.
- Funds will also need to clarify if they plan to exit investments that will not achieve impact-related goals. While many Funds are able to achieve impact and economic returns harmoniously, it is necessary for sponsors to include information for how they will handle conflicts of interest in order to make candid and fulsome disclosure to investors (the Fund documents should also specify whether an advisory committee must consent to such conflicts).
- How the manager will address other conflicts of interest, such as the allocation and co-investment issues described earlier. The manager should also include any other conflicts of interests, including, for example, if the Fund will use affiliated service providers or joint venture partners in pursuing its strategy. Because conflicts disclosure is fact-specific, it will vary greatly depending on the other activities of the funds sponsor, details about how the sponsor will operate the Fund, and the overall complexity of the sponsor's business.
- The fact that the Impact Fund may not achieve its investment objectives given its more circumscribed focus (e.g., if there are not sufficient available appropriate investments), difficulties in

obtaining impact reporting and measurements and other risks, such as those driven by the nascent state of the industry.

- Information about exit risk, both because impact investments may be less likely to have strong public or secondary markets and because an exit could undermine the impact thesis (e.g., if there is a chance that the exit from an affordable housing investment may be to sell it to a market-rate real estate operator). Investors may also try to seek general assurances from the sponsor about how it will consider exit risk as part of the impact thesis.

The sponsor will generally update the PPM throughout the life of the fundraise (typically through updates or stand-alone supplements) to reflect changes in the impact thesis or fund terms as a result of negotiations, updated investment performance (where applicable), to provide details about Fund investments for subsequent closing investors, and to discuss new potential conflicts of interest or risks that may arise in the context of the Fund.

Conclusion

There is virtually no question that the Impact Fund industry will continue to grow both inside and outside the United States as investors continue to demand ESG and impact products and as sponsors raise new Funds to meet that demand. That growth will bring increased regulatory scrutiny from U.S. and non-U.S. regulators and possibly more ESG- and impact-related lawmaking, as well as an increasing sophistication of both sponsors and investors. As the market matures, Impact Fund sponsors and investors, and especially their legal advisers, must take care to keep up with these developments and use that knowledge to help guide sponsors in their Fund documentation and overall decision-making.

5

Doing the Deal

Deborah Burand[1]

This chapter attempts to answer a simple, yet complex question. What does a lawyer negotiating an impact investment do differently from what a skilled deal lawyer does when negotiating more traditional market transactions?

Even as I ask this question, I worry that I am trying to explain how a hybrid car's engine differs from that of car running only on gas. That is to say, both types of cars can transport us at the same speeds. Both look a lot alike, at least until we raise the hood. And, neither are going to be around much once fully electric cars take to the roads. But, if today's technologies are likely to become obsolete, why learn how their mechanics differ? Or, to put it in the context of this chapter, if impact investing is likely to go mainstream in coming years, why examine how lawyering clients engaging in impact investments differ from advising clients engaging in more traditional market transactions?

I would argue that the more work we do now to understand the mindset and legal toolbox of today's impact investment lawyer, the more likely the legal profession will be able to navigate and add value to the business and finance deals of tomorrow, whether characterized as impact or otherwise. According to some, that tomorrow is coming fast. Look at the flood of money flowing into environmental, social, and governance (ESG) funds. Notice the generational transfers of trillions of dollars of wealth from baby boomers to millennials. If these trends continue, as seems likely, deal lawyers will need to shift their mindsets and retool their skills—fast.

1. Professor of Clinical Law, Director of International Transactions Clinic, Faculty Co-Director, Grunin Center for Law and Social Entrepreneurship, NYU School of Law.

Sir Ronald Cohen, in his 2020 book *Impact: Reshaping Capitalism to Drive Real Change*,[2] describes a world where impact will be at the center of our economic system. In that new world, decisions no longer will be made based on calculations of how to make as much money as possible with the lowest possible risk. Rather, decisions will be based on how to make "as much money as possible but in a way that is consistent with achieving the highest impact and with the lowest level of risk." In short, he envisions a society where impact is in its very DNA, and the world of business and finance turns on a "triple helix of risk-return-impact."[3]

Reshaping capitalism into "impact capitalism," he explains, requires a shift in mindsets. But, as he and others have observed, that mindset shift is already starting to take place among business and finance leaders. So, it should come as no surprise that professions that provide services to businesses and financial institutions also need to undertake a similar mindset shift. Lawyers are no exception.

I was trained as a young corporate associate in a Wall Street law firm during the mid-1980s. One morning, a senior partner of the law firm started the weekly meeting of our corporate finance practice group by quoting Gordon Gekko from the 1987 movie *Wall Street*. "Greed is good," he told all of us. Bewildered, I darted looks at the rest of the lawyers around me. Some were smiling; others were laughing out loud. But some were furrowing their brows just as I was. I fled to the women's bathroom as soon as the meeting ended. There other young, female associates were gathering. We spoke in hushed tones, lest one of the firm's handful of female partners at the time also be nearby. Had we heard correctly? Were we really being told to embrace greed in our transactional practice of law? Looking back, I now think that what that senior partner was trying to say, albeit perhaps more shockingly direct than others might have, is that the motivations of the firm's corporate clients needed to be understood by the lawyers who served them.

Understanding greed as a motivation for doing business is relatively easy, as distasteful as that may have seemed to my idealistic younger self. Seen in that light, an exhortation like Gekko's greed is good can be viewed as but a pithy summary of the old business paradigm trumpeted by Milton Friedman in the 1970s and 1980s—that is, the business of business is to make as much money as possible with the lowest possible risk.

---

2. Sir Ronald Cohen, Impact: Reshaping Capitalism to Drive Real Change (2020).

3. *Id.* at 12.

My job as a corporate lawyer in the mid-1980s, that law firm meeting reminded me, was narrower than I hoped it would be. Changing the world for the better was to be confined largely to pro bono practice. When it came to billing clients, however, the overwhelming mindset of the time was that transactional lawyers were being paid to help clients pursue big profits with little risk. In short, I had been hired to be a professional worrier, paid handsomely by my clients to imagine all the possible risks that might beset a transaction and then find ways to avoid, mitigate, or transfer those risks to others who might be better suited to managing them.

I should have seen this coming, in retrospect. Months before that office meeting, I had pulled several consecutive all-nighters to help close a leveraged buyout of a company that manufactured car parts. Surprising even myself, I summoned the courage to ask the partner in charge what the social utility was of that leveraged buyout. After an uncomfortable pause, he told me that I was not being paid to ask that question. Then I received a lecture about Adam Smith's metaphor of the invisible hand and the efficiencies that come in a free market economy when individuals work to advance their own self-interests.

I wish I had been a better student of Adam Smith's work so that I could have responded more articulately to this impromptu lecture. As Sir Ronald Cohen reminds us, before Adam Smith published *The Wealth of Nations* in 1776, Smith wrote *The Theory of Moral Sentiments*, which provides a theory for how morals and ethics provide a foundation for human behavior. There Smith writes ". . . there are evidently some principles in [human] nature, which interest [humankind] in the fortune of others. . . ."[4]

Cohen and his G7 counterparts married these two ideas of Smith in a report published in 2014, entitled "Impact Investment: The Invisible Heart of Markets." This G7 report boldly predicted:

> The world is on the brink of a revolution in how we solve society's toughest problems. The force capable of driving this revolution is 'social impact investing,' which harnesses entrepreneurship, innovation and capital to power social improvement.[5]

Today deal lawyers are being paid to ask questions about the social and environmental utility of the transactions they support. I like to imagine

4. Adam Smith, The Theory of Moral Sentiments, 1759, pt. I, sec. I, chap. I, para. 1, http://oll.libertyfund.org/192/39008/908774.

5. G7 Report, *Impact Investment: Harnessing the Invisible Heart of Markets* (2014), Impact-Investment-Report.pdf (gsgii.org).

that somewhere, perhaps even in a conference room of my old law firm, a senior partner is telling young associates, "Impact is good." At the very least, a growing number of law firms are now recognizing and building practice areas to help clients that are focusing on the sustainability of their investments by looking at environmental, social, and governance (ESG) considerations.[6]

Now that a third dimension—impact—is being introduced into the investment transactions that we structure and document, our mindsets as deal lawyers have to change. Yes, we still are professional worriers. That is unlikely to ever change. But we need to add another perspective to how we look at deals. We need to put our imagination to work to look also at how these transactions will impact, for good and for bad, society. And we need to help our clients contract to achieve profits and desirable impacts, all the while managing risk.

So here is the good news. Achieving meaningful social and environmental impact can also help minimize the risks of a transaction. Thus, an impact-focused, transactional practice is not quite as foreign as it might first seem. This is not just a matter, as some seasoned deal lawyers might think, of putting a new brand on old skills or parroting impact lingo while conducting business no differently than before. Rather, it is necessary to shift our mindsets and expand our legal toolboxes, lest we jeopardize the goals of the impact investment transactions that we are negotiating, structuring, and documenting.

Shifting Our Mindsets—Spotting Blind Spots

To think differently about the roles to be played by deal counsel to an impact investment transaction, past modes of counselling clients may be informative, but not fully fit to purpose. So, what blind spots are most likely to surface for a lawyer engaging in an impact investment transactional practice?

6. *See* Dylan Jackson, *ESG Practice Groups Proliferate in Big Law, Driven by New Priorities*, Am. Law. (Feb. 11, 2021, 10:53 AM); *see also* Jenny B. Davis, *Corporate Lawyers Can Help Clients Change the World—And Bill for It—With This Growing Practice Area*, A.B.A. J. (Apr. 1, 2020, 3:40 AM), https://www.abajournal.com/magazine/article/in-this-growing-practice-area-corporate-lawyers-can-help-clients-change-the-world-and-bill-for-it (describing growing practice areas for corporate lawyers advising social entrepreneurs and impact investors).

Discerning Intentions

First, is the question of understanding the contracting parties' intentions. This is not just a matter of degree. Figuring out how much money the parties hope to make is a very different calculus from figuring out how much social or environment impact they hope to achieve in an impact investment. Financial returns are comparatively easy to define and then calculate. Not so with impact returns. One client's desired impact could be very different from another's. And clients' willingness to trade financial returns for impact also can vary widely.

Similarly, clients' perception of and tolerance for social and environmental risks also is changing. What might have been a tolerable risk in the past may no longer be acceptable. Accordingly, clients also can have different and evolving risk tolerances when it comes to avoiding negative or unintended societal or environmental impacts.

Even when impact goals have been agreed by the parties, those impact targets sometimes can be devilishly hard to measure, especially if the parties are looking to achieve impact outcomes, not more limited impact inputs or outputs. No wonder some pay for performance deals, like social impact bonds, often choose impact outcomes that involve beds. We can count how many people are in the beds of hospitals, homeless shelters, or jails. And, we can count how many fewer beds are occupied after interventions funded by our client's impact investment have been delivered. Other impact outcomes are much harder to define or measure. Hence, the growing focus today on collecting, measuring, and verifying impact data, as discussed in Chapter 3.

Identifying and Engaging Stakeholders

Another blind spot that can sink an impact investment is the question of how to define and engage affected stakeholders, particularly those beneficiaries whose interests are being directly touched by an impact investment. An impact investment negotiation that focuses only on advancing the interests of those sitting at the table runs the risk of missing much of the point of the transaction. To complicate matters even more, stakeholder interests may differ from those of both the impact investor and the investee.

Stakeholder engagement is tricky. While we lawyers might be skilled at discovering and articulating the interests of our respective clients, doing the same for a group not in the room (and possibly unrepresented by counsel) is much harder—particularly, if that group is not easily identifiable, changes over time, or speaks with many, possibly conflicting, voices.

Right-Sizing Contracts

A third blind spot that can limit the effectiveness of deal counsel in impact investing is the decision about how "completely" or "incompletely" to contract for impact.

Developing deal documentation that memorializes parties' expectations of each other certainly is important in advancing the likelihood of a successful relationship, be it in an impact investment or a more traditional market transaction. Where the goals of contracting parties are three-dimensional (e.g., make money and achieve impact while minimizing risks to both), these relationships can become even more complex. Hence, so might the contracts.

Right-sizing contracts and legal services to fit an impact investment's complex yet sometimes interrelated goals can be challenging, especially if that investment involves comparatively small amounts of money or is expected to generate relatively small financial returns. For some lawyers, the answer may be not to try to negotiate every possible corner of an impact investment, but to deliberately contract incompletely—particularly those provisions dealing with the achievement of impact. Nobel laureate, economist Oliver Hart's work on incomplete contracting is relevant here.[7] Just as compensation contracts and venture capital investments, to name a few, often make use of incomplete contracts, so too may this style of contracting suit impact investments. Knowing what to nail down *ex ante* in a contract, and what to leave to later decision-making processes is not always obvious in an impact investment, however.

Getting this calculation right is all the more important in those impact investments that prioritize contractual flexibility over certainty of outcomes or even enforcement—be it through litigation or arbitration. Accordingly, sharing experiences and contract approaches will be important in shaping how contracting for impact evolves.

Underestimating Legal Uncertainty

A fourth blind spot, which unfortunately plagues all lawyers working in the field of impact investing, is that much of what is being contracted for may be charting new ground, not only in the law but also for the legal cultures involved.

Our clients are facing evolving standard-setting and regulatory regimes in impact investing—formal and informal, mandatory and

7. Oliver Hart, *Incomplete Contracts and the Theory of the Firm*, Working Paper Department of Economics, Number 448, May 1987, Massachusetts Institute of Technology.

voluntary. And those regimes are not yet harmonized globally. Related, views are changing within the United States and in jurisdictions outside of the United States about what fiduciary duties will be imposed (or not) on our clients.

Additionally, our clients may be engaging with parties that are incorporated under one of the new legal forms created in the United States and beyond to house social entrepreneurial activities. Or our clients may have chosen to incorporate under one of these new forms themselves. (See Chapter 2 for a description of these forms.) Many of these new forms, like benefit corporations, low-profit limited liability companies (L3Cs), social purpose corporations, and public benefit limited partnerships, are untested both in the boardroom and in the courtroom.

Furthermore, within the United States, the state legislation authorizing such new forms can vary significantly from state to state. A public benefit corporation incorporated in Delaware, for example, faces significantly different obligations and restrictions than those confronted by benefit corporations incorporated in say, Ohio. And some of those state laws, and hence obligations, continue to change.[8] All of which confuses matters further.

In sum, legal uncertainty abounds as our clients privately contract in spaces that later may be shaped by government policy and judicial review.

Shifting Our Mindsets—Avoiding Blind Spots

How can a lawyer try to avoid these blind spots and consequent pitfalls? It may sound simple and obvious, but one place to start is to refine the questions to be asked when coming to the table to negotiate an impact investment. As one observer has said, "[i]n the old economy, it was all about having the answers. But in today's dynamic, lean economy, it's more about asking the right questions."[9]

What are the "right questions" to ask when preparing to start an impact investment negotiation? Here is a starting place. Get to know the: (1) language, (2) client, (3) counterparty(ies), (4) affected stakeholders/beneficiaries, (5) impact goals and related measurements, and (6) yourself. Easier said than done, particularly the last category.

8. *See* Forrest, Greggs & Yang, *State of Social Enterprise and the Law 2020–2021*, https://www.law.nyu.edu/sites/default/files/Tepper%20Report%20-%20State%20of%20Social%20Enterprise%20and%20the%20Law%20-%202020-2021.pdf.

9. Eric Ries, *What If Everyone in the Company Could Answer Their Own Questions? A More Beautiful Question*, https://amorebeautifulquestion.com/if-everyone-company-could-answer-their-own-questions-2/.

1. Getting to know the language of impact investing

Impact investing is rife with acronyms and with words that are misleading, to say the least. Perhaps the alphabet soup of acronyms cannot be helped given the relatively early stage of impact investing. New behaviors often spawn new language. Accordingly, it behooves a lawyer entering the field of impact investing to become familiar with the meaning of acronyms like SDGs (Sustainable Development Goals), KPIs (Key Performance Indicators), GIIN (Global Impact Investing Network), IRIS (Impact Reporting and Investment Standards), JII (Joint Impact Indicators) and SASB (Sustainability Accounting Standards Board), to name a few. Lest this soup not be murky enough, some acronyms have more than one meaning, thereby confusing matters still further. For example, "PRI" can refer to political risk insurance or it could be describing a program-related investment. Imagine the headaches that ensue when negotiating an impact investment that involves both types of PRI—political risk insurance and a program-related investment.

On the other hand, as lawyers are often the keeper of the words—the legal profession's tool of choice—it is up to us to insist that the words used in impact investing convey understandable meaning. When a client creates a new term to capture its newest impact investment instrument, we should not shirk from pushing back against misleading language.

Here are several examples of misleading terms that have crept into the impact investing field. A "demand dividend" is not a dividend. (It is a debt vehicle designed to improve the repayment cycle for impact investors and ease capital access for social enterprises.)[10] Just as "social impact bonds" and "development impact bonds" are rarely bonds. And, as I would have liked to advise the creators of a multistate essay examination question and model answer used by the New York State Bar that was administered in July of 2020, a company that is certified as a "B-Corporation" by the B Lab is not the same thing as a company that incorporates under state legislation as a "benefit corporation." Not even close.[11] It does the impact investing space no good to tolerate linguistic confusion of these sorts.

---

10. https://thegiin.org/assets/Santa%20Clara%20U_Demand-Dividend-Description.pdf.

11. Even those charged with developing bar examination questions, such as a multistate essay examination (MEE) question posed in July 2020 to those taking the bar examination in New York State and elsewhere, have been thrown by this linguistic confusion. In that instance, the MEE question provided a hypothetical fact pattern that ignored a recent change in the Model Business Corporation Act, which now explicitly provides for benefit corporations. Then, the model answer to this same MEE question erroneously interchanged the term "B-Corporation" for "benefit

2. Getting to know the client

Any client-focused lawyer will recognize that it takes work to fully know a client. When representing clients in the impact investing space, this knowledge can be vital to the success of a transaction. As noted, clients can vary—a lot—when it comes to discerning where they fall on the spectrum of impact and financial return expectations. And they can equally vary with respect to their appetite and tolerance for risks—impact and financial.

Some have tried to map client preferences in this regard, for example, identifying some investors as "impact-first," other investors as "finance-first," and still others as "catalyst-first."[12] But clients may defy easy categorization.

Moreover, clients can be slippery. It is not easy to neatly pin them down. How they identify themselves today may not mesh well with how they will want to act tomorrow. Distinctions of impact-first and finance-first can be quickly jettisoned when payment defaults are imminent. Take, for example, the impact-first lenders to a troubled microfinance institution that saw their borrower prepaying the more expensive loans of finance-first lenders ahead of the cheaper loans the impact-first lenders had provided. A financially sound decision by the troubled borrower no doubt, but that is not how many of the impact-first lenders saw it as they howled in protest over the unfairness of the borrower's treatment of its creditors. A possible, and perhaps not surprising, lesson from this example is that when impact investors espouse workout principles that call for the equitable treatment of similarly situated creditors, they do not necessarily mean equitable treatment of "like-minded" creditors.

---

corporation" for purposes of analyzing whether a shareholder of a winery could sue the winery for a violation of State A's laws (which has not provided for legislation authorizing benefit corporations) after it incorporates in State B (which has authorized the incorporation of benefit corporations). The model answer starts its analysis with a wrong assertion, saying that "State A does not allow B-Corporations while State B does allow B-Corporations." To be clear, should the drafter of that MEE question and its accompanying model answer ever read this rather nerdy footnote, a state should care no more about whether wineries (or any other companies) incorporated in its jurisdiction are certified as B-Corporations by the B-Lab than it would concern itself about whether those wineries are certified by an accredited certifying agent (ACA) who has verified that their wines meet all appropriate specifications in the USDA organic regulations.

12. *What Is Impact Investment?*, Morrison Foerster, https://www.mofo.com/special-content/impact-investing/what-is-impact-investing.html.

3. Getting to know the counterparties

If knowing your own client can be challenging, it is likely even harder to know the other parties at the table. Reputations matter in the field of impact investing. Impact investing is a small enough world, at least for now, to be able to provide some visibility on how other investors or investees have conducted themselves in negotiating and living within other impact investments. Like those who live in small towns, knowing that neighbors are watching (and, possibly, gossiping) can curb aggressive or inappropriate behaviors, at least some of the time. But the small-town feel of impact investing is likely to change as more players enter this market. Some of these new players may either not yet have a track record in impact investing or their past behaviors are not widely known within the field of impact investing. Consequently, it will likely be up to the lawyers to spark some of the harder conversations at the negotiation table about contracting parties' motivations and practices. And then it will be up to the lawyers to survey the resulting landscape, bandage any resulting wounds, and set up guard rails to shape and limit the range of acceptable, future behaviors by those contracting parties.

4. Getting to know the stakeholders/beneficiaries

Knowing the affected stakeholders/beneficiaries of an impact investment presupposes that this group is cohesive enough to be knowable. That is an assumption that might not prove true in an impact investment—particularly where the desired impact is likely to be dispersed across a broad spectrum of stakeholders. Yet, where a group can be identified, there is work to be done to solicit stakeholder input as impact investments are structured and, equally important, as those investments are managed going forward. It is no accident that the United Nation's guidance for issuers of SDG-bonds includes principles, such as:

a. Have "transparent mechanisms to identify stakeholders materially affected or likely to be affected by its decisions and activities and promotes stakeholder involvement in decisions like:
   i. Ensure meaningful agency in decision making and impact management practices that affect them;
   ii. Transparently keep stakeholders informed of actions, progress, and lessons;"

b. Establish "effective grievance and reparation mechanisms for affected [s]takeholders;" and

c. Manage "data ownership (stakeholders) and privacy issues and ethical and commercial issues regarding data gathering, use, and disclosure (acting on behalf of stakeholders)."[13]

5. Getting to know the impact goals and related measurements

Young deal lawyers today are often trained in not only the legal skills necessary to transact business deals, but also in basic financial skills, like reading a balance sheet. One can imagine that this training soon will extend, at least for those engaging in an impact investing practice, to introducing lawyers to the knowledge and skills needed to make sense of impact goals and the impact measurement systems being created to evaluate progress made in achieving those goals. While the heavy lifting for exercising impact management skills will rightfully remain the responsibility of clients, lawyers will need to develop insights into impact analysis, just as they now are expected to understand financial analysis, so that they can document how parties have agreed to define, measure, report, and verify impact data.

Pressure on lawyers, seasoned and more junior, to learn and become familiar with the collection and management of impact data is only likely to intensify as regulators around the world raise the bar and require more reporting on the positive and negative impacts of investments of any type. Impact transparency, as some have called it, is coming and it is unlikely to be confined to just those investments that self-identify as impact investments. Indeed, if the growth of ESG funds continues to outpace impact investment funds, as discussed in this book, it is likely that the establishment of ground rules for reporting on the ESG performance of investment funds will set a baseline for what impact investment funds also will be expected to report.

6. Getting to know yourself

Why does knowing yourself figure prominently in an impact investment practice? Based on my experiences practicing in this field, there are at least three reasons that increasing one's self-awareness can help a lawyer to better counsel clients conducting impact investments.

13. United Nations Development Programme, SDG Impact Standards: Bond Issuers, Version 1.0, March 2021, https://sdgimpact.undp.org/assets/SDG-Impact-Standards-for-Bonds-Version-1_0-FINAL_EN.pdf.

First, as should be clear by now, impact investments will be shaped by our clients' values and beliefs, perhaps values and beliefs that are quite different from a lawyer's personal values or beliefs. When a lawyer's belief system and values mirror that of a client, work often feels more meaningful. On the other hand, cynicism can take root if the impact target seems impossibly out of reach, or a client's commitment to achieving that impact target seems compromised or, worse, insincere. Self-awareness can help keep that cynicism in check. It also can help to flag ethical issues that may require a lawyer to walk away from a possible representation.

More practically, however, knowing yourself is also important for creating a negotiating style that is effective in transacting impact investments. Parties to an impact investment may have different expectations as to how collaborative, transparent, or adversarial they expect a negotiation to be. A lawyer's negotiation style that might be welcome or expected in a more commercial transaction might be frowned upon when negotiating an impact investment. As in all deals, it helps to take cues from a client when determining how hard to press a point. But that also requires a degree of self-awareness and self-control to be able to see those client cues, particularly if subtle or, even, masked. That is not to say that an impact investment negotiation will not evoke passionate disagreement among the parties. Far from it. In fact, it may very well be that impact investment negotiations are more passionate than deals in which the primary thing at stake is money. Keeping your cool as a lawyer in an impact investment negotiation can be hard to do, particularly when your client does not.

Finally, part of knowing yourself requires also knowing what you want to gain from engaging in an impact investment practice. Are you looking for a satisfying pro bono practice that makes use of and grows your transactional skills? Or are you looking to build a fully billable practice that allows you, as well as your clients, to do well financially by doing good in the world? Or are you somewhere in between—ready to provide pro bono services now but hoping that impact investing could become a practice area in the future, particularly as you gain more experience? Making clear your own intentions is important as you navigate your commitment to an impact investing practice. Of course, this is not a decision that can be made in a vacuum. Your law firm's pro bono policies may dictate what type, if any, impact investment transactions are eligible for pro bono or low bono services.[14] Even if a firm's policies do not constrain

14. Impact Investments, APCO Sustainability and Social Impact, https://apcoworldwide.com/services/sustainability-social-impact/.

a pro bono practice in impact investing, some practice areas may not be conducive to doing so for marketing/business development purposes. Consider, for example, a tax-exempt organization practice, fund formation practice, or other practice areas where serving some clients on a pro bono basis could cannibalize or make it hard to justify billing other similarly situated clients for comparable services.

Expanding the Toolbox—Making It Real

We are entering a new stage in impact investing. As the head of the International Finance Corporation (IFC) has put it, we've moved from the "what" to the "how" of impact investing.[15] Given that deal lawyers are very much about building the architecture of transactional relationships, our skills are particularly well-suited to facilitating the "how" of impact investing.

The IFC defines impact investments as "investments that are made in companies or organizations with the *intent* to *contribute measurable* positive social or environmental *impact*, alongside a financial return (emphasis added).[16] This definition shines a light on three aspects of impact investing that drive investors to behave differently than they might in a more commercial transaction. As they act differently, so too must their lawyers. These three aspects are (1) intentions, (2) contributions, and (3) measurement of impact.

First is the setting of *intentions*. Whose intentions matter—the investor, the investee, or both? Context matters here. While investor intentions are a necessary pre-condition to the making of an impact investment, the intentions of investees matter too. Accordingly, the extent to which parties agree on intentions and, hence, transaction goals can make or break an impact investment.

Some impact investors have not moved beyond the setting of intentions. They will ask their lawyers to memorialize the parties' intentions in the deal documentation by specifying the impact goals of the transaction in the recitals, but not do much more. Others may go a step further and set boundaries around the uses to which an investment can be put, but then stop there. Some "use of proceeds" bonds, like green bonds or social bonds, may fall into this category.

15. IFC Operating Principles for Impact Management, https://www.impactprinciples.org/.

16. *Id.*

Second is ascertaining the *contribution* that the investment is expected to make. Put differently, how does the making of this particular investment, and, related, the actions of the investor in managing this investment over its life likely contribute to the desired impact?

Investors that pay attention to how their investments contribute to impact may ask their lawyers to help them structure a transaction or modify traditional investment instruments to advance the likelihood of achieving impact. Examples are blended financings that aim to catalyze a variety of funding sources by purposefully using credit enhancements or building capital stacks that promise to de-risk elements of an impact investment, thereby attracting a broader range of funders with varying risk tolerances.

Similarly, just as the making of an investment and crowding in of more and varied funding sources might shape the extent to which an investment contributes to impact, so too can exiting from a transaction. This has given rise to discussions about what a "responsible" exit looks like in the context of an impact investment. A responsible exit will take into consideration the investor's motivation for making the investment in the first place. Consequently, a responsible exit from an impact investment will not be solely motivated by financial returns. Instead, a responsible exit from an impact investment will be structured to preserve, sustain, or even optimize the contributions made by that investment to desired social or environmental impacts. A performance aligned stock instrument provides an example of a structured exit used in impact investing. This instrument is designed to provide investors with desired and reliable liquidity but preserve founder control over the investee's mission and operations.[17]

Third is determining the appropriate *measurement of impact* (both desired and unexpected). How will investors monitor progress toward impact goals? When (and how) will investors take corrective action should this progress slow? And finally, how (and when) will the investor evaluate *ex post* achievement of the investment's impact goals? As these questions suggest, impact measurement is not static. Just as data gleaned from financial reports can shape investor behavior over the life of the investment, so too will the collection of impact data.

Lawyers can play an important role in forging each of these three components of impact investing—intention, contribution, and measurement. Common to all is the question of how to ensure that the interests

---

17. See description of performance aligned stock at https://www.womblebonddickinson.com/us/insights/alerts/new-investment-structure-performance-aligned-stock.

of contracting parties are aligned going into an impact investment. But the story doesn't end there. Lawyers can help in also figuring out how to maintain that alignment of interests over the life of the investment.

This question of how best to align and maintain alignment of interests in a contractual relationship is not unique to impact investing, of course. Even Adam Smith recognized that where there was a misalignment of interests across parties, they were unlikely to fully realize the gains of cooperation. In his case, he was looking at sharecropping arrangements and saw that the misalignment of interests in those arrangements often resulted in giving tenants insufficient reason to improve the land they tilled.[18]

Nor are impact investors the first to create incentives and disincentives to try to maintain an alignment of interests among contracting parties. Where impact objectives are inextricably linked to the financial success of an investment and vice versa, maintaining an alignment of interests is less complicated. Social impact bonds (SIBs) and development impact bonds (DIBs) are examples of impact investments that positively correlate financial return with the achievement of impact outcomes. If these transactions run their expected course, greater impact achievements of SIBs and DIBs typically will generate greater financial returns for their investors. But even these transactions have experienced challenges in maintaining an alignment of interests across all of the parties over the life of the transaction.

In other types of impact investments, financial returns and impact achievements are not so closely correlated, and, at times, require trade-offs. Here the challenges of maintaining an alignment of interests are magnified. In those instances, impact investors may decide to use financial rewards to encourage their investees to meet impact goals. For example, some impact investors have been willing to reduce interest rates charged on loans to borrowers if impact milestones are met. Or impact investors may tranche investments, investing more funds only when and if impact milestones are met. More rare, some impact investors aim to penalize (or more likely, to threaten the imposition of penalties on) investees for sub-standard impact performance. These penalties, real or threatened, can vary from increasing interest rates to imposing a mandatory prepayment or share redemption, depending on how seriously the investee underperforms or, worse still, ignores negative consequences affecting the intended beneficiaries of the impact investment.

18. For more on this issue, see Joseph D. Reid, Jr., *Sharecropping in History and Practice*, 49(2) Agric. Hist. 426–40 (Apr. 1975).

Whether positively correlated or inversely correlated, whenever financial rewards are linked to impact goals, there is a risk that perverse incentives might creep into the transaction that throw the parties' interests out of alignment. For example, investees may be tempted to "juice" the impact data if not verified by a third party, or they may cherry pick among beneficiaries so that the only those beneficiaries that are likely to show a demonstrable improvement are targeted for services or products.

This can happen more subtly too. For example, decisions might be made to slightly lower the quality of an impact service or product, for example, to reduce financial expenditures. To minimize the chances of this kind of impact performance "shading," it is useful to set clear performance standards *ex ante*, and then ensure that there is a good deal of visibility during the investment around how well those performance standards are being met.

Of course, it is not always investee behaviors to be worried about. Perverse incentives can shape investor behavior too. In this context, it is important to remember that, while the financial returns of an impact investment typically accrue to the investor, the impact benefits will likely be more broadly dispersed to others – namely affected beneficiaries. So, some impact investors may feel pressure to maximize financial returns, at the expense of impact returns. This can be particularly true when impact investors themselves are under pressure from funders to deliver financial returns. To respond to this issue, some investors in impact investment funds have started linking the fund manager's compensation to both the financial returns and the social returns of the fund (as described in Chapter 4).

It is not always easy to predict whether an alignment of interests around impact goals and financial returns will stand the test of time, particularly when events outside of the parties' control throw impact goals or financial returns off course. Take the SIBs and DIBs discussed earlier. Many of these investments have had to respond to fast-changing and unexpected circumstances that have taken place during the life of these transactions. Think pandemics, catastrophic climate events, or other acts of god that are outside of the contracting parties' control. These events can impede the actual achievement of the desired impacts, as well as hamper the extent to which impact can be measured.

It is at times like these that "boilerplate" contractual provisions may prove woefully inadequate to the job in an impact investment. Take, for example, a force majeure clause that excuses parties from performance for a designated period of time should an unexpected event outside of the parties' control take place. Excusing the financial performance of parties to an impact investment in such a circumstance may make good sense. But should these same parties be excused from impact performance too? What if the very impact objectives at the heart of the transaction are to protect vulnerable beneficiaries? Often folks will refer to the need to increase the flow of "patient" capital into impact investments. But aren't there times when the capital funding impact investments should be *impatient*—particularly when vulnerable lives are at stake? I continue to wrestle with these questions and suspect I am not alone among those who also counsel clients engaged in impact investments.

Given these complexities, how do lawyers embed impact into a transaction? Here are some of the more obvious opportunities for embedding impact throughout the life cycle of an impact investment from cradle to grave: (1) due diligence, (2) structuring, (3) documenting, (4) managing/governing, and, finally, (5) exiting.

1. Due Diligence

The goals of due diligence are many. As with commercial investments, impact investors will use the due diligence process to identify, measure, and consider how best to allocate risks and returns should the investment move forward. Due diligence in an impact investment context can perform other functions too, however.

The due diligence process provides an opportunity for the impact investor to learn how fully impact objectives and considerations are embedded in the DNA of the investee—its constituent documents, key personnel, strategy, and operations. Due diligence also can provide insights into how vulnerable the investee might be to pressures to let its mission drift. This information can be used to help an impact investor evaluate the extent to which guardrails are in place and are up to the job of minimizing such a drift. Or whether safeguards should be structured into the transaction.

This is an opportunity for the impact investor to come to agreement with the investee (and perhaps those funding the impact investor) about how to embed impact considerations into the investment terms so as to optimize the investee's future impact performance. Where there are obvious shortcomings in the investee's impact performance to date, this is also an opportunity to agree upon a program for rectifying or responding to these issues, and to determine whether improvements in impact performance are a condition precedent or condition subsequent to the impact investment going forward. For example, some impact investors use the due diligence process to identify existing impact data collection and management processes of the potential investee so as to inform what else might be required (or not) of the investee going forward.

2. Structuring

As noted previously, key to structuring an impact investment is paying attention to how effectively interests are aligned at the onset of the investment and then to develop mechanisms that can help maintain that alignment over the life of the investment. To put it more succinctly, here is an opportunity to "design to align."[19] Deal structures also can play a crucial role in revealing the extent to which interests stay in or move out of alignment. What can make an impact investment different from its more commercial counterpart is the three dimensions of interests that need to be aligned—profit, risk, and impact. Another related aspect of an impact investment, which may differ from more commercial transactions, is how its structure may need to make deliberate room for the engagement and feedback of affected stakeholders/beneficiaries.

3. Documentation

Documenting an impact investment is not easy for many of the reasons explored earlier. And there is a very real risk that the complexities of an impact investment will be compounded, not simplified, by the documentation used. As of yet, there is not much in the way of standardized impact investment agreements. Sometimes, there are not even templates. For example, one lawyer told me that when she drafted her first pay for success contract to undergird a SIB, she started with a blank page. On the other hand, there are plenty of opportunities for lawyers to think creatively about how to repurpose contractual provisions that are common to more commercial investments for use in impact investments.

For example, recitals may include statements of impact goals. Investment and repayment terms may reflect incentives to reward investees that meet or surpass impact milestones, or disincentives to penalize those that woefully miss the mark. Representations and warranties may address the investee's legal form of doing business, or the existence of a mission or purpose statement in the investee's charter or other constituent documentation. Covenants may require the regular submission of social or environmental performance reports and specify the impact-oriented purposes to

19. David Koch, co-founder of the law firm Plave Koch, coined this phrase in describing how he counsels clients that are developing social franchise relationships so that the interests of the social franchisor and its franchisees start and remain in alignment over the course of their relationship.

which investment proceeds may be used. Events of default or other remedies may address and attempt to limit any unintended, adverse consequences of the impact investment on its intended beneficiaries. Transfer and exit provisions may include provisions aimed at protecting the mission of the investee or the reputation of the investor, should negative or perverse impact outcomes take place. Early exit or wind-up provisions may attempt to ensure that vulnerable beneficiaries continue to receive important care and services, despite the premature termination of the impact investment. Dispute resolution mechanisms may be expanded to incorporate grievance processes for affected stakeholders/beneficiaries, or to seek the input of a knowledgeable ombudsman or third-party verifier should there be a dispute about the levels of impact reached. And the list goes on.

4. Managing/Governing

It is here, in the area of deal management and governance, that an impact investment may take a very different turn from what one might find in a more traditional market transaction. Impact investments are, by definition, trying to achieve something that is likely hard to do, or there would be no need for such an investment. There is a risk, however, that some parties to an impact investment may be paying only lip service to impact goals. The worst of them may be engaging in "impact washing" by overstating or falsely claiming that an investment is more impactful or is more committed to achieving impact than it is.

Fears of the backlash that impact washing might wreak on the impact investment field have given rise to a veritable rainbow of impact washing terms. There is green washing (overstating positive environmental impacts), pink washing (claiming unsubstantiated or inaccurate breakthroughs in gender inclusion), and blue washing (pretending to conform with UN principles), to name a colorful few.

Accordingly, standard-setters like the United Nations and international financial institutions like the IFC are creating standards that aim to inform how impact investment decisions get made, whose voices are heard, and, ultimately, what gets done, what gets prioritized and what gets communicated.[20] All of this is leading to the development of global standards to create what some call "impact integrity."[21]

---

20. United Nations Development Programme, SDG Impact Standards: Frequently Asked Questions, at 7, https://sdgimpact.undp.org/assets/SDG_Impact_Standards_FAQs.pdf.

21. ImpactAlpha, *Getting the Three Pillars of Impact and Integrity Right, Right at the Fund's Formation*, https://tideline.com/getting-the-three-pillars-of-impact-and-integrity-right-right-at-the-funds-formation/.

Many of the initiatives to advance impact integrity rely on shedding a light on how decisions get made and how progress is measured and verified in an impact investment. Consequently, impact investment transactions can be more transparent than more commercial deals—even when transactions are among privately-held parties that are not subject to formal disclosure requirements. In part this is driven by the need to include and inform stakeholder/beneficiaries of the progress and actions of the impact investment. Some impact investments may even provide for inclusive decision-making processes that go beyond the contracting parties to include affected stakeholders/beneficiaries (or those who can speak on their behalf).

Another driver of transparency in impact investing is the learning value ascribed to these transactions. Impact investments often are expected to share lessons learned with the broader impact investment community. Take, for example, the MicroBuild Fund, an impact investment fund sponsored by Habitat for Humanity to expand the funding available globally for housing microfinance. The MicroBuild Fund was created as a "demonstration" fund in hopes that its successes would spur others to also invest in housing microfinance. So seriously does Habitat take this demonstration effect that it has contributed to a growing number of case studies about the launch and scaling of this fund, going as far as to include the original deal documentation (debt and equity) in those case studies.[22]

Similarly, some impact investors are working to prompt learning within and across their investees. For these investors, care is often taken to ensure that tendencies toward dualistic (either/or) responses to the achievement of impact goals are tempered by a culture that instead foments continual and iterative learning and improvement. This more nuanced approach to evaluating the success of an impact investment can lead to decision-making processes and governance mechanisms, including contractual governance provisions, that prize impact insights over impact accomplishments.

5. Exiting

Impact investing is still largely taking place among privately held parties. Hence, exits can be challenging. This explains why so much of the early days of impact investing was in the form of debt, not equity. As noted earlier, where equity exits from impact investments take place, increasing

22. *See* MicroBuild Fund Case Study Series at Grunin Center Resource Library, N.Y. Univ., https://www.law.nyu.edu/node/35321.

attention is being paid to doing so responsibly, in ways that optimize or sustain desired impacts. The structures used for responsible exits from impact investments can vary. For example, transfer restrictions may be imposed on secondary sales to ensure that new investors will have the same level of commitment to the social or environmental impacts being advanced by the original investment as well as to the interests of the affected stakeholders/beneficiaries. As noted earlier, structured stock sales or variable loan repayment options that tie exits to an investee's revenues, cashflows or other milestones are another form of exit used in impact investing. Or exiting investors may attempt to tie their contractual rights to information or even control over the operations of the investee that extend far beyond the life of their respective investments. They may continue to ask to receive impact data that is gleaned after the investment has been repaid. They may even attempt to create perpetual rights, say through the licensing of valuable intellectual property or other key assets, that give them a say should the investee shift from its original mission or purpose.

Conclusion

This chapter is a beginning point for identifying what a lawyer negotiating an impact investment does differently from what a skilled deal lawyer does when negotiating more traditional market transactions. In doing so, it highlights some of the significant mindshifts that need to take place in lawyers when representing parties engaging in an impact investment. It also describes how a deal lawyer's legal toolkit may need to expand to respond creatively to the challenges and opportunities of an impact investment And, finally, it offers examples of how impact can be embedded into impact investment agreements.

This is but a start. As the field of impact investing evolves and grows, deal lawyers and their tools will need to continue to change and grow in order stay in step with their impact-seeking clients. If Sir Ronald Cohen's vision of impact capitalism is to come true, we lawyers will likely have played a vital role in making that happen. If that vision does not materialize, our inadequacies may be a contributing factor.

Part II

6

Social Enterprises Outside of the United States

Alan S. Gutterman[1] *and Robert L. Brown*[2]

It should come as no surprise that jurisdictions outside of the United States have also attempted to develop and/or otherwise support governance frameworks that might be suitable for sustainable entrepreneurs with interests that extend beyond profit making.[3] As we will see in this Part, many countries have structures that predate the United States and offer alternatives that are quite appealing and interesting.

The authors of a comparative study of legal framework for social enterprise published in 2016 noted that "those seeking a middle ground between the for-profit and non-profit sectors to enable social enterprise have found legal frameworks lacking," thus causing a number of countries to take steps to develop appropriate legal frameworks to support and stimulate the development of social enterprise.[4] Based on their assessment of multiple jurisdictions, the authors found that there appeared to

---

1. Of Counsel, Harvey Esquire, Los Angeles and Silicon Valley, California; President, Global Law Business, LLC.

2. Senior Counsel, Lynch Cox Gilman & Goodman, Louisville, Kentucky.

3. With regard to activities in Asia, *see* J. Defourny & S. Kim, *Emerging Models of Social Enterprise in Eastern Asia: A Cross-Country Analysis*, 7(1) Soc. Enterprise J. 86 (Spring 2011), and Social Enterprise in Asia Theory, Models and Practice (E. Bidet & J. Defourny eds., 2019).

4. A. Triponel & N. Agapitova, Legal Frameworks for Social Enterprise: Lessons from a Comparative Study of Italy, Malaysia, South Korea, United Kingdom and United States 7 (World Bank Group, 2016).

be agreement on the broad definition of social enterprises: "Social enterprises could be private for-profit, non-profit and hybrid organizations with a social mission that use business approaches to achieve their objectives." However, when deciding upon an appropriate legal framework, lawmakers have taken different approaches to addressing two fundamental related questions: should "social enterprise" be formally defined by the government or left to the opinions of academics, practitioners, and other commentators *and* should the government create specific legal structures that can and must be used to carry out recognized social enterprise activities or leave it to social entrepreneurs to design their own governance frameworks within an existing set of legal structures? Specifically, the authors found examples of each of the following:[5]

- Not define social enterprise, and leave it to social entrepreneurs to adapt preexisting legal structures to social enterprise (e.g., Malaysia and most other ASEAN nations)[6]
- Not define social enterprise, but create a range of legal forms that can be used for social enterprise (e.g., United States)
- Have the executive branch adopt a working definition of social enterprise and complement this working definition by creating a legal form specifically for social enterprise (e.g., United Kingdom)
- Have the legislative branch adopt a legal definition for social enterprise and create a legal form for social enterprise-type activities (e.g., Italy, South Korea)

As we will see in this Part II, in Europe, the European Commission launched a Social Business Initiative in 2011 that aimed to introduce a short-term action plan to support the development of social enterprises, key stakeholders in the social economy, and social innovation.[7] The initial priorities of the Commission were organized around three themes: making it easier for social enterprises to obtain funding, increasing the visibility of social entrepreneurship, and making the legal environment

5. *Id.* at 8.

6. See ASEAN Social Enterprise Structuring Guide (UN Economic and Social Commission for Asia and the Pacific, British Council and others, February 2018) for a summary of the legal frameworks for social enterprises among the ASEAN nations.

7. Portions of the discussion of "social enterprises" in Europe in this section are adapted from information appearing at http://ec.europa.eu/growth/sectors/social-economy/enterprises_en. *See also* A. Fici, Recognition and Legal Forms of Social Enterprise in Europe: A Critical Analysis from a Comparative Law Perspective (Euricse Working Papers No. 82|15 (2015)).

friendlier for social enterprises. The Commission described "social enterprises" as follows:

> A social enterprise is an operator in the social economy whose main objective is to have a social impact rather than make a profit for their owners or shareholders. It operates by providing goods and services for the market in an entrepreneurial and innovative fashion and uses its profits primarily to achieve social objectives. It is managed in an open and responsible manner and, in particular, involves employees, consumers and stakeholders affected by its commercial activities.

As opposed to U.S. benefit corporations, which are distinguishable legal entities, the social enterprise that the Commission has in mind does not follow a single legal form, and the Commission noted that many social enterprises operate in the form of social cooperatives, some were registered as private companies limited by guarantee, some were mutual, and a lot of them were nonprofit organizations such as voluntary organizations, charities, or foundations. Regardless of form, social enterprises should be understood to include businesses for which the social or societal objective of the common good is the reason for the commercial activity, often in the form of a high level of social innovation; businesses in which profits are mainly reinvested to achieve this social objective; and businesses that have adopted a method of organization or ownership system that reflects the enterprise's mission, using democratic or participatory principles or focusing on social justice. Common fields of operation for social enterprises according to the Commission include work integration, personal social services, local development of disadvantaged areas, recycling, environmental protection, arts, culture or historical preservation, science, research and innovation, and consumer protection.[8]

An important trend to watch is the movement of the benefit corporation concept to Europe and the recognition of a European Benefit Corporation. The first steps were taken in Italy in December 2015 when the Italian parliament adopted the Stability Act of 2016, which provided for the creation of a "Società Benefit," a separate legal entity formed and organized for the pursuit of one or more "common benefit" purposes

8. The lack of a single legal form, even though a number of European countries have recognized and regulated social enterprise activity, has been criticized as leading to the use of inappropriate forms and unnecessary restrictions that ultimately harm the advance of social purpose and development of social enterprises. For further information, see the website of the Legal Network for Social Impact (https://esela.eu/legal-concept-maps).

as well as an economic activity. The move was notable for the fact that it was the first benefit corporation created in a civil law legal system and commentators have noted that while the new entity has many of the characteristics of U.S. benefit corporations, it was created in a completely different legal and social context given that directors in Italy and in other civil law countries were already allowed to take into consideration stakeholder interests and thus it was not necessary to be too concerned about protecting directors.[9]

The main objective of the European benefit corporation movement seems to be promoting a completely new model of conducting business that supports pursuit of both economic and social purposes simultaneously. The Stability Act describes a Società Benefit as a company that aims at the distribution of profits, but, at the same time, pursues one or more common benefit goals in favor of other stakeholders in the business, including people, communities, territories and the environment, cultural heritage, social activities, entities and associations, by working in a responsible, sustainable, and transparent manner. Designation as a Società Benefit is available to any for-profit company, and although the model has borrowed many of the main characteristics of a U.S. benefit corporation there are important differences: the Società Benefit must list in the bylaws the specific benefit activities; the annual report must be more detailed than the U.S. benefit corporation; directors are not eligible for limitation of their liabilities with respect to third-party lawsuits, and the scope of the law applies not only to for-profit companies but also to limited-profit companies.[10]

In the UK, lawmakers have already begun to take a more progressive approach with regard to the fiduciary duties of directors of traditional corporate entities. For example, section 172(1) of the UK Companies Act 2006 (the "Act") states that

> [a] director of a company must act in the way he considers, in good faith, would be most likely to promote the success of the company for the benefit of its members as a whole, and in doing so have regard (amongst other matters) to—(a) the likely consequences of any decision in the long term, (b) the interests of the company's employees, (c) the need to foster the company's

9. A. Pelatan & R. Randazzo, *The First European Benefit Corporation: Blurring the Lines Between "Social" and "Business,"* https://view.officeapps.live.com/op/view.aspx?src=https%3A%2F%2Fesela.eu%2Fwp-content%2Fuploads%2F2016%2F06%2FBenefit-Corporation-Article-June-16.docx.

10. *Id.*

business relationships with suppliers, customers and others, (d) the impact of the company's operations on the community and the environment, (e) the desirability of the company maintaining a reputation for high standards of business conduct, and (f) the need to act fairly as between members of the company.

The British Academy commented that the language in the Act enshrines what is sometimes termed "enlightened shareholder value," but also noted that it does not permit directors to further interests of stakeholders at the expense of shareholders or provide protection to companies that promote purposes beyond shareholder value.[11] As such, directors must proceed cautiously, although it does appear that they can and should take into account the factors in the Act as part of their overall deliberations on strategy and in making specific operational decisions.

One of the most popular legal forms for pursuit of social enterprise in the UK is the community interest company (CIC), which was first established in 2005 and has since grown considerably in terms of both numbers and the diversity of their activities, ranging from small local projects to larger undertakings across all industry sectors. CICs are subject to the approval of, and ongoing regulation by, the UK's CIC Regulator, and also required to register as either a company limited by shares or a company limited by guaranty with the Companies House. CICs are also subject to additional requirements to ensure that their primary purpose for operation is to provide a benefit to the communities that they serve including prescribed provisions, including a statutory asset lock, in the articles of association. CICs are not nonprofit entities and they are allowed to deliver financial returns to their investors as long as those returns are balanced and reasonable. For example, the UK's CIC Regulator noted that some CICs deliver their benefits through the provision of a service to a specific community, such as a welfare service to vulnerable people, whereas others focus on generating profits from their activities that are used to support a specific purpose (e.g., a cafe that uses the profits it generates to benefit the community). Each CIC is required to submit on a yearly basis a report detailing the activities undertaken and how these have benefitted the community.[12]

---

11. *Principles for Purposeful Business: How to Deliver the Framework for the Future of the Corporation* 20 (The British Academy Future of the Corporation, 2019).

12. For detailed discussion and guidance relating to CICs, see https://www.gov.uk/government/publications/community-interest-companies-how-to-form-a-cic. *See also* Triponel & Agapitova, *supra* note 4, at 20–22 and 41–42.

In 2019, Canada amended its business corporation statutes to integrate the holdings of that country's Supreme Court that in evaluating the best interests of a corporation, directors could look beyond the interests of shareholders and consider the interests of a broader array of stakeholders, including employees, creditors, consumers, and others. Specifically, the Canada Business Corporations Act (CBCA) now provides that when acting with a view to the best interests of the corporation, directors and officers may consider, but are not limited to, factors such as the interests of shareholders, employees, retirees and pensioners, creditors, consumers, and governments; the environment; and the long-term interests of the corporation. The amendments also imposed new disclosure requirements on companies organized under the CBCA with respect to executive pay, corporate diversity, and employee well-being.

The first and only legal definition for social enterprise in Asia comes from South Korea, which defined the term in Article 2 of its 2006 Social Enterprise Promotion Act (SEPA) as an enterprise certified in accordance with Articles 7 and 8 of SEPA "that pursues a social objective, such as raising local residents' quality of life, etc., by providing vulnerable groups with social services or jobs while conducting business activities, such as the production and sale of goods and services, etc." Among the requirements for certification are pursuit of a social objective, provision of social services or jobs to vulnerable groups or contribution to local communities, employment of paid workers and conduct of business activities (e.g., the production and sale of goods and services), spending of at least two-thirds of distributable profits on social objectives, and use of a participatory decision-making structure. The Ministry of Employment and Labor must certify each social enterprise and the social enterprise must take a specific legal form, although organizations are allowed to choose from among a range of for-profit and nonprofit forms. Regardless of the legal form selected, there must be a restriction on how the enterprise's assets are distributed upon dissolution.[13]

13. The description of social enterprises in South Korea is adapted from TRIPONEL & AGAPITOVA, *supra* note 4, at 25–26.

North America

7

Canada

Stephen Erlichman[1] *and Lisa DeMarco*[2]

This chapter discusses the state of impact investing in Canada and provides two impact investing case studies that illustrate the unique legislated carbon pricing and indigenous context in Canada. Unless otherwise noted, dollar figures in this chapter refer to Canadian dollars.

Market Overview and Impact Investing Growth

According to Canada's Responsible Investment Association (RIA), impact investing assets have grown quickly in Canada, from $3.8 billion at the end of 2012 to $14.8 billion at the end of 2017 to $20.3 billion at the end of 2019.[3]

The RIA reports the following characteristics of the Canadian impact investing market:

- Organization type. The top three organization types ranked by impact assets under management are impact funds/managers with 54 percent of reported impact assets, then credit unions with 31 percent, followed by Quebec solidarity-based finance investment organizations with 8 percent.
- Jurisdiction. The top three provinces for impact investing are Ontario with 43 percent, then British Columbia with 32 percent, and Quebec with 20 percent.

1. Partner, Fasken Martineau DuMoulin LLP, Toronto, Canada.
2. Senior partner and CEO at Resilient LLP.
3. 2018 Canadian Impact Investment Trends Report, RIA (Feb. 2019), https://www.riacanada.ca/research/2018-impact-trends-report/; see also 2020 Canadian Impact Investment Trends Report, Responsible Investment Association (Nov. 2020), https://www.riacanada.ca/research/2020-canadian-ri-trends-report/.

- Asset allocation. The top three impact investing asset classes are public equity with 41 percent, then private equity with 34 percent, and private debt with 10 percent.

Another organization that provides data on impact investing in Canada is the Sauder Centre for Social Innovation & Impact Investing at the University of British Columbia (Sauder Centre). Using methodologies differing from that used by the RIA, its February 2019 impact investing report (Sauder Report)[4] adds the following market data regarding Canadian impact investee companies in its database:

- Age. Sixty percent of the investee companies are less than five years old while only 13 percent were older than ten years.
- Employees. Sixty-three percent of the investee companies had zero to ten employees, with the median company having seven.

RIA's 2018 Canadian Impact Investment Trends Report states that there is no dominant sector for impact investments in Canada, with investors identifying the following sectors as ones in which they invest: food/agriculture and housing/real estate each at 10 percent; energy at 9 percent; environment and nonprofits/social enterprise each at 8 percent; community development at 7 percent; clean technology, education, and employment each at 6 percent; healthcare at 5 percent; and various others at lower percentages. On the other hand, the Sauder Report states that of the investee companies in its database, 44.8 percent are in the health-related sector, 24.8 percent are in the climate-related sector, 10.7 percent are in the food-related sector, 9 percent are in the education-related sector, and 10.6 percent are in other sectors.

Policy Framework and Government Initiatives

There is no comprehensive or coherent regulatory framework in Canada for impact investing. Rather, there are a myriad of laws, stakeholders, and initiatives across Canada. Despite the lack of focused legislation, impact investing in Canada is gaining impetus, such as from federally legislated carbon pricing under the Greenhouse Gas Pollution Pricing Act,[5] pursuant to which carbon prices are scheduled to rise from $40/

4. Social Venture Impact Investing: The Canadian Landscape, Centre for Social Innovation & Impact Investing (Feb. 2019), https://www.sauder.ubc.ca./sites/default/files/2019-03/SVII_Canada_S3i_FINAL_Report.pdf.
5. Greenhouse Gas Pollution Pricing Act, S.C. 2018, c. 12, s. 186.

tonne excess carbon in 2021 to $170/tonne excess carbon in 2030. This section discusses some of the other activities in Canada's impact investing ecosystem.

Government Initiatives

Canada has various government initiatives that relate directly or indirectly to impact investing, some at the federal government level and others at the provincial governments level. Some of the initiatives at Canada's federal government level are described next.

In 2017, the federal government created the Social Innovation and Social Finance Strategy Co-Creation Steering Group[6] with the mandate to guide the development of a social innovation and social finance strategy for Canada. In the steering group's 2018 report, it noted that "social finance differs from responsible investing in that those making and receiving social finance investments intend to create tangible social and environmental impacts through their activities." The steering group stated that the government "has a strategic role to play in supporting the development of social innovation and social finance ecosystems" across the charitable and nonprofit, public, and private sectors and made 12 recommendations that the steering group believed "would, collectively, unleash the potential of social innovation to address Canada's most pressing social and environmental challenges."[7]

Later, in 2018, the federal government announced that it was proceeding on one of the steering group's key recommendations to create a new social finance fund of up to $755 million over the next ten years (with $85 million being provided annually for the first four-year period starting in 2020), and that it would also make available an additional $50 million over the next two years, as described next.

The federal government launched its Investment Readiness Program (IRP) in 2019.[8] The IRP is a two-year $50 million pilot program designed to help advance social innovation and social finance in Canada by building on existing supports to help catalyze community-led solutions to

6. Social Innovation & Social Finance Strategy, ESDC-Consultations (last visited Feb. 3, 2022), https://esdc-consultations.canada.ca/social-innovation.

7. Inclusive Innovation: New Ideas and New Partnerships for Stronger Communities, Gov't of Canada (last visited Feb. 3, 2022), https://www.canada.ca/en/employment-social-development/programs/social-innovation-social-finance/reports/recommendations-what-we-heard.html.

8. About irp-ppci.ca, Investment Readiness Program (last visited Feb. 3, 2022), https://irp-ppi.ca/en/about-the-program/.

persistent social and environmental challenges. The pilot program is designed to provide a learning opportunity to inform future direction on how best to support and mobilize the social finance sector. Among other things, it will allow eligible social purpose organizations to access a broad range of expert services in areas such as strategic impact focus and impact sustainability.

The federal government created the Expert Panel on Sustainable Finance in 2018 to present a set of recommendations to scale and align sustainable finance with Canada's climate and economic goals. The Expert Panel issued its final report in 2019 (Expert Panel Report),[9] setting out what it described as 15 "practical, concrete recommendations focused on spurring the essential market activities, behaviours and structures needed to bring sustainable finance into the mainstream" in Canada. Several of the Expert Panel Report's recommendations tie directly or indirectly into impact investing, including:

- 2: Provide Canadians the opportunity and incentive to connect their savings to climate objectives.
- 2.1: Create a financial incentive for Canadians to invest in accredited climate-conscious products through their registered savings plans.
- 9: Expand Canada's green fixed income market, and set a global standard for transition-oriented financing.
- 9.1: Convene key stakeholders to develop Canadian green and transition-oriented fixed income taxonomies.
- 9.2: Work with financial sector leaders to accelerate Canada's supply of liquid green and transition-linked fixed income products.
- 11.3: Use blended finance models to mobilize private investment in areas of strategic priority.
- 13.4: Develop a regional green bank network to facilitate an "on the ground" retrofit market.
- 15: Engage institutional investors in the financing of Canada's electricity grid of the future.

9. Final Report of the Expert Panel on Sustainable Finance: Mobilizing Finance for Sustainable Growth, Gov't of Canada (last visited Feb. 3, 2022), https://publications.gc.ca/collections/collection_2019/eccc/En4-350-2-2019-eng.pdf.

Although these initiatives are relatively current and deal with the domestic impact investing ecosystem, Canada's federal government was involved with impact investing for many years before the term "impact investing" was commonly used. For example, as part of the government's objectives to assist private sector development in emerging economies outside of Canada, one of this chapter's authors acted for the Canadian government in 2005 when it sponsored and agreed to invest, on a basis that matched third-party investors dollar for dollar up to $100 million, in the Canada Investment Fund for Africa (CIFA).[10] CIFA was an impact investing private equity fund focused on providing risk capital for private sector development in Africa with social, environmental, and health and safety objectives. In reviewing the results of this fund, the government reported that CIFA was successful in creating impact in Africa by "contributing to the creation and development of long-term viable businesses that have sustainable economic and social benefits, such as: sustainable job creation, improved infrastructure, long-term mobilization of capital, technology transfer, increased tax revenues, increased foreign exchange, and improved business practices."[11]

Some of Canada's provinces also have impact investing initiatives. A notable example is the Community Economic-Development Investment Fund (CEDIF)[12] regime established by the Province of Nova Scotia more than 20 years ago. CEDIF is intended to create impact via community economic development by investing in for-profit local businesses in Nova Scotia. The CEDIF regime provides Nova Scotia tax incentives and a securities regulatory framework for CEDIFs offered for sale to Nova Scotia retail investors.

Two case studies of impact investing projects underway in Canada are set out in the Appendix at the end of this chapter. They illustrate the importance of indigenous equity structures and the role of local and regional climate impacts in Canadian impact investing.

---

10. Canada Investment Fund for Africa LP, CDC Investment Works (last visited Feb. 3, 2022), https://www.cdcgroup.com/en/our-impact/fund/canada-investment-fund-for-africa-lp/.

11. Project Profile—Canada Investment Fund for Africa, Gov't of Canada (last visited Feb. 3, 2022), https://w05.international.gc.ca/projectbrowser-banqueprojets/project-projet/details/a032944001?Lang=eng.

12. Community Economic-Development Investment Funds (CEDIFs), Nova Scotia Sec. Comm'n (last visited Feb. 3, 2022), https://nssc.novascotia.ca/corporate-finance/community-economic-development-Investment-funds.

Canadian Legislation

There is legislation at both the federal and provincial government levels relating to impact investing, a few of which laws are described in this section.

As noted earlier, the Province of Nova Scotia enacted securities and tax laws more than 20 years ago to enable the creation of CEDIFs. In addition, in 2016 Nova Scotia enacted the Community Interest Companies Act, which allowed new and existing businesses incorporated under the Companies Act (Nova Scotia) to apply for designation as a Community Interest Company.[13]

In 2020, the Province of British Columbia became the first jurisdiction in Canada to pass legislation allowing for the establishment of for-profit benefit companies that can pursue both an economic and a social mandate,[14] thus joining more than 35 U.S. states that already enacted benefit company legislation. The introduction of benefit companies is the most recent step in the province's commitment to social enterprise, following upon legislation passed in 2013 to permit the formation of for-profit community contribution companies.[15]

The federal government amended the Canada Business Corporations Act (CBCA)[16] in 2019 to expand upon and codify the duties of directors as enunciated by the Supreme Court of Canada in its 2008 *BCE Inc. v. 1976 Debentureholders* decision.[17] Although the CBCA amendment is not focused directly on impact, it relates to environmental, social, and governance (ESG) matters and sustainability and ties into impact. The new provision added to the CBCA states in relevant part as follows: "When acting with a view to the best interests of the corporation . . . , the directors and officers of the corporation may consider, but are not limited to, the following factors: (a) the interests of (i) shareholders, (ii) employees, (iii) retirees and pensioners, (iv) creditors, (v) consumers, and (vi) governments; (b) the environment; and (c) the long-term interests

13. Community Interest Companies Act, Bill No. 153, Chapter 38 of the Acts of 2012.

14. What Is a Benefit Company, bc centre for soc. enter. (last visited Feb. 3, 2022), https://www.centreforsocialenterprise.com/benefit-company/.

15. Community Contribution Companies (C3), bc centre for soc. enter. (last visited Feb. 3, 2022), https://www.centreforsocialenterprise.com/community-contribution-companies/.

16. Canada Business Corporations Act, R.S.C., 1985, c. C-44.

17. 2008 SCC 69 (CanLII), [2008] 3 SCR 560.

of the corporation."[18] The amendment applies to the many Canadian companies, both public and private, that are governed by the CBCA and may provide directors of these companies with greater latitude to consider factors in their decision making that in the past were not top of mind.

Canadian Organizations

There are many organizations of varied types in Canada involved in impact investing and the broader area of ESG and sustainability, including think tanks, universities, profit and nonprofit enterprises, and government agencies. A few of the prominent Canadian organizations are described next.

The Sauder Centre is focused on "leveraging business tools to advance social innovation and sustainability, through research, incubation, and application" and states that it "works closely with impact investors to advance the market in Western Canada, by providing high quality research, advisory work on capital allocation strategies, and building a pipeline of innovative social ventures."[19] The Sauder Centre hosts the Impact Investment Forum, which "intends to build the Canadian impact investing community by showcasing the thought leadership of Canadian experts."[20] The Sauder Report mentioned earlier is an example of the research prepared by this organization.

The Institute for Sustainable Finance at the Smith School of Business at Queen's University states that it is "the first-ever cross-cutting and collaborative hub in Canada that fuses academia, the private sector, and government with the singular focus of increasing Canada's sustainable finance capacity. The institute's mission is to align mainstream financial markets with Canada's transition to a prosperous sustainable economy."[21]

The MaRS Centre for Impact Investing in Toronto was founded in 2011 to create new funding models that channel more money and bring more stakeholders together to work on society's toughest problems, such as providing affordable housing, good educations and jobs, quality healthcare, and clean technology. MaRS states that they "connect the

---

18. Canada Business Corporations Act, R.S.C., 1985, c. C-44 (s. 122).

19. Centre for Social Innovation & Impact Investing, UBC Sauder Sch. of Bus. (last visited Feb. 3, 2022), https://www.sauder.ubc.ca/thought-leadership/research-outreach-centres/centre-social-innovation-impact-investing.

20. Impact Investment Forum: What Is Impact Investing, IIF (last visited Feb. 3, 2022), https://www.impactinvestmentforum.com/.

21. Shaping the Future of Sustainable Finance, Inst. for Sustainable Fin. (last visited Feb. 3, 2022), https://smith.queensu.ca/centres/isf/index.php.

public, the private, the non-profit and the charitable sectors and draw them together to push social progress."[22]

Common Funding Products and Sourcing Opportunities

There are many investment funds in Canada that focus on sustainability and ESG factors, some of which specifically have an impact focus. These funds were created as private equity funds and private debt funds as well as publicly offered closed-end funds, open-end mutual funds, and exchange-traded funds (ETFs). Following is an example of some listing sources.

The previously mentioned RIA database lists many responsible investment funds available to Canadian investors, including more than 30 retail offered funds that the RIA characterizes as impact funds. That number is conservative, however, because there are other Canadian databases listing impact investing products and opportunities not shown in the RIA database.

SVX is an online impact investing platform for Canadian ventures, funds, and investors seeking social or environmental impact alongside the potential for financial return.[23] This platform lists a large number of privately offered impact funds not shown on the RIA's publicly offered impact fund list.

OpenImpact describes itself as an uncurated online platform and currently lists more than 100 Canadian funds that are self-reported as impact investments. Most of the listed funds are either private equity or private debt, with the rest being split among public equity, public debt, and real assets.

The Sustainable Development Investments Asset Owner Platform, of which Canadian pension fund manager British Columbia Investment Management Corporation is one of the four owners, was created in 2020 with the "primary objective of accelerating market adoption of investments aligned with the Sustainable Development Goals (SDGs)."[24] This platform focuses on potential portfolio companies, rather than on investment funds, and currently classifies more than 8,000 companies around the world according to their contribution to the SDGs.

---

22. Every Dollar Should Make a Difference, MaRS Centre for Impact Investing (last visited Feb. 3, 2022), https://impactinvesting.marsdd.com/.

23. Seeking Positive Change through Impact Investing, SVX (last visited Feb. 3, 2022), https://svx.ca/.

24. A Global Standard for Investing into the Sustainable Development Goals, SDI Asset Owner Platform (last visited Feb. 3, 2022), https://www.sdi-aop.org/.

One new fund deserves mention because of its magnitude. In February 2021, Canadian asset manager Brookfield Asset Management Inc. announced its plan to raise US$7.5 billion for Brookfield Global Transition Fund, but as a result of investor demand Brookfield announced an increase in the size of the fund to US$15 billion in December 2021.[25] This fund, which is part of the ESG and impact investing business that Brookfield is building led by former Bank of Canada and Bank of England Governor Mark Carney, will focus on renewable power and other investments in Canada and around the world to assist in reducing carbon emissions.

Challenges and Opportunities

There are various challenges—like those in other countries—to growing the impact investment market in Canada. Such challenges include, in no particular order: performance concerns, shortage of high-quality investment opportunities with track records, lack of investment professionals with relevant skills, lack of common nomenclature for impact investing, lack of research and data on products and performance, inadequate impact measurement practices, and lack of a coherent organized market for impact investment funds and investment opportunities.

Many of these challenges should be overcome, however, as the Canadian impact investing market matures and as impact investing infrastructure continues to be built. For example, following upon Recommendation 9.2 of the Expert Panel Report described earlier, effective March 1, 2021, the Toronto Stock Exchange began to list certain green, social, and transition sustainable bonds for trading, thereby filling a previous void by creating a more liquid, transparent, and efficient marketplace in Canada to improve access to sustainable fixed-income investments. With an increasing focus in Canada on ESG, resulting from major worldwide problems such as climate change and employee health and wellness issues arising out of the COVID-19 pandemic, as well as from Canadian institutional investors continuing to focus on integrating ESG factors into investment and voting decisions, the impact investing market is expected to continue to grow robustly in Canada in the years ahead.

25. Brookfield Announces Initial US$7 Billion Closing for Brookfield Global Transition Fund, Brookfield Asset Mgmt. (July 27, 2021), https://bam.brookfield.com/press-releases/brookfield-announces-initial-us7-billion-closing-brookfield-global-transition-fund; see also Brookfield Sees Raising over $15 Billion for New Impact Fund, Bloomberg (Dec. 8, 2021), https://www.bloomberg.com/news/articles/2021-12-08/brookfield-ceo-flatt-says-impact-fund-upsized-to-15-billion.

APPENDIX

The following two Canadian impact investment initiatives illustrate the importance of indigenous reconciliation and local and regional climate change mitigation as drivers of Canadian impact investment.

Lower Mattagami River Project

The Lower Mattagami River Project (Project) is the largest hydroelectric project in Northern Ontario in 50 years. It was completed in January 2015 and added an additional 438 megawatts of clean, renewable hydro capacity with six new units at four redeveloped stations, including the Little Long, Harmon, Kipling, and Smoky Falls stations in northeastern Ontario. The Project is noteworthy, not just for the sizeable investment but for its precedent-setting equity sharing with the indigenous community upon whose traditional territory the Project was built. It advances indigenous reconciliation by creating an equity partnership that expressly recognizes the harm done by previous hydro projects that flooded the indigenous community's lands.[26]

Earlier in 2010, Ontario Power Generation Inc. (OPG) embarked on the $2.6 billion redevelopment Project to build additional capacity in Northeastern Ontario. OPG partnered with Moose Cree First Nation (MCFN) on the Project, which is located on the traditional territory of MCFN and on Treaty 9 lands. OPG and MCFN entered into the Amisk-oo-Skow Agreement which provided MCFN with a 25 percent equity stake in the Project in recognition of past flooding of the traditional territory.

Amisk-oo-Skow Agreement. The Amisk-oo-Skow Agreement provides environmental protections and supports business and employment opportunities for indigenous businesses and MCFN community members. The Amisk-oo-Skow Agreement resulted in the creation of the Amisk-oo-Skow Finance Corporation, which is owned by MCFN and holds its equity interest in the Project. In addition, the Amisk-oo-Skow Agreement provides for an aboriginal employment program ensuring access to both jobs and training for MCFN members as well as for MoCreebec, Taykwa Tagamou Nation, and the Métis Nation of Ontario—all indigenous communities identified during the environmental assessment process. The

26. Amisk Fine Jan 12 2016 H264 3Mbps, Mushkeg Media Inc. (Jan. 20, 2016), https://vimeo.com/152577855.

Project created more than 450 person years of construction employment for indigenous communities, exceeding the target of 200 person years specified in the Amisk-oo-Skow Agreement. It also is resulting in lasting community benefits through the development of skilled trades, investment, and project management with the community.

Funding. As a result of the Amisk-oo-Skow Agreement, which set aside 9 percent of subcontracted work for MCFN businesses, MCFN businesses were awarded more than $300 million in Project subcontracts. Throughout the Project development and construction, more than 250 community and indigenous workers were employed. By partnering and receiving an equity stake in the Project, MCFN will have a consistent and reliable revenue stream over the service life of the Project, which is expected to be at least 90 years.

Low Carbon Cities Canada

Low Carbon Cities Canada (LC3) is a partnership between the Federation of Canadian Municipalities (FCM) and seven urban climate centres (LC3 Centres) across Canada in Vancouver, Calgary, Edmonton, Toronto/Hamilton, Montreal, Halifax, and Ottawa. While the LC3 is funded through an initial federal budget allocation, it is uniquely structured to create seven regional, self-perpetuating not-for-profit investment vehicles that fund private climate impact investments in local projects. The unique structure is meant to provide climate investments in commercial urban projects that respond to the diversity of Canada's regional and local communities. LC3 provides investment funding tailored to local and regional circumstances by the LC3 Centres and was modeled on the Atmospheric Fund in Toronto. LC3 Centres will seek to provide solutions to reduce greenhouse gases (GHGs) through impact investing, grant making, and demonstration programs in three key areas: (1) energy efficiency in buildings, (2) urban renewable energy, and (3) transportation solutions.

Source of funding. The federal government's budget, released on March 19, 2019, provided a $350 million investment in LC3, which is administered through the FCM's Green Municipal Fund.

Structure. LC3 Centres have the objective of facilitating local private investments, strategic grants, demonstration projects, and other programs that address barriers and accelerate the adoption of local emissions reductions solutions, while operating in collaboration with municipalities and local stakeholders. Local engagement also enhances capacity building in the community and catalyzes further impact investments and projects. Through each LC3 Centre, an endowment is created to facilitate investing in eligible projects that result in meaningful reductions of GHG emissions, environmental improvements, and impactful local community benefits. LC3 Centres act independently, are largely autonomous in investment decisions, and are not-for-profit corporations or trusts.

Project and initiatives funded to date. To date, all regional centres and related investment vehicles have been created with the endowment seed funding flowing to the Metro Vancouver Zero Emission Innovation Centre, Climate Innovation Fund hosted by the Alberta Ecotrust Foundation in Calgary and Edmonton, the Atmospheric Fund in the Greater Toronto and Hamilton area, the Ottawa Community Foundation, the Greater Montreal Climate Fund, and the Halifax Climate Investment Centre.

8

United States

Robert L. Brown and Eli Bronn[1]

Market Overview and Impact Investing Growth

The U.S. Forum for Sustainable and Responsible Investment (US SIF) produced a 2020 Trends Report describing where impact investing money is allocated within the marketplace. The report analyzed 1,500 money managers and community investing institutions, representing $16.6 trillion in assets. Due to the lack of information on impact investing in the United States, it represented a positive step toward transparency.

As briefly discussed earlier, impact investing is generally comprised of environmental, social, and governance (ESG) factors. In America, environmental and governance factors are the leading criteria for impact investing. Since 2018, environmental impact investing increased by 58 percent. Over that same time period, governance impact investing increased by 47 percent.

Within those sectors, certain areas garnered more attention than others. In the environmental sector, for example, climate change/carbon emissions and sustainable natural resources garner the most attention. Overall, climate change is now the most asset-weighted impact investment sector considered by money managers. Sustainable natural resources impact investing grew 81 percent since 2018, now topping $2.4 trillion,[2] although it was not even in the top ten environmental criteria in 2018. Further changes have been seen within the governance factors

1. Lynch Cox Gilman & Goodman. Preliminary work on this chapter was contributed by Kristina Aiad-Toss.

2. Deborah Nason, *"Sustainable Investing" Is Surging, Accounting for 33% of Total U.S. Assets under Management*, CNBC (Dec. 21, 2020, 8 AM), https://www.cnbc.com/2020/12/21/sustainable-investing-accounts-for-33percent-of-total-us-assets-under-management.html.

as well. For example, factors related to executive pay saw monumental growth since 2018, increasing 122 percent to a whopping $2.2 trillion. Within the governance sector, anti-corruption and board issues are also being more heavily addressed.

The SIF report went deeper into specific investors and surveyed 530 institutional investors. Those investors had $6.2 trillion in ESG assets, 54 percent of which included public funds. Among institutional investors, social factors were applied to more than 92 percent of assets. Further, among institutional investors, policies focused on conflict risk[3] were the single most prominent ESG criterion, holding $2.7 trillion in assets. However, these institutional investors did not ignore environmental issues. Criteria related to climate change and carbon emissions remained the most significant environmental issues among institutional investors, with $2.6 trillion in assets.

As always in a capitalistic market, shareholders drive growth, as well as where that growth should take place. From 2018 to 2020, corporate political activity was a hot button issue among shareholders interested in impact investing. These investors specifically cared about company contributions aimed at influencing elections, as well as corporate lobbying for the purpose of influencing laws and regulations. As a result, shareholders targeted companies that supported lobbying organizations opposing regulations to curb greenhouse gas emissions. Other mainstream shareholder concerns included fair labor issues, equal employment opportunity issues, and carbon assets.[4]

Where does all of this money for impact investing come from? In the GIIN 2019 Impact Investor survey,[5] fund managers were asked to identify their main source of supply for impact capital. They answered that family offices, or high net worth individuals, were the main sources of such funding. Generally, impact investors are not expecting outrageous returns on their investments. For example, two-thirds of impact investors sought market-rate returns, adjusted for risk. However, 19 percent of such investors expect below-market returns that are close to the market rate, while the remaining 15 percent of such investors expect returns closer to

3. Terrorist or repressive regimes.

4. *Report on US Sustainable and Impact Investing Trends 2020*, US SIF Found. (last visited Jan. 25, 2022), https://www.ussif.org/files/Trends%20Report%202020%20Executive%20Summary.pdf.

5. *Annual Impact Investor Survey 2019*, GIIN (June 2019), https://thegiin.org/assets/GIIN_2019%20Annual%20Impact%20Investor%20Survey_webfile.pdf.

a capital-preservation rate. Presumably, the latter group of investors are investing for philanthropic reasons.

Institutional investors based in the United States also invest in emerging markets abroad, which are defined as countries having some characteristics of a developed market, but not yet fully developed. Many of the countries falling within this category are experiencing or have just experienced rapid growth and industrialization, which makes them attractive due to the potential high returns (even though accompanied by high risk).[6] In emerging markets, U.S.-based investors mainly fund enterprises that work on poverty, gender equality, and economic growth issues. They also focus their efforts and investments toward institutional issues, climate issues, and making communities sustainable. In 2019, 181 high-profile CEOs signed the Business Roundtable's pledge, vowing to pursue long-term value not only for their shareholders but for all *stakeholders*, including customers, employees, and the community at large.[7]

History of Impact Investing Industry

World War II caused a surge of technological advancements,[8] but it also fundamentally changed the way people perceived and acted on world affairs. Following World War II, the U.S. government began providing political risk insurance to private investors doing business abroad.[9] This caused greater investment by U.S.-based investors throughout the world. In 1961, some 16 years after the end of World War II, President Kennedy established the U.S. Agency for International Development (USAID), primarily to fund global development. In 1968, The Ford Foundation, created by Edsel Ford—son of Henry Ford of Ford Motor Company—began

6. *Emerging Markets: Introduction*, GLOBALEDGE (Feb. 15, 2021), https://globaledge.msu.edu/econ-class/emerging-markets#:~:text=Emerging%20markets%20are%20countries%20that,yet%20a%20fully%20developed%20market.&text=These%20countries%20are%20experiencing%20rapid,premium%20over%20already%20developed%20countries.

7. *Annual Impact Investor Survey 2019*, *supra* note 5; *see also Business Roundtable Marks Second Anniversary of Statement on the Purpose of a Corporation*, BUSINESS ROUNDTABLE (Aug. 19, 2021), https://www.businessroundtable.org/business-roundtable-marks-second-anniversary-of-statement-on-the-purpose-of-a-corporation#:~:text=%E2%80%9CTwo%20years%20ago%2C%20Business%20Roundtable,which%20they%20operate%2C%20and%20shareholders.

8. Becky Little, *6 World War II Innovations That Changed Everyday Life*, HISTORY (Apr. 26, 2021), https://www.history.com/news/world-war-ii-innovations

9. *Political Risk Insurance*, NAIC, https://content.naic.org/cipr_topics/topic_political_risk_insurance.htm, (last updated Feb. 25, 2021).

experimenting with program-related investments, which had potential for social change, while still retaining investment principal for future use.[10] Also in the 1960s, the federal tax code was amended to recognize "program related investments." These programs are typically concessionary, and are treated as charitable grants, but can be made to for-profit or nonprofit entities. By 1971, international aid, generally, had grown, and USAID began developing finance operations abroad. This culminated in the creation of the Overseas Private Investment Corporation, which is now known as the U.S. International Development Finance Corporation. It currently offers many products and services, including debt financing, equity investments, feasibility studies, investment funds, and political risk insurance.[11]

In 1976, the "Grameen Bank" was established in Bangladesh.[12] The Grameen Bank is a microfinance organization and community development bank. What is unique about Grameen Bank is that it makes small loans (sometimes called "microcredit" or "grameencredit"[13]) to the impoverished without requiring collateral,[14] a new concept at the time. During apartheid, what we would now call impact investors diverted their capital away from South Africa to pressure its leaders into capitulation, which helped to end apartheid in South Africa. The United States followed this trend in 1977, when Congress passed the Community Reinvestment Act, which required the Federal Reserve and other federal banking regulators encouraging financial institutions to help meet the credit needs of the communities in which they do business, including low- and moderate-income (LMI) neighborhoods.[15]

During the 1980s and into the 1990s, the average investor began to think more about socially responsible investments. By 1994, Congress passed the Riegle Community Development and Regulatory Improvement Act, whose purpose was "[t]o reduce administrative requirements

---

10. *Our Origins*, FordFoundation, https://www.fordfoundation.org/about/about-ford/our-origins/ (last visited Feb. 23, 2022).

11. *Our Products*, U.S. Int'l Dev. Fin. Corp., https://www.dfc.gov/what-we-offer/our-products (last visited Feb. 23, 2022).

12. *Grameen Bank*, Britannica, https://www.britannica.com/topic/Grameen-Bank (last visited Feb. 23, 2022).

13. *Microcredit definition*, Grameen Bank (Sept. 25, 2008), https://www.grameen-info.org/microcredit-definition/.

14. Bank for the Poor Grameen Bank, https://grameenbank.org/.

15. *Community Reinvestment Act (CRA)*, Bd. of Governors of the Fed. Rsrv. Sys., https://www.federalreserve.gov/consumerscommunities/cra_about.htm (last updated on Sept. 28, 2020).

for depository institutions to the extent consistent with safe and sound banking practices, to facilitate the establishment of community development financial institutions, and for other purposes."[16] It was passed to ensure that people had greater access to capital and credit, and promoted local economic growth through community development financial institutions.[17]

In 2000, the New Markets Tax Credit (NMTC) was established.[18] The NMTC provides an incentive for investment in low-income communities based on the U.S. Department of the Treasury allowing intermediaries to select investment projects. Investors in such projects receive a tax credit against their federal income tax. The NMTC has supported more than 5,300 projects in all 50 states, and parceled out credits worth $26 billion (in 2020) between 2003 and 2020.[19] The New Markets Tax Credit, as implemented in 2002, was designed to incentivize new or increased investment in low-income areas by permitting institutions or individuals to receive federal income tax credits for making equity investments in specialized financial institutions, known as Community Development Entities.[20] These Community Development Entities invest in primarily nonresidential operating businesses and real estate projects being carried out by new or existing for-profit or nonprofit entities (referred to as Qualified Active Low-Income Community Businesses).

Foundations have played an important role in impact investment. Recognizing the increase of socially minded investors, in 2007, the Rockefeller Foundation called for a meeting between leaders of the finance and philanthropy industries that coined the term "impact investing." In 2010, The Foundation Center (a nonprofit which acts as a database on U.S. nonprofits) tracked its 427 investments. It found that foundations had invested in nearly 4,000 "program-related investments," totaling more

---

16. *FDIC Law, Regulations, Related Acts*, FDIC, https://www.fdic.gov/regulations/laws/rules/8000-5400.html (last visited Jan. 23, 2022).

17. Office of Financial Institutions Policy, *Summary of The Riegle Community Development and Regulatory Improvement Act*, ECONOMIC INCLUSION IN THE CLINTON ADMINISTRATION, https://clinton.presidentiallibraries.us/exhibits/show/economic-inclusion-in-the-clin/item/101203 (last visited Jan. 23, 2022).

18. *What Is the New Markets Tax Credit, and How Does It Work?* TAX POL'Y CTR.), https://www.taxpolicycenter.org/briefing-book/what-new-markets-tax-credit-and-how-does-it-work (last visited Jan. 23, 2022.

19. *Id.*

20. *New Markets Tax Credit (NMTC) Program Evaluation*, CDFI, https://www.cdfifund.gov/sites/cdfi/files/documents/nmtc-program-evaluation-executive-summary.pdf (last visited Jan. 23, 2022).

than $3 billion.[21] In comparison, the nation's top foundations gave more than $200 billion in grants over the same time period.

Funds have changed along with the impact investment market. For example, in 2010, the ten largest funds held 70.6 percent of sustainably invested assets under management.[22] In 2020, the ten largest funds only comprised 38 percent of that total. This fundamental shift suggests a large growth in numbers of new, sustainable funds.[23] However, these numbers may be a bit misleading. Henry Shilling, founder and director of research at Sustainable Research and Analysis LLC, stated, "About 85% of the growth in assets managed by sustainable mutual funds and ETFs is attributable to fund rebranding—existing funds that formally modified their strategies to use sustainable approaches. . . . [I]t's not net new money." In fact, between January 2019 and September 2021, 799 funds were *rebranded* as sustainable.[24]

Recent events have accelerated impact investments. In 2016, countries began adopting the Paris Climate Accord,[25] which caused many investors and asset managers not already doing so to think more about sustainability. Additionally, by then, social justice had emerged on the forefront of society. Finally, studies were emerging that indicated investors do not have to give up returns to work toward positive societal outcomes. Investors can achieve both high returns and invest in social initiatives. These events have led impact investors working together to create industry infrastructure and centers of investment activity, such as the Global Impact Investing Network (GIIN) and the Global Impact Investing Rating System (GIIRS).[26]

Key Stakeholders

The United States has a diverse pool of impact investment stakeholders, including boutique consulting firms, incubators and accelerators, professional networks, universities, and competitions, all of which seek to advance the impact investment economy. Robust philanthropic support in

21. *Private Capital Public Good*, U.S. NAT'L ADVISORY BD. ON IMPACT INVESTING (June, 2014), https://www.bridgespan.org/bridgespan/Images/services/impact-investing/Private_Capital_Public_Good.pdf.
22. Nason, *supra* note 2.
23. *Id.*
24. *Id.*
25. *Id.*
26. *Private Capital Public Good*, *supra* note 21.

the United States has enabled the development of a strong field-building ecosystem.

The key funders of impact investing in the United States include the Omidyar Network, the Rockefeller Foundation, the Ford Foundation, the MacArthur Foundation, the Heron Foundation, and the Sorenson Impact Foundation. Of course, there are many other stakeholders in this market. For example, the U.S. Impact Investing Alliance facilitates ecosystem development, while the Global Impact Investing Network (GIIN), as cited earlier, is mainly focused on knowledge exchange. Private foundations have been reliable impact investing stakeholders since the 1960s, when the tax code was amended as noted previously. As an example of the financial might of some of these foundations, the Gates Foundation manages a $1.5 billion dollar commitment to income-generating program-related investments, and the MacArthur Foundation's program-related investments grew to more than $300 million by 2013.[27]

Businesses in the United States, from start-ups to Fortune 500 companies, are increasingly seeking opportunities to participate in industries that have social impact. As people become more socially conscious, so do the businesses they work for and represent. An example of this would be Google, which has invested more than $1 billion in renewable energy projects. Coca-Cola has made similar investments, putting $1 billion into a training program that helps millions of women-owned and minority-owned suppliers develop business skills and acumen.

Direct investment is not the only approach, however. Patagonia and Etsy became Certified B-Corporations (sometimes referred to as Benefit-Corporations or B-Corps). These are for-profit entities that consider societal and environmental aspects in their day-to-day and long-term business decisions. See Part I for more on B-Corps and these companies.

Large financial institutions can potentially be one of the biggest drivers of impact investing in the United States. Institutions such as Goldman Sachs and Morgan Stanley are seeking ways to improve their impact investing standards. Many of these financial institutions utilize impact investing to diversify their portfolios across multiple sectors, an investment strategy popularized by Harry Markowitz.[28] This encourages pension funds, and funds generally managed by institutional investors, to allocate portions of their investments to impact investing.

Impact investing is also quite popular among high-net-worth individuals. High-profile entrepreneurs and investors, such as Steve and Jean

27. *Id.*
28. Harry Markowitz, *Portfolio Selection*, 7(1) J. FIN. 77–91 (1952).

Case, Vinod Khosla, Pierre Omidyar, and George Soros have made significant contributions to impact investing to address social and environmental problems. Other big-name individuals, such as Charly and Lisa Kleissner, have created portfolios that show impact investing's ability to compete with traditional investments. This type of work is extremely important, as it encourages others to invest when they realize impact investing is not only moral but financially sound. In the next generation, this could have a major impact, as millennials, who are more likely than prior generations to align investment decisions with their values, are poised to become the recipients of an intergenerational wealth transfer of more than $68 trillion by 2030.[29]

Growing Market Initiatives and Opportunities

As a relatively young marketplace, there are constant streams of new initiatives and opportunities in impact investing. For instance, as unconventional as it was 50 years ago, pension funds have become more active in the impact investing market, both as investors and as intermediaries. For instance, in 2001, the California Public Employees' Retirement System (CALPERS) created the California Initiative, which invests private equity in traditionally underserved markets. Between 2001 and 2017, the initiative invested approximately $1 billion in 569 private entities across the state.[30] Wisconsin has a similar initiative. There, the state of Wisconsin Investment Board allocated more than $16 billion toward businesses with ties to the state who promote equitable economic development.[31]

Compared to the rest of the world, the United States has aggressively embraced so-called green bonds. Green bonds are structured like normal bonds, in that they are fixed-income instruments, but they differ from typical bonds in that they are used exclusively to finance environmental and sustainable projects.[32] Since 2007, the U.S. green bond market had a cumulative issuance of $118.6 billion, comprising 20 percent of the world

29. Jack Kelly, *Millennials Will Become Richest Generation in American History as Baby Boomers Transfer Over Their Wealth*, Forbes (Oct. 26, 2019), https://www.forbes.com/sites/jackkelly/2019/10/26/millennials-will-become-richest-generation-in-american-history-as-baby-boomers-transfer-over-their-wealth/?sh=275c2426c4b9

30. *The California Transparency in Supply Chains Act*, State of Cal. Dep't of Just., https://oag.ca.gov/SB657 (last visited Jan. 25, 2022).

31. *SWIB Makes Investments in Wisconsin Businesses*, ETF (May 1, 2017), https://etf.wi.gov/news/swib-makes-investments-wisconsin-businesses.

32. Alana Benson, *Green Bonds: What They Are and How to Invest*, Nerdwallet (Nov. 5, 2021), https://www.nerdwallet.com/article/investing/green-bonds.

green bond market. In 2018 alone, the United States issued $34.1 billion in green bonds, more than double the volume of any other country.[33]

Some areas of the country have implemented carbon-pricing programs. For example, the Regional Greenhouse Gas Initiative (RGGI), aimed at reducing carbon emissions through a cap-and-trade program, was formed among 11 states in the Northeast and Mid-Atlantic regions. California implemented a similar cap-and-trade program.[34] These 12 states account for one-third of the U.S. gross domestic product (GDP), and thus their investment decisions have a sizeable impact on the rest of the country and the world. The RGGI was the first mandatory cap-and-trade program in the United States to limit carbon dioxide emissions from the energy and power sector,[35] and helped those states to reduce emissions.

The environment for outcome-based contracting has also become favorable in the United States. Outcome-based contracts are results based, focusing on the outputs, quality, or outcomes of the contract.[36] The contracts are with a public sector or governing authority that pays for better social outcomes in certain areas and passes on part of the savings achieved to investors.[37] These types of contracts are becoming more common in the United States, with 21 commissioned in 12 states, and an additional 60 deals in development. Supporting the trend, in 2018, the U.S. government created the Commission on Social Impact Partnerships to administer a federal outcomes fund for initiatives promoting cost savings.

Another growing market in the domestic impact investing market is gender-lens investing (GLI). GLI is an approach to investing that considers gender-based factors in the investment process to advance gender

33. *Green Bonds the State of the Market 2018*, CLIMATE BONDS INITIATIVE (2019), https://www.climatebonds.net/files/reports/cbi_gbm_final_032019_web.pdf.

34. *California Cap and Trade*, CTR. FOR CLIMATE & ENERGY SOLUTIONS, https://www.c2es.org/content/california-cap-and-trade/ (last viewed on Jan. 25, 2022).

35. *The Regional Greenhouse Gas Initiative*, RGGI, https://www.rggi.org/ (last visited Jan. 25, 2022).

36. Chris McFall, *Outcome-based Contracts—Adding Value to the Contract Life-cycle*, PWC (Aug. 25, 2015), https://pwc.blogs.com/deals/2015/08/outcome-based-contracts.html.

37. James Chen, *Social Impact Bond (SIB)*, INVESTOPEDIA, https://www.investopedia.com/terms/s/social-impact-bond.asp#:~:text=Key%20Takeaways-,A%20social%20impact%20bond%20(SIB)%20is%20a%20contract%20with%20the,the%20savings%20achieved%20to%20investors (last visited Feb. 23, 2021).

equality and better inform investment decisions.[38] Generally, GLI is comprised of two broad categories. The first is investing with the intent to address gender issues or promote gender equity. The second involves utilizing an investment approach that focuses on gender, from pre-investment activities to post-deal monitoring, or a strategy that examines investee enterprises' vision or mission to address gender issues, their organizational structure as it relates to gender issues, their use of data and metrics for the gender equitable management of performance, and how their financial and human resources signify overall commitment to gender equality.[39]

Bloomberg has established the sector-neutral, Bloomberg Gender Equality Index (ticker GEI), comprised of more than 100 listed companies across ten sections in 24 countries. This index tracks the performance of public companies committed to disclosing their efforts supporting gender equality through policy development, representation, and transparency.[40] Investing in this index allows investors to pool their money toward entities that embrace a gender-lens, without having to individually research all the companies themselves. The U.S. International Development Finance Corporation, mentioned earlier, also utilizes a gender-lens approach in their 2X Women's Initiative. Through the initiative, the U.S. International Development Finance Corporation has catalogued more than $7 billion of investments in projects "owned by women, led by women, or provide a product or service that empowers women. . . ."[41]

Disadvantaged groups in the United States have historically been, and continue to be, one of the main subjects of impact investing. Native Americans, women, and people with disabilities are examples of such subjects. The U.S. government has well-established federal procurement requirements for those within disadvantaged groups. Beyond the United States, the 2018 BUILD Act, which passed through Congress with broad bipartisan support, seeks to "crowd-in" vitally needed private sector investment toward low- and lower-middle income countries.[42] By

38. *Gender Lens Investing Initiative*, GIIN, https://thegiin.org/gender-lens-investing-initiative (last visited Jan. 23, 2022).

39. *Id.*

40. *Gender-Equality Index*, BLOOMBERG, https://www.bloomberg.com/gei/ (last visited Jan. 23, 2022).

41. *2X Women's Initiative*, U.S. INT'L DEV. FIN. CORP., https://www.dfc.gov/our-work/2x-womens-initiative (last visited Jan. 23, 2022).

42. Daniel F. Runde & Romina Bandura, *The BUILD Act Has Passed: What's Next?* CSIS (Oct. 12, 2018), https://www.csis.org/analysis/build-act-has-passed-whats

crowding-in private investment, the act will support countries through their transitory stage from non-market to market economies.

Another legal development, the Social Impact Partnerships to Pay for Results Act (SIPPRA), largely administered by the Department of Treasury, was also signed into law in 2018.[43] SIPPRA is intended to improve the effectiveness of social services by only paying for a project if predetermined project outcomes have been met and validated by an independent evaluator, in a system called a "pay for results partnership."[44] Congress appropriated $100 million to the program, which goes toward implementing Social Impact Partnership Demonstration Projects and the related feasibility studies to prepare for those projects.

Another significant program is the Opportunity Zones, which provides tax benefits to investors in low-income distressed areas within the Unites States that spur economic and job growth.[45] Opportunity Zones were created under the Tax Cuts and Jobs Act of 2017, with thousands of low-income communities, located in all 50 states, being designated as Qualified Opportunity Zones.

In addition to tax credits for investments in environmentally friendly projects, new legal structures for impact business have been created. For example, B-Corps, as discussed in Part I, are now allowed in more than 40 states.[46]

Challenges in Impact Investing

The United States has done many things to improve its standing in the world of impact investing, but much remains to be done for it to compete on the world stage. One of the biggest challenges, not only for the United States but for other countries, as discussed in Part I, is the lack of a standardized measurement system of the impact of projects. Both public and private actors want to measure the change created by their investments.

-next#:~:text=A1%3A%20The%20BUILD%20Act%20of,and%20lower%2Dmiddle%20income%20countries.

43. *SIPPRA—Pay for Results*, U.S. DEP'T OF THE TREASURY, https://home.treasury.gov/services/social-impact-partnerships/sippra-pay-for-results (last visited Jan. 23, 2022).

44. *Id.*; note the similarities between this and outcome-based contracting, discussed earlier.

45. *Opportunity Zones*, IRS, https://www.irs.gov/credits-deductions/businesses/opportunity-zones (last visited Jan. 23, 2022).

46. *Country Profile USA*, GSG, https://gsgii.org/reports/country-profile-usa/ (last visited Jan. 25, 2022).

More specific to the United States, unlike the European Union, and despite increasing pressure from large institutional investors, the U.S. Securities and Exchange Commission (SEC) has been reluctant to adopt ESG-specific guidelines. Rather, the SEC only mandates that disclosure of ESG risks be made if such risks are "material." Not totally opposed to the idea, in 2016, the SEC published a concept release on business and financial disclosures, which mentioned sustainability themes. Certain sectors, however, such as conflict minerals, payments by resource extraction companies to foreign governments, and health and safety violations at mining-related facilities, were categorized as required disclosures regardless of their materiality. However, when the SEC had the chance in 2020 to publish rulemaking policy in the ESG arena, it declined to do so.[47]

The lack of disclosure requirements in the United States impact investing market has prompted the formation of a coalition aimed at Fidelity Charitable, called "Unmasking Fidelity."[48] Fidelity Charitable is an independent, 501(c)(3) public charity, and the largest grant maker in the United States. In 2020, Fidelity Charitable granted $9.1 billion to 170,000 charities.[49] Fidelity Charitable is alleged to have funneled $4.9 million to 31 different hate groups between 2015 and 2017. This revelation spurred the Unmasking Fidelity movement, which began in February of 2019.[50] The coalition alleges that Fidelity Charitable has a role in "funneling millions of dollars through Donor Advised Funds to white supremacist, anti-Muslimism, anti-Black, anti-LGBTQ, anti-immigrant organizations and institutions."[51] Unmasking Fidelity's first demand was for Fidelity Charitable to publicize the last five years of contributions

47. *Sustainable Finance: A Global Overview of ESG Regulatory Developments*, CLEARY GOTTLIEB (Oct. 22, 2020), https://www.clearygottlieb.com/-/media/files/alert-memos-2020/sustainable-finance-a-global-overview-of-esg-regulatory-developments.pdf.

48. Marigo Farr, *Fidelity Charitable Exposed for Funding Hate Groups, Activists Demand Disclosure*, THE BOSTON SCOPE (Oct. 1, 2021), https://thescopeboston.org/7120/news/fidelity-charitable-exposed-for-funding-hate-groups-activists- demand-disclosure/.

49. *Fidelity Charitable Donors Doubled Down with a Record $9.1 Billion Granted to 170,000 Charities in 2020—24 Percent More Dollars than 2019*, FIDELITY CHARITABLE (Feb. 17, 2021), https://www.fidelitycharitable.org/about-us/news/fidelity-charitable-donors-doubled-down-with-a-record-9-1-billion-granted-in-2020.html.

50. *About Us*, UNMASKING FIDELITY, https://unmaskingfidelity.org/about-us/ (last visited Jan. 25, 2022).

51. *Id.*

to certain grantees. It also called for disclosing any screening tools that Fidelity Charitable uses to decide which charities are grant eligible. Currently, these data metrics are not publicly available. It is difficult to predict where this conversation may go in the future, but more people are becoming aware of the complexities related to impact investing, and how required disclosure standards can have an effect on the public discourse.

As just discussed, one of the main issues with the impact investing framework in the United States is that the disclosure standards are weak. For example, while many voluntary ESG disclosure standards have been created, and some have been incorporated into mandatory reporting regimes by public and private regulators, U.S. companies that choose to implement an ESG disclosure framework are primarily doing so voluntarily. Proposals espoused by federal legislators in 2019 regarding ESG requirements were essentially ignored when the SEC's January 2020 proposed amendments to the MD&A (Management Discussion and Analysis) rules did not include requirements for ESG or climate-related disclosures.[52] This leaves public companies in a difficult situation as investors seek out companies who promote ESG factors, but the regulations do not require the disclosure of such factors.

As usual, the free market is outpacing the government's ability to keep up with the newest innovations. Many influential investors, such as Black Rock, Vanguard, and State Street are trying to get ahead of the changing sentiment of U.S. investors by making public statements in support of companies making ESG disclosures aligned with the Sustainability Accounting Standards Board and Task Force on Climate-Related Financial Disclosures.[53] These reporting frameworks have gained in popularity among U.S. investors and, while not required, are used voluntarily by some U.S. entities.

The SEC's policy on ESG is heavily critiqued within the investor community. The main reason is that the SEC gives minimal guidance as to which impacts should be addressed, and more importantly, *how* those impacts should be addressed. This critique is especially poignant now as it comes in the midst of increasing prescriptive disclosure frameworks worldwide, specifically within Europe and from nongovernmental

---

52. Sec. & Exch. Comm'n, *Management's Discussion and Analysis, Selected Financial Data, and Supplementary Financial Information*, 17 C.F.R. pts. 210, 229, 230, 239, 240, and 249, https://www.sec.gov/rules/final/2020/33-10890.pdf.

53. *BlackRock, Vanguard and State Street Update Corporate Governance and ESG Policies and Priorities for 2022*, Gibson Dunn (Jan. 25, 2022), https://www.gibsondunn.com/blackrock-vanguard-and-state-street-update-corporate-governance-and-esg-policies-and-priorities-for-2022/.

organizations. While federal legislators have responded with various proposals with respect to climate change and social disclosure,[54] the United States still lags behind Europe in its disclosure policy.

Conclusion

In the United States (and even abroad) the impact investing market is still coming out of its infancy. The United States is well-positioned for connecting private investors to high-priority, sector-oriented initiatives, and there are significant emerging opportunities in those areas.[55] The question is whether it will take advantage of that position.

The social and financial innovation that takes place in America can continue to act as a catalyst for motivating private capital to be pushed toward public purposes. Challenges still remain, and regulation may be less restrictive than elsewhere, but as U.S. investors shift their funds to impact investing vehicles, the government will presumably adapt at some point, even if it is not as soon as some would like.

The impact investing market has grown at a nearly exponential rate year-over-year since it began, and investors are constantly shifting capital into funds that advance social justice, combat climate change, address gender disparities, and foster growth in the developing world. The future of the impact investment market in the United States is one of continued growth, improvement, and innovation.

---

54. *The U.S. Regulatory Framework for ESG Disclosures*, Paul Weiss (July 31, 2020), https://www.paulweiss.com/insights/esg-thought-leadership/publications/the-us-regulatory-framework-for-esg-disclosures?id=37633.

55. *The U.S. Impact Investing Ecosystem*, Soc. Impact Inv. Taskforce (Apr. 2014), https://www.pacificcommunityventures.org/wp-content/uploads/sites/6/2017/08/US-Ecosystem_Final-2014-04-24.pdf.

Latin America

9

Argentina

Hernan Slemenson and Jacqueline Berkenstadt[1]

Market Overview and Impact Investing Growth

Impact investments in Argentina have been adversely affected during the last several years due to foreign exchange restrictions in place since September 2019, together with Argentina declaring, in January 2020, a public emergency in economic, financial, fiscal, administrative, social security, utility prices, energy, public health, and social matters by means of the Social Solidarity and Productive Reactivation Law No. 27,541. That law led to a government debt restructuring process. Although successful in negotiations with private creditors, the national government is still in negotiations with the International Monetary Fund.

Even though Argentina has one of the best human talent pools in the region, with a well-educated population and a good number of quality entrepreneurs, it is an underdeveloped market concerning impact investments due to the devaluation of the Argentine Peso, the foreign exchange restrictions currently in force, and its inability to obtain financing from international markets, among others.

In Argentina, according to a report developed by the Impact Investment Group for Argentina (Impact Investment Group) together with Austral University, between 2013 and 2017, eight impact investors struck 16 deals worth $7.4 million; and for the period 2018 to 2022, 16 investors planned to invest $71 million in 139 deals.[2] This can be contrasted with numbers for Brazil, for instance, which in 2018 reported total

1. Marval O'Farrell Mairal, Buenos Aires, Argentina.

2. Grupo de Inversión de Impacto and Austral University, *Inversión de Impacto en Argentina 2013-2022* [*Impact Investment in Argentina 2013-2022*], http://inversiondeimpacto.net/wp-content/uploads/2019/07/Market-Size.FINALFINAL-1.pdf.

impact-related assets under management of $343 million.[3] A summary of major deals is listed below.

Major Deals			
Issuer	**Type of Bond**	**Amount**	**Term and Rate**
CP Los Olivos SAU and CP Manque SAU	Green	ARS 1,109,925,000	1 year 0.97%
FF FECOVIT	Social	$3,000,000	1 year 2%
Plaza Logistica S.R.L.	Green	$27,062,528	3 years 6.25%
Banco Ciudad de Buenos Aires	Social	ARS 3,999,999,950	30 months 1.80%
CP Manque S.A.U. and CP Los Olivos S.A.U.	Green	$35,160,000	3 years 0.00%
FF Proyecto Vida - Laboratorios Richmond	Sustainable	$85,000,000	20 years
Genneia S.A.	Green	$17,300,00	36 months 0%
Genneia S.A.	Green	$50,000,000	120 months 5.65%
Genneia S.A.	Green	$15,605,674	3 years 6.00%
Genneia S.A.	Green	$366,118,638	72 months 8.75%
Genneia S.A.	Green	$48,971,674	2 years 3.50%
Luz de Tres Picos	Green	$30,000,000	36 months 0%

3. Global Steering Group for Impact Investment, *Country Profile Brazil*, https://gsgii.org/reports/country-profile-brazil/.

Company	Total Funding	Investor	Sector
Digital House (AR)	USD 200 mn	TPG Rise, Omidyar, Endeavor, Kaszek	Education
Afluenta (AR)	USD 17 mn	IFC, Elevar Equity, NXTP Labs, IGNIA	Health
Bankingly (UR)	USD 5.3 MN Omidyar	TPC Rise, Endeavor, Elevar Equity	FinTech
Proyecta tu Fulturo SIB (AR)	USD 1.5 mn	IRSA, Organizacion Roman, Banco Cludad, Banco Galicia, Private Investor + IADB LAB Loan	Employability of underprivileged youth
Afluenta (AR)	USD 1.5 mn	Phitrust, Seed Capital Bizkala, Creas SL, Ship2B, Oltre Venture	Logistics
KIADBox (UR)	>USD 1 mn	NXTP Labs, Startup Chile, Fondo Emprendedor	Education
CPSGAY (UR)	>USD 1 mn	Infocorp Ventures, Agora Dove, Seedstars	Community development

Still, over the past few years and taking into consideration the necessity to develop cultural, habitat, and service investments, the Argentine government is creating a more favorable environment for investors.

Argentina's Commitments to Sustainability

Over the past five years, Argentina has taken important steps to recognize sustainably as a central pillar in the administration of resources. Earth.Org now ranks Argentina 104th in the Global Sustainability Index, an index that examines the environmental policies and actions of every country by combining global indexes on pollution, climate change, policy, energy, oceans, and biodiversity.[4]

In October 2015, an amendment to the Renewable Energy Promotion Law No. 26,190 encouraged the use of renewable energy sources for power generation through several government policies and tax incentives. It set ambitious objectives, with the goal that renewable energy sources would become 8 percent of total power consumed in Argentina by December 31, 2017, and 20 percent by December 31, 2025. To achieve this objective, new tax incentives and exemptions were introduced, and a federal trust fund was created to act as a public benefit fund granting loans, issuing securities, investing in renewable energy companies, and providing guarantees to renewable energy producers.

Following its approval in 2016, Argentina ratified the Paris Climate Agreement,[5] and created a national commission to implement and supervise the Sustainable Development Goals (SDGs) of the United Nations.[6] Moreover, Argentina declared in 2019, through its Senate, a state of climate emergency.[7] The nation also extended the applicability of Biofuels Law No. 26,093, which regulates and promotes sustainable production and use of biofuels.[8]

And, in 2018, Bolsas y Mercados Argentinos S.A. (BYMA, after its Spanish acronym), Argentina's most relevant market, developed an index for pricing companies that comply with sustainable practices. The index was designed to promote their regional and international visibility. Currently, there are fifteen companies in the BYMA index.[9]

First Impact Investment Projects in Argentina

Although Argentina has not been able to fully develop its market, major milestones in the development of impact investment have been achieved.

In 2009, the first impact investment financial trust in Argentina, called Equitas I, was created by Equitas Venture S.A., a company that brought together investors with entrepreneurs and focused on financing

4. Owen Mulhern, *Argentina—Ranked 104th in the Global Sustainability Index*, Earth.Org. (June 10, 2020), https://earth.org/global_sustain/argentina-ranked-104th-in-the-global-sustainability-index/.

5. Law No. 27,270.

6. Decree No. 499/2017.

7. Argentine Senate, DR-1079/19.

8. Decree No. 456/2021 and Law No. 27,640.

9. For more detailed information, see https://www.byma.com.ar/emisoras/indice-de-sustentabilidad-esp/.

projects with environmental impact. Ultimately, ten investors (eight individuals and two institutions, including a local bank) participated, with venture capital and debt allocated to social and environmental projects. Unfortunately, devaluation and foreign exchange (FX) restrictions made it difficult and sometimes impossible for entrepreneurs to honor their payments in U.S. dollars, and certain fiscal measures for financial trusts harmed the project. Still the fund was a start.

In 2012, Njambre was funded, an impact company builder supporting entrepreneurs that co-creates and accelerates impact companies by giving financial support, among other activities.

In 2013, the B System arrived in Argentina, which is a global organization connecting B-Corporations all over the world. These corporations are characterized as businesses meeting the highest standards of verified social and environmental performance, public transparency, and legal accountability to balance profit and purpose.[10]

In 2017, the Provinces of La Rioja and Jujuy issued the first two green bonds in Argentina. In the case of La Rioja, it issued bonds for a total of $300 million through an initial offer of $200 million in February 2017 and an additional $100 million in October 2017.[11] It also agreed to use a significant portion of the net income to partially finance the development of the Parque Arauco wind park, and to invest in projects having positive environmental impacts. The Jujuy province[12] green bonds were issued in September 2017 for a total sum of $210 million and were listed in the Luxemburg Stock Exchange. The proceeds were used to co-finance a solar plant called Cauchari complex.

In 2018, the government of the City of Buenos Aires, together with the Inter-American Development Bank, the nonprofit consultancy Social Finance of the United Kingdom, and impact advisory Acrux Partners issued its first Social Impact Bond (SIB)[13] to finance a program called *Proyectá tu Futuro* that inserts young people in vulnerable situations into the labor market. The contract was awarded to a group of social

10. Certified B Corporation, *About B Corps*, https://bcorporation.net/about-b-corps.

11. Bolsar, *Technical Description*, https://www.bolsar.com/Vistas/Investigaciones/FichaTecnicaEspecie.aspx?Id=614766&UrlVolver=.

12. Bolsar, Prospectus, https://www.bolsar.com/Downloads.aspx?Id=303136.

13. Beccar Varela Law Firm, *Beccar Varela asesora en el lanzamiento del primero Bono de Impacto Social de Argentina* [*Beccar Varela Acts as Advisor in the Launching of the First Social Impact Bond in Argentina*], Abogados.com.ar, https://abogados.com.ar/beccar-varela-asesora-en-el-lanzamiento-del-primero-bono-de-impacto-social-de-argentina/22727.

investors, including Banco Ciudad, Banco Galicia, IRSA, and Organización Román.[14] At the mid-point and despite the worsening economic situation in Argentina, an expert committee revealed the success rate for the SIB was 18 percent, compared to 14 percent by government-run equivalent projects in 2018.[15]

Also, in 2018, Banco Galicia, one of the leading financial institutions in Argentina, was the first financial institution to issue green bonds (worth $100,000,000) in Argentina, the proceeds of which would be used to finance environmental projects related to energy efficiency, renewable energies, and sustainable construction. The International Finance Corporation was the lead investor.[16]

Current Market Structure

In Argentina, as well as rest of the Southern Cone, entrepreneurship is important for economic growth and thus attractive to investors.[17] Nowadays, several impact companies in Argentina, such as Njambre, Xinca, Arbusta, Umana, Inclúyeme, Guayaki, Interrupción, Semptive, among others, have proven this new way of doing business. These companies usually focus on projects related to labor inclusion, environmentalism, fair market, agriculture, generation of inclusive services and products, and value chain.

Since the Argentine Securities and Exchange Commission (CNV, after its Spanish acronym) regulation was passed in 2019,[18] there has been some interest in the market for issuances of green and social bonds.

For instance, so-called green securities (CP Manque SAU, CP Los Olivos SAU, and Plaza Logistica SRL) and two so-called social impact securities (Banco de la Ciudad de Buenos Aires and FF Fecovita Fiduciario Banco de Valores) were issued between 2019 and 2020. The proceeds of the issuances focused mainly on green construction and job opportunities:

---

14. *Id.*

15. Environmental Finance, *Impact Project/Investment of the Year—Education: Argentina's First Social Impact Bond*, (Sept. 14, 2020), https://www.environmental-finance.com/content/awards/impact-awards-2020/impact-project/investment-of-the-year-education-argentinas-first-social-impact-bond.html.

16. Nicholson y Cano Law Firm, *Nicholson y Cano asesoró emisión de primer bono verde* [*Nicholson & Cano Acts as Advisor in the Issuance of the First Green Bond*]. Press release, https://www.nicholsonycano.com.ar/nicholson-y-cano-asesoro-en-la-emision-del-primer-bono-verde/.

17. Maria Laura Tinelli in *Inversiones de Impacto: el Venture Capital ante un cambio de paradigma*, [*Impact Investiments: Venture Capital under a Paradigm Shift*], https://www.youtube.com/watch?v=vAAiYBUJnKA.

18. See Regulatory Framework and Government Initiative, *infra.*

- CP Los Olivos SAU and CP Manque SAU co-issued in September 2020 green bonds for the total amount of ARS 1,109,925,000 destined for the construction of wind parks and, to a lesser extent, to finance working capital linked to the renewable energy sector.
- Plaza Logistica SRL issued bonds for $27,062,528 in September 2017 and then re-labeled them in 2019 as green bonds after BYMA regulation was passed as funds were destined for green construction.
- Banco de la Ciudad de Buenos Aires aimed at granting credit lines to alleviate or prevent impacts of the COVID-19 pandemic, including but not limited to financing health sectors, companies, SMEs, and microenterprises to sustain employment levels of these sectors. Social bonds were issued in September 2020 for a total amount of almost ARS 4 billion.
- FF Fecovita was the first Financial Trust to issue social securities, which it did for $3,000,000 in December 2020. Overbidding was four times the amount offered. Destination of the funds is financing and refinancing of purchases and delivery of agricultural inputs for the maintenance or improvement of vineyards of its associated producers and third-party processors, and of oenological (science of making wine, also called viniculture) inputs for the production of wines and/or musts (from Latin for "young wine," it refers to freshly crushed fruit juice—usually grape juice—containing the skins, seeds, and stems of the grape).

Finally, in July 2020, the Centro de Innovación Tecnológica, Empresarial y Social S.A (CITES, after its Spanish acronym) created a Financial Trust and issued securities for a total amount of ARS 24,000,000. Although securities were not qualified as green, social and sustainable securities (SVS Securities, after its Spanish acronym) is important as CITES is an organization that identifies, develops, and brings to the market new technology-based companies with positive social impact.

Regulatory Framework and Government Initiatives

In March 2019, CNV published Guidelines for the Issuance of Social, Green, and Sustainable Bonds (Guidelines)[19] aiming to promote, through the capital markets, development of financial instruments with a positive social, environmental, and/or governance impact together with attractive

19. CNV General Resolution 788/2019.

instruments for investors. CNV's Guidelines followed the international standards of the Green Bond Principles of the International Capital Market Association and the International Climate Bonds Standard of the Climate Bonds Initiative.

The CNV Guidelines established three categories of securities:

- Green bonds. Proceeds used to finance or refinance, in whole or in part, new or existing projects with environmental benefits. Projects can be related to renewable energy, energy efficiency, prevention and control of pollution, sustainable management of natural resources, conservation of terrestrial and aquatic biodiversity, clean transportation, climate change adaptation, ecological buildings, and so on.
- Social bonds. Proceeds used to finance or refinance, in whole or in part, new or existing projects with social benefits. Projects can be for affordable basic infrastructure and housing, access to essential services, employment creation, food security, socioeconomic development and empowerment, and gender equality.
- Sustainable bonds. Proceeds used to finance or refinance, in whole or in part, new or existing projects with environmental and social benefits.

SVS Securities are structured in a similar way to traditional securities. The main difference is that proceeds obtained through the issuance of SVS Securities will be exclusively used to finance social, green, or sustainable activities or projects. According to CNV, SVS Securities can be issued through the following structures:

- Bonds
- SME's bonds
- Simple bonds
- Project bonds
- Mutual investment funds
- Financial trusts

In the case of renewable energy projects, issuing green bonds allows the issuer to obtain various tax benefits, including VAT refunds, accelerated depreciation for income tax purposes, extension to ten years of the set-off term for tax credits and debits, tax credits, and exemption of the minimum income tax and income tax on payments of dividends.

Issuance of the Guidelines led to an increase in sustainable financial products and, with the goal of increasing investments in sustainable products, CNV submitted for public consultation Resolution No. 879/2021 on

January 14, 2021. It created a special regime for sustainable collective investment products. This regime, approved by Resolution No. 885/2021, creates open and closed investment funds and financial trusts whose special investment purpose is investment in securities with environmental, social, and governance impact. Proceeds of the issuance of these products must be allocated directly or indirectly to the financing or refinancing, totally or partially, of social, green, or sustainable activities or projects.

BYMA also created a special panel for green bonds and issued guidelines and instructions for the listings of securities.[20]

Additionally, in March 2017, the Argentine Congress passed Support for Entrepreneurial Activity Law No. 27,349, which provides tax benefits to encourage investors interested in such projects, creates a Fiduciary Fund for Entrepreneurial Capital Development, regulates Crowdfunding Systems, and creates a new legal entity, Simplified Corporation (SAS, after its Spanish acronym).

- The Support for Entrepreneurial Activity Law provides two main fiscal benefits for investors in projects, whether or not in existence. The first benefit provides for the possibility for legal entities or individuals duly registered with the Registry of Entrepreneur Institutions to deduct from their income tax up to 85 percent of capital contributions made to entrepreneurships or institutions whose only corporate purpose is to provide resources to entrepreneurships. The deductible amount can be no more than 10 percent of net taxable income during a given fiscal year, or pro rata if less than a full year. The second benefit is that the amount exceeding 10 percent off may be carried forwarded to the following five fiscal years, which is consistent with the current losses' mechanism available for commercial companies.[21]
- The Fiduciary Fund for Entrepreneurial Capital Development (FONDCE, after its Spanish acronym) was created as an administrative and financial trust to provide financing for entrepreneurs and/or entrepreneurial capital institutions. It will be funded by a variety of resources (both public and private), including granting loans, non-reimbursable contributions, and capital contributions.
- Crowdfunding was authorized to provide financing for entrepreneurs. Investors can participate in a crowdfunding project by investing in shares of a Corporation (SA, after its Spanish

20. For more detailed information, see https://www.byma.com.ar/bonos-svs-esp/.

21. For more detailed information, see https://www.marval.com/publicacion/ley-de-apoyo-al-capital-emprendedor-12979&lang=en/.

acronym) or a SAS, loans convertible into shares of an SA or a SAS, and certificates of participation in a trust.

- The main characteristic of SAS is its low complexity and administration cost, and wider flexibility for internal corporate affairs. Its main objective is to fulfill the needs of entrepreneurial capital.[22]

After the Support for Entrepreneurial Activity Law, CNV issued General Resolution No. 717/2017, which created additional rules regulating crowdfunding. It required crowdfunding platforms to comply with their authorized purposes and to register with the CNV. They were also given reporting requirements. In addition, crowdfunding projects must qualify as "Argentine Entrepreneurship" under the regulations established by the Ministry of Production.[23]

With the objective of improving the crowdfunding system, in December 2019, CNV submitted for public consultation Resolution No. 822/2019, which modifies certain aspects actually in force. For instance, the resolution updates the amount of the minimum net worth of the Platform, the maximum amount that the Platform can issue, and investment limits in the collective financing system, among others.

Key Stakeholders

The key impact investment players in Argentina, as listed below are:

- Argentine government. Since impact investment is still in its early stages, government initiatives are key not only to creating an effective regulatory framework but also in offering investment products, subsidies, and making public investments. In this sense, the Argentine government has started taking measures to promote impact investment (see Government Initiatives to Support or Promote Impact Investing).
- Impact investment group. Different key stakeholders from finance/investment sector, academy, governments, impact companies, among others, formed this group to promote a unified vision on impact investment and to create a space to exchange ideas and promote changes.
- Multilateral organizations. Inter-American Development Bank (IADB), Latin American Development Bank, United Nations

22. *Id.*
23. *Id.*

Development Program, and World Bank have provided financing. For instance, in 2018, IADB invested in the first Social Impact Bond in Argentina.

- Big companies and corporations. In Argentina corporations play a key role in impact investment using diverse strategies, in particular through corporate venture capital funds. Some examples worth mentioning are Mercado Libre, Globant Ventures, and Patagonia creating Tin Shed Ventures.
- Entrepreneurs and small businesses. There are more than 1,066,351 small businesses in Argentina.[24] In addition, according to B Systems organization, 20 percent of youth entrepreneurs in Argentina are social and environmental entrepreneurs.[25] Therefore, this sector can be a key to the development of the impact market in the country.

Key Players		
Asset Owners	**Asset Managers**	**Impact Entrepreneurs**
Organizacion Roman	NXTP Labs	Arbusta/Njambre
IRSA	Potencia Ventures	Arquelite
IFC	Elevar Equity (AR)	Agua Segura
Potencia Ventures	Thales Lab (UR)	Mamotest (AR)
IADB Lab	Tokal Ventures (UR)	Afluenta (AR)
Banco Galicia		
UNDP		
Mercado Libre		

Government Initiatives to Support or Promote Impact Investing

Although impact investment is still incipient in Argentina, the Argentine government took several measures in recent years to foster the market. Examples include:

24. Ministry of Production, *PyMEs Registradas* [*Registered SME*], https://www.produccion.gob.ar/pymesregistradas/.

25. BSystems, *Ley BIC: El Congreso Argentino podrá reconocer legalmente y potenciar a las empresas de triple impacto* [*BIC Law: The Argentine Congress May Legally Recognize and Empower Triple Impact Companies*], http://sistemab.org/ley-bic-el-congreso-argentino-podra-reconocer-legalmente-y-potenciar-a-las-empresas-de-triple-impacto/.

- In 2016, a bill was submitted to the Argentine Congress to create Benefit and Collective Interest Entities (*Sociedades de Beneficio e Interés Colectivo*). The bill was approved in 2018 but lost its parliamentary status because it was not discussed in the Senate.
- The Entrepreneurs Program for Sustainable Development was launched in 2016 with the objective to spot, promote, and strengthen high-impact ventures that promote sustainable development through the use of new technologies.
- First steps toward fiscal incentives in relation to renewable energy projects, implemented through Law 27,191.
- Generation of the first Impact Investment Vehicles such as first Social Impact Bond (see First Impact Investment Projects in Argentina).
- At a local level, the government of the City of Buenos Aires launched "Incuba Social," a project that aims to help entrepreneurs with sustainable businesses based on the sale of goods and/or services that have a social impact business model and contribute to innovatively solving a social problem.
- Since the creation of FONDCE, the Argentine government has launched several programs offering credit lines for entrepreneurs and entities that provide incubation services, acceleration, expansion, technical assistance, mentoring, among others, to entrepreneurs, including programs for impact projects, such as *Fondo Aceleración*, launched in September 2017;[26] *Fondo Semilla* launched in October 2019;[27] and *Programa Redes Para Emprender*, launched in December 2020.[28]
- In November 2019, Argentina hosted the GSG (Global Steering Group) Impact Summit.

Challenges in Impact Investing and Growing Sector Opportunities

There have been challenges and opportunities in the development of impact investment in Argentina: fiscal framework, regulation of impact

26. Resolution 434/ 2017 of the Ministry of Production, Secretariat for Entrepreneurs and Small and Medium Enterprises.

27. Resolution 437/2019 of the Ministry of Production and Labor, Secretariat for Entrepreneurs and Small and Medium Enterprises.

28. Resolution 159/2020 of the Ministry of Productive Development, Secretariat for Small and Medium Enterprises and Entrepreneurs.

investment companies, and underdeveloped private and entrepreneurial capital market.

Fiscal Framework

Argentina needs to update its fiscal framework in order to attract investments. Today, certain fiscal regulations discourage investments and philanthropy (such as a 5 percent haircut applied to income from donations).

The Impact Investment Group suggested measures that could help foster impact investment, such as exemptions on the payment of income tax by investors, impact investment funds, and companies, and increasing the nontaxable income on donations to organizations, impact funds, and NGOs.[29]

Regulatory Framework of Impact Investment Companies

In Argentina's current legal framework, entities may be categorized as public entities, private entities, nonprofit associations, and foundations. Different regulatory frameworks apply in each case.[30] An impact investment company in Argentina, therefore, must opt to fit into a for-profit entity or a nonprofit entity (i.e., an NGO).

However, today many companies could fit in a middle ground, where both private but also social, ethic, and environmental objectives intermingle. Therefore, it would be useful to include new legal entities that contemplate objectives of impact investment companies, since today there is no legal recognition for them.

In this sense, as mentioned earlier, in 2016, a bill was submitted to the Argentine Congress to create Benefit and Collective Interest Entities, but it has not yet been adopted.

Underdeveloped Private and Entrepreneurial Capital Market

Much of the lack of progress in impact investment framework can be attributed to the fiscal and regulatory challenges mentioned earlier, but also to corruption and other factors that may create a lack of long-term trust.

The Argentine government has worked to create a more credible environment for investment in the last few years, but this has yet to lead

29. Grupo de Inversión de Impacto, *Inversión de Impacto en Argentina 2017, Oportunidades y Desafíos* [*Impact Investment in Argentina 2017, Opotunities and Challenges*] at 65 and 66, http://inversiondeimpacto.net/.

30. Private Corporations are regulated in Law No. 19550 while nonprofitable entities are regulated in the Civil and Commercial Code.

to a strong rise of investments. Still, Argentine's entrepreneurial class is very sophisticated and, despite the economic and political concerns, is still attracting new investments.[31]

Argentina, as other countries of the Southern Cone, faces the challenge of bringing new players and actors to the market,[32] involving investors, and improving information skills to communicate ideas on new projects and products.

31. Maria Laura Tinelli, *supra* note 17.
32. *Id.*

10

Brazil

Walter Stuber[1]

Market Overview and Impact Investing Growth

In addition to financial return, impact investments seek measurable socio-environmental results, not only private activities on socio-environmental issues but projects by companies, foundations, institutes, and governments. They seek to reconcile economic results with the possibility of generating positive social impact. It is a category within the ESG (environmental, social, and governance) category. Interest in these investments has created a new industry that operates in the unexplored area between philanthropy and a focus on profit maximization.[2]

These impact investors seek companies in which to invest that have concern about social and/or environmental aspects, as well as, worry about ensuring good parameters of corporate governance and transparency. Generally, these investments are made in corporate stocks or debt securities.

Policy Framework and Government Initiatives

In Brazil, there are regulatory frameworks in several sectors promoting social values in parallel to obtaining profit, such as:

1. Walter Stuber, of Walter Stuber Consultoria Jurídica, São Paulo, Brazil.

2. See report on "Já ouviu falar em investimento de impacto? Conheça a mais nova tendência entre os mais ricos" (Have You Ever Heard of Impact Investing? Meet the Newest Trend among the Richest) by the journalist Naiara Bertão, published in Valor Investe, a section of the leading Brazilian financial newspaper Valor Econômico on July 17, 2020.

- CMN Resolution no. 4,327, of April 25, 2014 (CMN Res. 4,327/2014),[3] issued by the Brazilian Monetary Council (*Conselho Monetário Nacional,* CMN), which adopted mandatory guidelines under the Social and Environmental Responsibility Policy (*Política de Responsabilidade Socioambiental,* PRSA) which must be followed by financial institutions and other institutions authorized to operate by the Central Bank of Brazil (*Banco Central do Brasil,* Bacen);
- Federal Decree no. 9,571, of November 21, 2018 (Decree 9,571/2018),[4] which established guidelines for the government and companies promoting respect for human rights and establishes the "Companies and Human Rights" label for companies that voluntarily comply with the guidelines;
- Federal Decree no. 10,387, of June 5, 2020 (Decree 10,387/2020),[5] which authorized financing incentives for infrastructure projects that generate environmental and social benefits;
- Law no. 13,986, of April 7, 2020 (Law 13,986/2020),[6] known as the Agrobusiness Law (*Lei do Agro*), which expanded access to finance for rural producers who preserve the environment; and
- Normative acts issued by the Brazilian Securities and Exchange Commission (*Comissão de Valores Mobiliários,* CVM),[7] that promote financial best practices in sustainability through regulation of financial instruments, ensuring transparency, consistency, and efficiency to the Brazilian capital market.

Prominent rules supporting impact investment adopted by CVM are:

- CVM Instruction no. 588, of July 13, 2017 (ICVM 588/2017), which exempts from registration small business public offers using electronic participatory investment platforms (e.g., crowd-

3. CMN Res. 4,327/2014 is available at Bacen's web page, https://www.bcb.gov.br/, in the part entitled *Busca de Normas* (*Search for Norms*).

4. Decree 9,571/2018 is available at Brazilian Federal Government—Presidency of the Republic web page, https://www.gov.br/planalto/pt-br, in the part entitled *Legislação* (*Legislation*).

5. Decree 10,387/2020 2018 is available at Brazilian Federal Government—Presidency of the Republic web page, https://www.gov.br/planalto/pt-br, in the part entitled *Legislação* (*Legislation*).

6. Law 13,986/2020 2018 is available at Brazilian Federal Government—Presidency of the Republic web page, https://www.gov.br/planalto/pt-br, in the part entitled *Legislação* (*Legislation*).

7. All the normative acts mentioned herein are available at CVM's web page, https://www.gov.br/cvm/pt-br, in the part entitled *Normas* (*Standards*).

funding) if they generate positive socio-environmental impacts; and

- CVM Instruction no. 480, of December 7, 2009 (ICVM 480/2009), covering registration of traders in the securities regulated markets, which was amended by CVM Resolution no. 59, of December 22, 2021 (CVM Res. 59/2021) to require reporting of material information on socio-environmental aspects of companies under CVM's supervision (*formulários de referência*).

Analyzing Opportunities

Although there are many methods to measure the financial return of impact investments, one approach receiving increasing attention is based on indicators of high relevance to the impact project with the addition of verification. This method measures not only the result of the project itself but also what would have happened to the target population without the investment. This measurement model is based on two pillars: indicators that have high relevance to impact of the project and comparison with similar control groups that were not contemplated by the investment.

The first step in any impact investment is choosing where to invest. For any investor, regardless of the size of the investment, impact investment must make sense not only for a diversified investment portfolio but also as an issue where investors actually see value. It may be, for example, lack of basic education, use of technology to scale small businesses, bringing basic sanitation to more Brazilians, or any other topic they genuinely want to address. Topics of interest to investors range from general to specific ones. What matters is the degree of affinity and relation to the subject.

The second step is choosing which investment instruments to use when achieving the goal. One can choose from equity funds that invest in companies such as moving to a low-carbon economy, to purchasing corporate debt such as "green bonds" and "blue bonds."

The third step is to allocate these assets according to the need for liquidity, asset preservation, and risk tolerance. Finally, the fourth step is to be aware that it is a long-term investment.

In the case of the impact investment market, it is necessary for investors to have an appetite for the intended goal, projects, and companies. The appetite must be genuine and not merely so-called social washing, a term made popular because of the COVID-19 pandemic. Social washing refers to a company using impact investing to appear more sustainable, socially concerned, and committed to solving society's problems than it really is. An example would be a company that donates masks and food to needy families but does not take care of its employees.

Transforming Companies

In 2013, Altimeter, a consulting and research firm, released a study, "The Evolution of Social Business: Six Stages of Social Business Transformation," which describes steps for transformation of companies into "social interaction environments."[8] The research notes there is a big difference between companies that are implementing a social media strategy and true social business. The six basic steps for a company to become a social enterprise are:

1. **Planning.** In the first stage, it is important to ensure that the foundation for development of the social business strategy is sound. The alignment of the organization, the training of people, and the effective execution of tasks must be constantly improved. Companies that spend considerable time at this stage tend to pursue sustainability more successfully.
2. **Presence.** At this stage, planning moves to action. It includes establishing a presence on social media, which may involve creating a YouTube channel, creating an internal blog, promoting a Facebook page, or investing in a corporate social network. These actions need to be based on strategies set up in the previous stage. They should focus on generating value for the company.
3. **Engagement.** Here, the presence on social platforms (whether internal or external) is no longer an "appendix," something extra, but is a critical element of relationship formation. One may encounter negative comments or difficulty engaging employees. It is up to the company to know how to deal with these situations and realize that investment in this type of contact channel with customers (or employees) can influence the entire consumer life cycle.
4. **Formalization.** With the possibility of rapid growth of access through the company's platforms, it is important to establish formal responsibility for this process. If this formalization does not happen, the organization may end up communicating differently,

8. This report of the Altimer Group is dated March 5, 2013, and may be accessed at https://pt.slideshare.net/Altimeter/the-evolution-of-social-business-six-stages-of-social-media-transformation.

and hindering development of the company's image and customer engagement.

5. **Strategy.** In the fifth stage, the use of social interaction technologies spreads throughout the company and its role becomes much more strategic, impacting the organization in several aspects. This is where social platforms get the attention of the company's leaders, who come to see great opportunities from these means.
6. **Convergence.** The use of social platforms does not necessarily transform a company into a social enterprise but contributes to migration of the business. Organizations at this stage are concerned with articulating digital tools to improve their relationship with the market and the environment in which they are inserted.

Transforming a company into a social enterprise is not a simple task. It takes planning and a lot of work. It is important that the search for this cultural characteristic be aligned with the company's objectives and strategy. The goal is to engage customers and employees with the ideals of the company and improve the relationship with all participants in the environment in which the organization is operating.

Case Studies

Within impact entrepreneurship, environmental issues are popular investment and business goals. Examples of successful Brazilian social enterprises that are worthwhile are:

- *SOS Mata Atlântica* has 40 years of experience in the third sector and is one of the most professional organizations in Brazil.[9] It adopts transparent and professional processes and metrics to allocate investment money it receives from foundations, investment funds, companies, and families. It was the first company in Brazil to have an investment committee and an unbureaucratic structure managing investments, ensuring that money reaches the ultimate goal. It is most interested in sustainable agribusiness, involving reforestation, containment of deforestation, especially in the Amazon, and valuing family agriculture to generate income for those who need it and to improve the quality of food people consume. It also sees an opportunity with forest restoration or agroforestry to contribute to improvement of the

9. For more information on *SOS Mata Atlântica*, see sosma.org.br.

environmental issue in Brazil, not only to give people more quality of life but also to honor Brazil's commitments to the global climate issue, such as the Paris Climate Agreement[10] and carbon production reduction targets.

- Cosmetics company *Natura* is in virtually all ESG portfolios in Brazil and is part of the Business Sustainability Index (ISE, *Índice de Sustentabilidade Empresarial*) of *B3 S.A.—Brasil, Bolsa, Balcão* (the Brazilian exchange).[11] Natura is known for stimulating local income and employment and using, in a sustainable way, the resources of forests to develop products with added value while being profitable.

Challenges in Impact Investing

Brazilian entrepreneurs need resilience to be successful. Such undertakings in Brazil are very difficult, but undertaking with impact is even more difficult because it requires a cultural transformation from the Brazilian traditional emphasis on profits. The main mistake for impact entrepreneurs is to invest in a business that ends up not being impact oriented. For this reason, it is particularly important for investors to know the impact goal of the company and its team, and understand the impact being proposed.

Another key factor is the level of professionalism within companies and organizations operating in the third sector. As noted in the Italy chapter, this sector covers a range of organizations that belong neither to the public sector (i.e., the state) nor to the traditional private sector (profit-making private enterprises). Leading third sector organizations include charities, voluntary and community organizations, social enterprises, and think tanks and private research institutes.

In Brazil, it will also be necessary to remove any stigma of lack of professionalism and even corruption that environmental NGOs had in the past.

---

10. The Paris Agreement is a legally binding international treaty on climate change. It was adopted by 196 Parties at COP 21 in Paris, on December 12, 2015, and entered into force on November 4, 2016, and may be accessed at the web page of the United Nations Climate Change: https://unfccc.int/process-and-meetings/the-paris-agreement/the-paris-agreement.

11. This index is available at B3's web page: https://www.b3.com.br/pt_br/market-data-e-indices/indices/indices-de-sustentabilidade/indice-de-sustentabilidade-empresarial-ise-b3.htm.

Opportunities for a Growing Market (Future of the Market)

To anticipate the future of impact investment in Brazil, it is necessary to understand the mistakes of the past and the present. One of them is Brazil's tendency to isolate itself from discussions in the world. It was only with the rise of the theme of sustainability in international events, such as the World Economic Forum,[12] and the decision-making power of new generations that impact investing is coming into sharper focus in Brazil.

As yet, few investment houses in Brazil follow international impact investment trends by offering products that align profit with positive impact. Such investments are still associated with the third sector and viewed as philanthropy. In a country with so many problems, the range of impact issues can be a daunting challenge from which to select. Nevertheless, it has been predicted that in a few years there will be no clear distinction among traditional, ESG, or impact investment.[13] The proof of this is that impact investing is beginning to interest smaller and less philanthropic investors. If a few years ago the capital came from families with high purchasing power and foundations, it now begins to arrive from institutional investors.

After the pandemic, even in Brazil, shareholder returns may not be the only thing being considered. Investors may look beyond how companies distribute resources and may also look at how they invest to improve the world. It will be a growing world of shareholders, society, and governments. The future of investment in Brazil? The answer is likely through impact investment.

12. The World Economic Forum (the Forum) is the International Organization for Public-Private Cooperation, and it engages the foremost political, business, cultural, and other leaders of the society to shape global, regional, and industry agendas. It was established in 1971 as a nonprofit foundation and is headquartered in Geneva, Switzerland. Its web page is https://www.weforum.org/.

13. HSM—The Power of Knowledge, a Brazilian corporate education platform that has consolidated itself as an international reference in management and business, points out: "While ESG investments have an approach to identifying nonfinancial risks that can affect the value of the asset, being part of an analysis process, impact investments say about the type of investment that the manager is seeking and its intentionality." This information is available at https://hsm.com.br/blog/investimentos-esg-e-de-impacto-qual-a-diferenca/.

11

Chile

Cristián Eyzaguirre, Francisco Guzmán, and Benjamín Saa[1]

Market Overview and Impact Investing Growth

Impact investing and social enterprises may be considered novel in Chile, but over the past few years they have expanded significantly, generating strong interest among leading local investors. These investors have included family offices, financial services companies, investment funds, and also nonprofit organizations and companies that pursue the growth of social enterprises.[2] Many have adopted environmental, social, and governance (ESG) factors when developing their business plans.[3]

The growth of the social investment sector has brought new concepts into the equation when analyzing whether to invest in a project. Some private investors are beginning to consider the social impact and pursuit of objectives other than pure profit, since the exclusive pursuit of monetary gain, at the expense of the surrounding community or the environment, is no longer tolerated by public opinion.

Growing Sector Opportunities

There are several projects in Chile attesting to the increased influence of the social impact trend. A good example is the first social impact contract carried out in Chile in 2018. The project was led by Fundación San Carlos de Maipo, a reputed nonprofit organization with self-sustaining

1. Partners, and associate, respectively, Carey, Santiago, Chile.

2. https://fisameris.cl/wp-content/uploads/2019/06/Gui%cc%81a-de-Inversio%cc%81n-de-Impacto-y-ABC-FINAL.pdf.

3. https://servicioscms.bolsadesantiago.com/Biblioteca%20de%20Archivos/Extension/Documentos/2019_ESG_Investment_Practices_Comunicado_FINAL.pdf.

resources.[4] This organization, with financing from private investors, launched the project to improve the reading and writing abilities of children from vulnerable boroughs of Santiago.[5] Since this project was the first of its kind in Chile, it was carried out without the participation of any government authority or the contribution of public resources, unlike most social impact projects. The traditional role taken by the state as outcome payer in this kind of finance mechanism was taken by nonprofit organizations. The investors were mainly family offices, who joined the project within a surprisingly short term. Unfortunately, because of the suspension of in-person classes to prevent the COVID-19 spread, not all the objectives were met, meaning that only intermediate payments were made by the outcome payers, which allowed the investors to recover part of the initial investment. This outcome, though not optimal, demonstrated that the risk is borne by the private investor, being an efficient alternative to allocate public or private resources destined to solve social problems with difficult solutions.

The project proved that there are viable alternatives to fund endeavors that aim to generate a desirable social outcome, while obtaining a monetary return, connecting the different incentives from the private and public sector.[6] Moreover, the successful execution of this project inspired the creation of a working group formed by officers from the Chilean development agency CORFO, the Inter-American Development Bank and representatives from the private sector.[7] Together, they designed a viable and attractive structure to implement social impact contracts that includes the Chilean State as an outcome payer, as they realized that there was a lot of interest from the private sector in participating in this kind of mechanism.

Another relevant case study for impact investing in Chile is the Social Investment Fund (FIS, its acronym in Spanish), an investment fund managed by Ameris Capital, a company focused on corporate finance, asset management, and institutional fund distribution.[8] The FIS was the first social impact private investment fund created in Chile, in 2010.[9] Ameris

4. https://www.fsancarlos.cl/.

5. https://www.fsancarlos.cl/impulsan-primer-contrato-de-impacto-social-en-chile/.

6. https://portal.nexnews.cl/showN?valor=gcs7f.

7. https://publications.iadb.org/publications/spanish/document/Bonos-de-impacto-social-en-America-Latina-El-trabajo-pionero-de-BID-Lab-en-la-region-Lecciones-aprendidas.pdf.

8. https://fisameris.cl/.

9. https://fisameris.cl/fis-ameris/.

Capital raised USD 4.5 million for the fund. Since the money was rapidly invested, Ameris Capital launched a second fund (FIS 2.0) in 2017 raising USD 9.5 million for that fund. Until October 2021, the funds have directly impacted more than 1,350,000 people from the bottom of the socio-economic pyramid[10] in Chile, along with recovering more than 24,300 tons of waste, and the portfolio's companies contribute, with 1,600 jobs of which 1,100 are for women,[11] and Ameris Capital is raising funds for its third FIS, aiming to raise USD 10 million.

Doble Impacto is a crowdlending platform specializing in financing social projects, that together with Quest, a corporate finance advisory firm and asset manager, launched the first public investment fund dedicated to impact investing, mostly through debt financing.[12] In addition to its crowdlending, Doble Impacto is committed to becoming the first purpose-driven bank in Chile, by replicating the model of Triodos Bank in Europe with the support of Fundación Dinero y Conciencia. On December 2021, it requested a banking license from the Commission for the Financial Market (Chilean Securities Regulator).[13]

In addition, Chile has impact investments related to debt securities, such as sustainable bonds issued by the state of Chile (green bonds since 2019[14] and social bonds issued in November of 2020).[15] There is also the social commercial paper program, with proceeds to be used in microfinance focusing on women entrepreneurs, issued by Fondo Esperanza in December of 2020 with the International Finance Corporation as the anchor investor. Fondo Esperanza's securities are the first debt issuance of commercial paper in Latin America pursuant the Social Bond Principles of the International Capital Markets Association.[16,17]

---

10. Bottom of the Pyramid is a concept from CK Prahald and Stuart Hart's book The Fortune at the Bottom of the Pyramid (2004). Such a concept is used by FIS in several reports, including their 2010–2020 impact report available at https://fisameris.cl/wp-content/uploads/2020/11/Memoria-FIS-2010-2020.pdf.

11. *Supra* note 9.

12. https://www.questcapital.cl/fondos-de-inversion/quest-doble-impacto/.

13. https://www.dobleimpacto.cl/solicitud-de-licencia-bancaria-ante-la-cmf/.

14. https://www.hacienda.cl/english/work-areas/international-finance/public-debt-office/sustainable-bonds/green-bonds.

15. https://hacienda.cl/index.php/english/work-areas/international-finance/public-debt-office/esg-bonds/sustainable-bonds

16. https://www.fundacionmicrofinanzasbbva.org/en/la-fmbbva-a-traves-de-su-entidad-lanza-la-primera-emision-de-deuda-social-de-una-microfinanciera-en-chile/

17. The Social Bond Principles of the International Capital Markets Association are a "voluntary framework with the stated mission and vision of promoting the role that global debt capital markets can play in financing progress towards environmental

In relation to social enterprises, Sistema B has certified more than 180 companies as B-Corporations in Chile, from start-ups to publicly listed companies, including all kinds of businesses from many different sectors.[18] Likewise, Fundación Purpose arrived in Chile a few years ago to promote Steward-Ownership[19] and challenge the traditional capital-driven power structures of companies, aiming for integrated systems among the different stakeholders.[20]

Sourcing Opportunities

The enterprises receiving impact investment capital come from several industries and sectors. They include financing companies dedicated to granting credits for small businesses or individuals that cannot access traditional bank funding, recycling companies, technology and software, sustainable energy, and even a bottled water company.[21] The options are limitless, since most industries have businesses that are potential targets for impact investing, depending on how those businesses establish and pursue their goals and objectives and how they govern themselves and run their operations.

Policy Framework and Government Initiatives

In the public sector, there are governmental bodies that work to expand the pool of impact investment capital, encourage the adoption of ESG factors, and increase the number of social enterprises. On November 2021, the CMF (*Comisión para el Mercado Financiero*, the Chilean

---

and social sustainability" (https://www.icmagroup.org/assets/documents/Sustainable-finance/2021-updates/Social-Bond-Principles-June-2021-140621.pdf); in summary, those principles are (1) use of proceeds for eligible social projects, which should provide clear social benefits; (2) process for project evaluation and selection; (3) management of proceeds; and (4) reporting.

18. https://www.sistemab.org/en/welcome/.

19. Steward-ownership is an alternative to the shareholder-ownership, aiming to incorporate all stakeholders into the property of the company, and being committed to two principles: (1) self-governance, meaning that control remains inside the company in people linked to the operation; and (2) profits serve purpose, profits are reinvested in the company, stakeholders or donated (and investors or founders are compensated with capped returns or dividends (https://purpose-economy.org/en/whats-steward-ownership/).

20. https://purpose-economy.org/en/who-we-are/.

21. Some of those companies are Quest Capital and Doble Impacto (https://www.questcapital.cl/fondos-de-inversion/quest-doble-impacto/), TriCiclos (https://triciclos.net/en/), AllRide (https://www.allrideapp.com/) and Latte (https://late.cl/).

banking, securities, and insurance regulator) issued Rule 461,[22] secondary legislation, which eliminated the Social Responsibility and Sustainable Development section from the annual report of listed companies, replacing it with the obligation to report ESG factors throughout all sections of the annual report.[23] CORFO has programs to strengthen social impact initiatives and environmental conservation. They include several credit programs with attractive payment terms, such as the FT Program, which has a special reduced interest rate for funds dedicated to impact investing or to promoting social innovation, allowing a leverage of up to 3:1 debt-to-equity ratio, granting lines of credit from USD 2 million up to USD 14 million.[24] Another example is InvestChile, the Foreign Investment Promotion Agency in alliance with Sistema B, which has a program to encourage overseas companies operating in Chile to adopt best practices with a triple impact (economic, social, and environmental).[25]

The public sector procurement process also plays an important role in encouraging businesses to consider and adopt ESG factors in Chile. ChileCompra is a decentralized public service that operates a web platform named Mercado Público. All governmental agencies are required to purchase services or supplies through this platform, usually by means of a public tender process.[26] ChileCompra has issued guidelines for public procurement, suggesting that public agencies consider sustainability[27] and the level of inclusion[28] of the bidders when gauging the best offers, as this is the first step for social enterprises seeking to enter the large public procurement market. Even though these guidelines are only recommendations, ChileCompra has also developed certain certifications granting a preferred status for sustainable companies or companies owned by women.[29] Having governmental entities consider ESG factors, especially those incorporated

22. https://www.cmfchile.cl/normativa/ncg_461_2021.pdf.

23. https://www.carey.cl/en/commission-for-the-financial-market-publishes-regulation-on-esg-content-in-annual-reports/.

24. https://www.bcn.cl/leychile/navegar?i=1101783.

25. https://investchile.gob.cl/investchile-launches-program-for-overseas-companies-to-improve-sustainable-development-practices/.

26. https://www.bcn.cl/leychile/navegar?idNorma=213004.

27. https://www.chilecompra.cl/wp-content/uploads/2016/11/directiva-n25.pdf.

28. https://www.chilecompra.cl/wp-content/uploads/2021/07/459-B-Directiva17.pdf.

29. Those certifications are Women Enterprise Certification (to companies that are controlled by women, i.e., more than 50 percent of the company is owned by women and that the CEO is a woman); Clean Production Agreement Certificate (to those companies that are certificate by the Sustainability and Climate Change Agency); and Cooperative Certification (for the companies that are structured as cooperative entities,

in the certifications, when acquiring services or supplies boosts the competitiveness of social enterprises, which can have higher costs than entities focused exclusively on the maximization of profits.

There is no special regulatory framework for impact investing or social enterprises in Chile. There are no tax incentives or benefits either. CMF has issued regulation (Rule 461) concerning ESG reporting, referred to earlier, but they are only mandatory for listed companies.[30] However, there are a number of listed companies that exceed the minimum legal requirements when preparing their sustainability reports, by trying to measure the impact of their different projects.[31] Recently, the Chilean Stock Exchange participated in the creation of the Dow Jones Sustainability Index (DJSI Chile) and the Stakeholders Sustainable Index Chile (SSIndex Chile).[32] The Santiago Stock Exchange has also adopted the Sustainable Stock Exchanges (SSE) initiative and has been an active ESG advocate. Moreover, some companies that are not regulated by the CMF have begun to voluntarily include the sustainability and social impact section in their annual reports, including finance services companies, investment funds, asset managers, private NGOs, and also public organizations.[33] Public opinion and interest from investors over the last few years has increased the pressure on both private and public companies to adopt ESG criteria.

Social Enterprise Legal Structuring Options

The most common vehicle used for structuring a for-profit social enterprise or for receiving impact investment capital is a commercial legal entity called a stock corporation (*Sociedad por Acciones*, or SpA). An

which is a special kind of legal entity), https://ayuda.mercadopublico.cl/autoatencion/secciondeayuda/articulo/?c=CAT-01003&s=CAT-010031&a=KA-01686.

30. https://www.cmfchile.cl/normativa/ncg_461_2021.pdf.

31. For example, CMPC S.A. (https://www.cmpc.com/pdf/Reporte_Sostenibilidad_2020.pdf), Empresas Copec (https://www.empresascopec.cl/wp-content/uploads/2021/07/Reporte-de-Sostenibilidad-2020-1.pdf), CCU S.A. (https://www.ccu.cl/wp-content/uploads/2021/07/Resumen_Informe_Sustentabilidad_2020_CCU.pdf).

32. https://www.bolsadesantiago.com/sostenibilidad_compromiso; https://www.bolsadesantiago.com/sostenibilidad_guiayrecomendaciones; https://www.bolsadesantiago.com/sostenibilidad_indices.

33. Empresas Carozzi S.A. (https://www.carozzicorp.com/wp-content/themes/carozzi/pdf/Reporte_Sostenibilidad_Carozzi_2020.pdf); Metro S.A. (https://www.metro.cl/corporativo/reporte/); Clínica Alemana S.A. (https://d51h1y0hva8v.cloudfront.net/docs/default-source/reportes-de-sustentabilidad/reporte-sustentabilidad-clinica-alemana-2020.pdf?sfvrsn=3d3d79d3_2).

SpA may have only one shareholder and is primarily governed by its bylaws.[34] This provides plenty of flexibility. SpAs are regulated as close corporations.[35] Such flexibility has important practical implications, since it enables virtually any kind of corporate governance, share transfer limitations, or preferences, as well as multiple series of shares.

However, since SpAs are for-profit commercial entities, counsel must maintain the for-profit essence of the entity when drafting the bylaws. This has two key implications that are particularly relevant when structuring a social enterprise. First, the ultimate purpose of the company must be profit creation for the shareholders (or at least the capability of profit creation), so the bylaws cannot contemplate a series of shares with zero economic rights. Second, the resources of the corporation must be dedicated to developing the business purpose indicated in its bylaws. This last point may cause difficulties from a tax perspective, since the expenses that are not deemed by the Chilean Tax Authority as directly related to the business purpose or not potentially capable of generating profits cannot be deducted, and the taxpayer could be subject to a 40 percent penalty tax for those expenses.[36]

The potential penalty tax does not apply when the enterprise is a nonprofit entity since it is not possible to distribute dividends or profits from a nonprofit entity, and the board members cannot be remunerated because the entity's primarily purpose is not a commercial one but rather a social, environmental, educational, or other purpose that may be considered beneficial for a group of people or society as a whole.[37] In Chile, nonprofit entities normally do not have a more beneficial tax treatment than for-profit companies.

Combining a nonprofit foundation with an SpA subsidiary creates a blended structure. The SpA acts as an operational company, and distributes dividends to the foundation, which ultimately pursues its social purposes with the revenues obtained by the operational subsidiary. This structure allows a combination between for-profit and nonprofit, since the SpA can have more shareholders, such as the founders or equity investors. It grants flexibility to obtain funding and to remunerate the founders, and even makes a successful exit feasible.

---

34. SpAs are ruled by the Chilean Commercial Code and subsidiarily by Law 18,045 about Anonymous Corporations.

35. Article 424 of the Chilean Commercial Code.

36. Article 21 of the Income Tax Law.

37. Article 545 of the Civil Code.

Currently, there is a bill in Congress that would create a new kind of company: the Companies of Benefit and Collective Interest (commonly known as BIC, its acronym in Spanish).[38] A BIC will not be a new form of legal entity, but a status or category for existing companies. Any company could become a BIC without changing its legal form or significantly amending its bylaws.

In the proposed legislation, the "benefit and collective interest" is defined as a positive impact or as a reduction of a negative effect in the community or the environment. Such interest must be specifically included in the bylaws of the company, stating that those who manage the company commit to pursue that interest. Other requirements include public disclosure of how such interest is actually pursued or achieved; identification in the bylaws of the mechanism for reporting progress in pursuit of the interest to the rest of the stakeholders; and how the impact will be supervised and measured. BIC companies shall also issue sustainability reports detailing the resources employed and efforts expended to seek the social or environmental objective, which shall be available to the public. The reports shall describe the companies' sustainability policies and other commitments to the community, an explanation of what the company did to fulfill its objectives, and the actual effects on the environment or community.

Challenges in Impact Investing

Although Chile is off to a good start, there are still obstacles to overcome before it becomes a world player in impact investing. First, the lack of data on social problems makes improvement difficult, since without a starting point it is hard to measure the real impact of philanthropic activity or impact investing. The state and private NGOs operate many social programs in Chile, so attributing results to one particular intervention is challenging. Also, the creation of a hybrid legal entity would dispense with the current need to maintain both for-profit and nonprofit enterprises simultaneously, which would result in lower operational costs. Tax benefits or incentives could also help boost social impact investing in Chile, since competing with traditional for-profit businesses puts the social enterprise at a significant disadvantage.

The tension between the development of the business purpose in order to maximize the shareholders' profit, with the pursuit of socially

38. https://www.camara.cl/legislacion/ProyectosDeLey/tramitacion.aspx?prmID=11789&prmBOLETIN=11273-03.

desirable objectives, is proof of an old-fashioned legal framework, which was created long before these new investment mechanisms or consideration of ESG factors even existed.

Opportunities for a Growing Market (Future of the Market)

Impact investing and the emergence of social enterprises are growing trends in Chile, which is moving from a purely philanthropic approach to social problem-solving to a more sustainable and integrated economy, with support from both the public and private sectors. Private sector participants come from countless industries and investment sources, although the most interested actors in the investment world are presently family offices and investment funds. Notwithstanding the challenges that impact investment is facing, including skepticism from the most traditional investors, the increasing attention this approach is receiving from government agencies and many elements of the private sector is leading to the creation of an ecosystem in Chile that could also help provide a bridge for impact investment in other countries of the region.

12

Colombia

José Francisco Mafla, Luis Gabriel Morcillo, and Guillermo Tejeiro[1]

Market Overview and Impact Investing Growth

Impact investing, or rather the idea of allocating economic resources toward change and impact, is present in Colombia, but in a scattered, un-uniformed way. Regulation-wise, there are many laws, decrees, public policies, social programs, among others, that one way or another seek to promote or develop investment with social and/or environmental impact. The scope is so wide that it ranges from programs such as Familias en Acción[2] to the Peace Treaty signed with The Revolutionary Armed Forces of Colombia—People's Army[3] (FARC) in 2016.

The former sought to impact the lives of families and children living below the poverty line by giving them economic incentives. Families were given additional money to supplement their monthly incomes, provided they made certain commitments aimed at spending the money to stimulate change in various ways. The latter, in one of six main agreements, sought to transform Colombia's rural areas most affected by the armed conflict, by integrating the regions and fomenting social and economic development. Furthermore, in the scope of international law, Colombia is member of the Paris Climate Agreement,[4] a signatory to the

---

1. Jose and Luis are partners, and Guillermo is a director, of Brigard Urrutia, Bogotá, Colombia.

2. Familias en Acción, https://prosperidadsocial.gov.co/sgpp/transferencias/familias-en-accion/.

3. Spanish: Fuerzas Armadas Revolucionarias de Colombia—Ejército del Pueblo, (FARC–EP or FARC).

4. Paris Agreement to the United Nations Framework Convention on Climate Change, Dec. 12, 2015 (entered into force Nov. 4, 2016), https://unfccc.int/sites/default/files/english_paris_agreement.pdf.

UN's environmental, social, and governance (ESG) objectives,[5] as well as the OECD's Principles of Corporate Governance.[6]

Growing Sector Opportunities

Colombia has many entrepreneurs, small- and medium-sized social enterprises with potential to become high-impact sustainable businesses. According to the Global Entrepreneurship Monitor (GEM) 2018–2019 report, Colombia ranks seventh worldwide in the birthplace of entrepreneurs. An example of the potential of local investment opportunities is the recent issuance of social bonds made by the Business Development Bank of Colombia (Bancoldex) in the domestic market. On May 24, 2018, the first issuance was made of approximately $111,871 million dollars, which was acquired by 103 investors with an overdemand of 1.2 billion pesos, that is, 4.1 times the value offered. The purpose of the money raised was to grant loans to micro and small entrepreneurs seeking to promote financial and labor force inclusion, as well as gender equality and local economic development. The social bonds benefitted:

- 104,721 microenterprises and 1,355 small businesses
- 16,909 companies located in rural and dispersed rural areas
- 58,227 women business owners
- 20,134 victims of armed conflict who own businesses in 623 municipalities
- 20,097 microenterprises (99.8 percent of the total number of enterprises)

The investments in micro and small enterprises were located in the following economic sectors: commerce (45 percent), industry (15 percent), services (22 percent), and agribusiness (7 percent).[7]

The approach of impact investing, by its nature, is multi-sectoral; however, in Colombia, the impact investment and innovative finance sector is tied to the same legal regime as traditional sectors such as capital markets, financial regulation, and banking intermediation. In Colombia, entities and companies seeking to make impact investments must, therefore, comply with significant regulatory burdens, such as minimum capital requirements,

5. United Nations, Sustainable Development Goals, https://www.un.org/sustainabledevelopment/sustainable-development-goals/.

6. Organization for Economic Co-Operation and Development (OECD), Principles of Corporate Governance, https://www.oecd.org/corporate/principles-corporate-governance/.

7. Familias en Acción, *supra* note 2.

stringent compliance, and security standards, which are not necessarily proportionate to the size and operation of the entities and companies. Since the impact investment and innovative finance sector has characteristics different from the traditional banking and financial sector, these companies and entities must adjust and make great efforts to adapt to such regulation, which translates into fewer opportunities for real impact on society.

Policy Framework and Government Initiatives

Currently, Colombia does not have a regulatory framework that defines the rules governing impact investments. There are, however, rules that separately cover and define related aspects and benefits, such as tax benefits to increase the number of local impact investors.

The main points of the Colombian regulatory framework are:

- Decree 1625 of 2016, modified by Decree 2205 of 2017 creates a 25 percent income tax discount for investments in environmental control, conservation, or improvement. Additionally, it establishes a gross income tax deduction for investments in the agricultural sector for construction, repair, foundation, expansion, and improvement of rural farms, subject to various requirements.
- Law 1558 of 2012 seeks promotion, development, and regulation of tourism as well as sustainable development and establishment of mechanisms for participation and coordination of public and private sectors. Additionally, it establishes the principle of "Tourism of Social Interest" with the purpose of providing accessible tourist services to less-favored populations and promoting development of places capable of raising their standard of living through tourism.
- Decree 1650 of 2017 grants tax benefits for companies doing business in zones most affected by Colombia's armed conflict. Its main purpose is to recover and promote economic development of more than 344 zones by granting companies a progressive income tax rate for a period of ten years. This mechanism provides investors the possibility of paying up to 50 percent of their income tax through direct investments in areas most affected by violence and poverty. In 2019, 41 companies with a total of 42 projects valued at $69 million dollars were approved.[8]

8. Agencias de Renovación del territorio, ABC Obras por Impuestos-OxI, https://portal.renovacionterritorio.gov.co/descargar.php?idFile=23509 .

- Decree 2112 of 2019 regulates the special tax regime created by the national government to attract domestic and foreign investment and generate employment in cities with high unemployment rates. The regime is called Special Economic and Social Zone and grants special income tax rate benefits for those creating a business in departments of Norte de Santander, La Guajira, Arauca, and the capital cities of Quibdó and Armenia.
- Circular 005 of 2022, issued by the Financial Superintendency, has made Colombia the first country in the Americas to adopt a green taxonomy. This document seeks to provide instructions and parameters to all market players to build an environmentally friendly market and to set the guidelines for an investment to be considered sustainable from an environmental point of view, also consolidating the government's commitment to achieve a balance between sustainable growth, the welfare of the population and environmental conservation, encouraging other Latin American countries to follow this path.
- Circular 031 of 2021 modified the disclosure regime for issuers of securities in relation to social and environmental matters, including climate issues, under a criterion of environmental and social materiality, adopting the international standards of the Task Force for Climate Related Financial Disclosure and the SASB Standards of the Value Reporting Foundation (*Estándares SASB de la Value Reporting Foundation*). This information must be disclosed by issuers by 2024 at the latest.
- Circular 008 of 2022 established the legal regime applicable to the offering of sustainable linked bonds (SLBs). In this sense, issuers must include in the offering memorandum information related the selection of key indicators, the calibration of sustainable performance objectives, the particular characteristics of such bonds and the external verification and reporting of the issuer.
- Law 2112 of 2021 established the obligation for pension fund managers to invest at least 3 percent of their resources in private equity funds, debt funds and/or funds of funds that in turn invest in Colombian companies or productive projects in Colombia in order to strengthen entrepreneurship and the scaling of the country's businesses. Additionally, pension funds managers must report the compliance with this obligation on a quarterly basis to the Colombian regulator.

In addition, within the framework of the initiative "Pact for Colombia, Pact for Equity" developed by 45 guilds and more than 60 public sector entities, agreements for growth and generation of employment were reached regarding the following sectors: business process outsourcing (BPO), commerce, processed food, tourism, software and information technology (IT), chemicals, fashion, transportation, construction, forestry, meat, and agriculture (especially growing oranges).

Common Funding Products and Vehicles

Common funding products and vehicles for impact investment in Colombia include impact funds, social impact bonds (SIB), green and social bonds, and blended finance.

Impact funds. Structurally, similar to traditional funds, although their investment strategy is different, impact funds seek projects with long-lasting impact. Examples of impact funds in Colombia are *Capital Fértil*, Ewa 2, Inversor, SEAF, and Acumen. These funds are generally structured as private equity funds and thus are regulated by Part 3 of Decree 2555 of 2010, but can also be structured as trust or investment agreements reflecting and incorporating conditions of impact funds. Nonetheless, structures are flexible enough to adapt corporate governance, fee structure, investment policy, and return metrics to function as a private equity impact fund.

Social Impact Bonds (SIB),[9] also known as results-driven agreements,[10] share the characteristics of other SIBs, meaning they are not truly bonds but rather results-driven agreements: investors are paid if the social outcome of the program funded by the SIBs is achieved.[11] In this sense, SIBs are not negotiated securities but rather private agreements among private and/or public entities. Parties are free to negotiate terms and conditions that suit investors' needs and social necessities, and thus are only regulated by the norms of the Civil and Commercial Codes and not by securities and capital market regulations. The first SIBs were established in 2017 and invested in a project called *Empleando Futuro* (Employing the Future) with the objective of employing and retaining 766 people for at least three months.[12] The second BIS was established

---

9. Sir Ronald Cohen. Impact: Reshaping Capitalism to Drive Real Change (2020).

10. Alma Agusti Strid & James Ronicle, *Social Impact Bonds in Latin America: IDB Lab's Pioneering Work in the Region: Lessons Learnt* (IDB Technical Note; 2087). Inter-American Development Bank. IDB Lab. (2021).

11. *Id.*

12. Youtube Video. Programa de Bonos de Impacto Social en Colombia. (SIBs. Co). (2020).

in 2020 with a similar purpose: employing vulnerable populations but retaining them for at least six months.[13]

Green and social bonds have the same structure as other common bonds. As fixed-income securities, they are regulated by securities and capital markets regulations. Their issuance and placement must be registered with the National Registry of Securities and Issuers, and must follow public offerings norms.[14] Although a third party must certify the bonds as being "green" or "social," the placement process is the same as other bonds.

In 2018, Celsia Empresa de Energía (Celsia), an electric power distribution company in Colombia, placed green bonds up to 420,000 million Colombian pesos (around $120 million). The bonds targeted institutional investors, with two corporations, International Financial Corporation and the *Financiera Nacianal de Desarrollo*, buying all the bonds. The money raised was destined for solar farms generating unconventional renewable energy that were expected to eliminate approximately 3.44 million tons of carbon dioxide.[15]

Other companies, such as *Bancolombia* and *Banco de Bogotá*, have also issued green and social bonds, in 2019 and 2020, respectively. Unlike green bonds issued by Celsia, these targeted retail investors. Given that banks (*Bancolombia* and *Banco de Bogotá*) lend to sustainable and environmentally friendly projects, instead of investing the funds directly, they are considered second-degree bonds.

To date, green bonds worth more than $1 billion Colombian pesos[16] (around $300 million) have been issued, an amount that continues to grow and is comparably much larger than other Latin American countries. The market for green bonds continues to grow because their returns

13. Heidy Monterrosa Blanco, *Colombia ha lanzado dos bonos de impacto social, uno a nivel nacional y otro en Cali. La República* (Mar. 5, 2020), https://www.larepublica.co/responsabilidad-social/colombia-ha-lanzado-dos-bonos-de-impacto-social-uno-nacional-y-otro-en-cali-2973210.

14. The general legal framework for the public offering of bonds can be found in Part 5 and Part 6 of Decree 2555 of 2010, and well as the Circular 029 of 2014 of the Superintendency of Finance.

15. *Epsa primera compañía del sector real en Colombia en emitir bonos verdes para financiar proyectos de energía solar con el apoyo de la IFC y la FDN* (July 5, 2018), https://www.celsia.com/en/noticias/epsa-primera-compania-del-sector-real-en-colombia-en-emitir-bonos-verdes-para-financiar-proyectos-de-energia-solar-con-el-apoyo-de-la-ifc-y-la-fdn/.

16. Andrés Felipe Gómez, Bonos Verdes en Colombia: compromiso con la sostenibilidad, (Sept. 22, 2020), https://www.grupobancolombia.com/wps/portal/empresas/capital-inteligente/mercado-capitales/bonos-verdes-colombia-sostenibilidad.

are similar to ordinary bonds,[17] and because institutional investors are shifting their paradigm and demanding that companies and projects also consider impact returns.

Blended finance, the strategic use of public and/or private/philanthropic funds to make projects sustainable[18] and achieve Sustainable Development Goals[19] is a common vehicle for impact investing in Colombia. Moreover, Colombia's administrative law allows public entities to associate with private companies through cooperation agreements that allow private parties to administer public funds or vice versa. Local public entities structure the agreements in such a way that for every dollar they invest, a private/philanthropic investor must agree to double that amount. FINAGRO[20] has recently incorporated blended finance in the investment policies of its private equity funds. It invests in funds that finance impact projects in the agricultural sector, with the fund manager agreeing to raise at least double FINAGRO's investment.

Sourcing Opportunities

In essence, sourcing opportunities for impact investment are the same as return-seeking investments. The key players of the Colombian capital market are pension funds (institutional investors) and private investors. These are mainly the kind of investors targeted to invest in traditional investments, and they are also targeted when seeking funds for impact investment.

The government has taken action to facilitate sourcing by pension funds. The Superintendency of Finance enacted a Good Practice Guide[21] that promotes socially responsible investments for pension funds to consider when building their portfolios. Although the Guide is not legally binding, it serves as a sourcing vehicle and starting point for unification and transparency.

Government funding and public-private associations are also sourcing opportunities that must be considered. In addition, companies frequently obtain social development through their charitable foundations,

17. *Id.*

18. Cohen, *supra* note 9.

19. The State of Blended Finance, *Convergence and Business & Sustainable Development Commission* (July 2017).

20. Fondo para el Financiamiento del Sector Agropecurio.

21. The guide, *Mejores Prácticas en el proceso de inversión en Fondos de Capital Privado*, published Feb. 12, 2020, can be accesed through the webpage of Superintendecy of Finance: https://www.superfinanciera.gov.co/jsp/10089706.

but are now opting to do it directly through impact investing. Also, some companies have taken actions demonstrating their interest in investing in projects or assets that not only seek financial returns but also impact returns by becoming signatories of the Principles of Responsible Investment (PRIs).[22]

Challenges in Impact Investment[23]

The leading challenges facing Colombia's impact investment ecosystem are impact measurement and an insufficient pipeline of investments.

Impact Measurement in Light of ESG Criteria

An investment policy or decision incorporating ESG and impact criteria must have a measurement metric that allows verification that the investment achieved the desired impact, as well as a report that allows communicating the results efficiently. The report can be prepared by the company or by the investor, under international standards such as Sustainability Accounting Standards Board (SASB), Global Reporting Initiative (GRI), Climate Disclosure Project (CDP), Climate Disclosure Standards Board (CDSB), or the International Integrated Reporting Council (IIRC).[24]

Impact assessment data is used, in turn, for evaluating investment portfolios by market ratings such as MSCI[25] or Sustainalytics.[26] From a project management perspective, the data also allows managers, investors, and governments to identify ways to improve typologies and strategies to improve evaluation of environmental and social interventions.

---

22. Such players include asset owners such as Porvenir, Skandia Administradora de Fondos de Pensiones y Cesantía SA, and Protección SA; investment managers like Altra Investments, Sura Investment Managers, and Bancolombia; and service providers such as MTS and Compartamos con Colombia, all Colombian companies.

23. Author of this section is Guillermo Tejeiro, director of the Environment and Sustainable Business Practice Group of Brigard Urrutia.

24. Please note that IIRC and SASB have merged into the Value Reporting Foundation since June 2021. Furthermore, during the COP26 in Glasgow, the International Financial Reporting Standards (IFRS) Foundation Trustees announced the creation of the International Sustainability Standards Board (ISSB). By January 2022, the ISSB has already issued a draft climate standard and expects to release two reporting protocols on disclosures in the second half of 2022. For more information: https://www.ifrs.org/groups/international-sustainability-standards-board/ and https://www.integratedreporting.org/the-iirc-2/.

25. https://www.msci.com/.

26. https://www.sustainalytics.com/.

In other words, measuring and reporting impact of investments is important for the development of an impact investment ecosystem, as well as for the development of projects that effectively incorporate ESG and impact criteria. In the "measurement and reporting ecosystem" identified by the World Economic Forum (WEF), challenges remain:[27]

- Complexity of environmental, social, and governance matters
- Lack of uniformity of data measuring environmental, social, and governance impacts
- Limited understanding of ESG ratings available in the market, as well as little interaction with them[28]

Unfortunately, according to recent studies in Colombia, at least 74 percent of impact investors mainly use their own methodologies to measure the impact of their investments.[29] The rest use internationally recognized methodologies such as the Impact Reporting & Investment Standards (IRIS), the Global Impact Investing Ratings System (GIIRS), or the Poverty Probability Index (PPI); or do not even measure the socio-environmental impact of their investments. These conclusions were confirmed by Luz Mila Lancheros and Gabriela Carrasco, who in a study conducted between November 2018 and May 2019, interviewed more than 90 actors in the impact investing sector in Colombia and Latin America.[30]

In Colombia, there is still no uniform measurement parameter defined by law, nor is there a guideline associated with the standardization of such impact measurement. Consequently, even when global standards are used in Colombia, doubts persist about metric uniformity, which makes it difficult to verify impact in a comparable way.

These problems are not inherent to the Colombian impact investment ecosystem but are common to all jurisdictions. It is important to

---

27. World Economic Forum, Alliaz SE, Boston Consulting Group, *White Paper, Seeking Return on ESG—Advancing the Reporting Ecosystem to Unlock Impact for Business and Society* (2019), http://www3.weforum.org/docs/WEF_ESG_Report_digital_pages.pdf.

28. *Id.* at 12.

29. Aspen Network of Entrepreneurs, LAVCA, *El panorama de la inversión de impacto en América Latina. Tendencias 2016 & 2017* (Octubre 2018), at 28, https://lavca.org/impact-investing-rep/el-panorama-de-la-inversion-de-impacto-en-america-latina-2016-2017/.

30. Luz Mila Lancheros Carvajal & Gabriela Carrasco, *Inversión de Impacto en Colombia: Ecosistema en Construcción*, (Sept. 12, 2019), https://www.linkedin.com/pulse/inversi%C3%B3n-de-impacto-en-colombia-ecosistema-lancheros-carvajal/?originalSubdomain=es.

understand that the criteria or metrics are not assimilable in all cases, all over the world. Thus, given the lack of uniformity in measurement, results obtained are not comparable with each other, making it difficult for decision makers (companies, investors, managers of socio-environmental projects, among others) to move forward with their investments, and for project sponsors to adequately determine the expected impact ratios and materiality.[31] Therefore, when referring to the lack of uniformity in the measurement criteria, James Magor from ACTIS, a leading global investor in sustainable infrastructure, echoes the need to establish uniform criteria for measuring impact, to create greater transparency and flow of capital for these investment projects.[32]

For these purposes, it is advisable, in our opinion, to consider the possibility of establishing uniform measurement standards and/or methodologies through regulations or principles, appropriate to the particular environment of the projects, and making use of tools such as the List of Green and Sustainable Businesses,[33] which incorporates local sustainability social and environmental criteria, evaluation of scalability, and return on investment of projects.

Insufficient Pipeline of Projects

This challenge can be subdivided into two common complaints, namely:

- Lack of projects,
- Lack of a unified pipeline of existing projects.

A frequent complaint of impact investors is lack of projects, since conditions and formalities providing security for investors must be met. In Colombia, where most impact projects are in rural areas, these formalities and requirements are, in most cases, difficult to achieve. The lack of capacities, knowledge, and experience interacting with investors, as well as lack of knowledge of standards and impact metrics associated with specific materiality criteria, are real hurdles.

---

31. Op. Cit. 4, at 13.

32. "(...) to allocate capital with the intention of generating positive impact, a broadly accepted framework does not yet exist. Instead of being greeted with a series of generally accepted principles and industry norms, asset owners are faced with a baffling array of unverified, opaque and incompatible measurement frameworks, leaving them little room to properly select between an increasing number of asset managers promising to generate positive impact" at https://www.reutersevents.com/sustainability/esg-investors-need-single-standard-measure-impact.

33. Ministry of Environment and Sustainable Development—Green Business Office.

As to the second point, availability of projects is related to availability of information on them. To date, there are a multiplicity of entities and asset managers who manage their own project pipelines, and independently seek support from investors. There is no unified directory of projects in the country, and, furthermore, there is no unified directory of projects with verified impact under uniform metrics.

Future for Growing Market

The legal framework of impact investing lacks unification and depth. The government must play a major role in reforming existing norms and set clear guidelines for impact investments, benchmarks to measure their real impact, and disclosure mechanisms that allow investors to make informed decisions.

Pension reform is unavoidable, as the current public budget cannot support the pension burden much longer. When and how it will occur remains a mystery, but the government will have to use the reform to include ESG and impact investing variables, related to financial statements and results, into the pension fund investment regime, as well as ease its restrictions. In this sense, not only should it be legally possible for pension funds to make socially responsible investments, but they should have incentives to do so.

To conclude, the Colombian market has responded positively to impact investing projects. Demand for socially responsible companies and projects has been growing and is expected to continue to grow, as people want change. The government must then catalyze that change by standardizing impact investments and establishing metrics to measure their results. The metrics and actual value of the impact must be incorporated in companies' and vehicles' accounting in such a way that it is classified as what it is: a value-creation asset and not a liability. Only then, will we see a true change in impact investing in Colombia.

13

Mexico

Carlos Velazquez de Leon and Daniela Garza[1]

Market Overview

Impact investing began to appear in Mexico approximately 21 years ago, in the beginning of the 2000s. Since then, these types of investments have grown in popularity and sophistication as Mexico's society seeks conscious solutions to its social and environmental challenges. According to a report by the Association for Private Capital Investment in Latin America, 80 percent of current actors made their first impact investment in Mexico after 2007 and more than half of those have continued to make impact investments in Mexico since 2012.[2]

The recent rise of impact investment in Mexico can be credited to the importance that recent generations have given to improving the nation's and the world's conditions. As in other countries, the notion that making a profit is not enough and that a social responsibility exists in each citizen has resulted in impact investment becoming more important than ever before. The increasing popularity of movements in Mexico such as social justice, social equality, feminism, environmentalism, among others, are examples of a society that has become more conscientious. This underscores why investors have begun to pay special attention to impact investment, which allows them to create a positive impact while also making a profit, especially in a country such as Mexico, where general conditions are in great need for improvement.

1. Mr. de Leon is a partner and Ms. Garza an associate at Basham, Ringe y Correa, S.C., Monterrey, Mexico.

2. Aspen Network of Development Entrepreneurs (ANDE), Latin American Private Equity & Venture Capital Association (LAVCA), & LGT Impact Ventures (2016, August), *The Impact Investing Landscape in Latin America* 106.

Case Studies

Rodrigo Villar, founding partner of New Ventures and president of the Alliance for Impact Investment in Mexico (AIIMx) stated that impact investment has shown financial returns that can be as good as traditional investment, with the additional element of addressing social and environmental problems.[3] To fully understand the positive impact that this type of investment has created, we can look to some cases that have been a success in Mexico.[4]

NATGAS

NATGAS, an alternative energy company, received an investment from Adobe Capital, an impact investing venture capital firm that uses tailored financing alternatives to support entrepreneurs who can create innovative, profitable, and scalable business models to address social and environmental challenges.[5]

Two years into Adobe's investment, NATGAS was able to secure larger investments from international firms. Adobe's investment generated a 22 percent internal rate of return (IRR) in USD.[6] During a period of five years, NATGAS received investments of more than USD 200 million, which allowed the company to fund the construction of five additional fueling stations and the conversion of more than 2,000 vehicles from gasoline to natural gas, which helped reduce carbon emissions by 136 tons.[7]

The positive environmental impact of this project is very relevant, since air pollution in Mexico has become a serious problem, which causes more than 14,000 deaths annually.[8] In Mexico, vehicles account for 36 percent of total particle emissions to the air[9] and the use of vehicles

---

3. C. Zepeda (2018, October 18), La inversión de impacto: El camino para revertir carencias en México con rentabilidad financiera. El Financiero.

4. These cases are in no way related to Basham, Ringe & Correa, S.C.

5. Adobe Capital, https://adobecapital.org/en/home-en/.

6. Global Impact Investing Network. *Adobe Capital's Exit from NATGAS*. https://thegiin.org/adobe-capital-exit-from-natgas (last visited June 17, 2022).

7. H. Schiff & H. Dithrich (2018, January). *The Lasting Impact: The Need for Responsible Exits*. Global Impact Investing Network.

8. ONU-Habitat. Contaminación, automóviles y calidad del aire, https://onuhabitat.org.mx/index.php/contaminacion-automoviles-y-calidad-del-aire#:~:text=En%20algunas%20zonas%20metropolitanas%20como,en%20nuestro%20pa%C3%ADs%2014%2C700%20personas.

9. L. Henández (2019, May 24). Vehículos particulares generan el 36% de los contaminantes: CAMe. *Excelsior*.

fueled by natural gas has been proven to reduce emission of carbon monoxide by approximately 90 percent, carbon dioxide by 30 percent, and particle emissions by 100 percent.[10] NATGAS found an opportunity to convert vehicles that used regular gasoline to natural gas and, additionally, established fueling stations across various Mexican cities, making it a sustainable and profitable business.

Clínicas del Azúcar

Clínicas del Azúcar is a Mexican company founded in 2011 that specializes in low-cost and easy-access medical attention to patients suffering from diabetes and high-blood pressure related diseases.[11] Chief Executive Officer (CEO) Javier Lozano Garza stated "I wanted us to become a convenience store for diabetes: there should be one on each corner, to give people cheap and easy access to treatment. And that's where the health clinic concept originated."[12]

Clínicas del Azúcar's operation began with one clinic in Guadalupe, Nuevo León, but through investments from institutions such as International Finance Corporation (IFC), Promotora Social México (PSM), and the Social Entrepreneurs Fund, it expanded to 17 clinics in six cities around the country by 2021.[13] In 2015, Clínicas del Azúcar received a platinum certification (the highest level of certification) as an impact business model from the Global Impact Investing Rating System (GIIRS), which led to BBVA Bancomer selecting the company for its "Momentum Project," which is an initiative that supports the development of social entrepreneurship.[14]

Since 2000, diabetes has been the leading cause of death for women in Mexico and the second leading cause of death for men.[15] For greater

---

10. P. Mentado (2019, Mar. 6). 60% de contaminación en el Valle de México por vehículos a gasolina, https://energiahoy.com/2019/03/06/60-de-contaminacion-en-el-valle-de-mexico-por-vehiculos-a-gasolina/.

11. Clinicas Del Azucar, https://www.clinicasdelazucar.com/clinica-de-diabetes-nosotros/.

12. BBVA Momentum/ Clínicas del Azúcar (n.d.), https://www.momentum.bbva.com/en/emprendimientos/clinicas-del-azucar/.

13. A. Pineda (2018, Nov. 14). Clínicas del Azúcar levanta más de 4 mdd para luchar contra la diabetes, https://expansion.mx/emprendedores/2018/11/14/clinicas-de-azucar-levanta-mas-de-4-mdd-para-luchar-contra-la-diabetes.

14. Clinicas Del Azucar, *supra* note 11.

15. DIABETES EN MÉXICO (2020, Aug. 26), https://www.insp.mx/avisos/3652-diabetes-en-mexico.html.

context, the average monthly salary for the Mexican worker is USD 300.[16] This means that most members of the population who suffer from this disease in Mexico do not have the economic resources to obtain treatment and medication. With the help of investors, Clínicas del Azúcar has made it possible to reduce costs for the patient by 70 percent and to reduce the time in which they get treatment by 80 percent.[17]

Alliance for Impact Investing in Mexico (AIIMx)

The Alliance for Impact Investing in Mexico was created in 2015. Since then, more than 45 companies, organizations, and institutions have joined in an effort to promote and strengthen the ecosystem for impact investing in Mexico.[18] AIIMx also seeks to remove the remaining obstacles that impede impact investing from evolving much faster.[19]

AIIMx is the largest and most important organization with a presence in Mexico relating to impact investment.[20] Various members of this alliance are top-tier and publicly traded companies, prominent universities, and banks, among others. Their presence strengthens the alliance and provides awareness for impact investment in Mexico. In 2017, AIIMx issued a report detailing current information regarding impact investment in Mexico.[21] This report, along with various related events carried out by this alliance, such as national conventions, brought attention and publicity to impact investment in Mexico, helping people realize the magnitude of the investments being made and the potential that this type of investment has in a country like Mexico.

Impact Investing Growth

Mexico is one of the largest markets in Latin America for impact investment.[22] Although Mexico still has a long way to go, the amount of invest-

16. G. Hernández (2019, Oct. 16), Trabajadores mexicanos ganan en promedio $6,000 mensuales, https://factorcapitalhumano.com/mundo-del-trabajo/trabajadores-mexicanos-ganan-en-promedio-6000-mensuales/2019/10/.

17. *Supra* note 12.

18. ¿QUÉ ES LA INVERSIÓN DE IMPACTO?, http://aiimx.com.mx/.

19. Disruptivo TV (2019, Feb. 5). *Entrevista a Rodrigo Villar, CEO de New Ventures y Presidente de la AIIMx* [Video file], https://www.youtube.com/watch?app=desktop&v=Hb4aQrXgjio.

20. Alianza por la inversión de impacto Mexico, http://aiimx.com.mx/publicaciones/.

21. Can be consulted at http://aiimx.com.mx/publicaciones/.

22. Aspen Network of Development Entrepreneur, https://www.andeglobal.org/wp-content/uploads/2021/02/LatAm-Impact-Investing-2018-2019-ES.pdf.

ment and the mechanisms by which the investments are made keep improving each year. In 2017, impact investments in Mexico amounted to more than USD 170 million.[23] The following year, the number increased and, according to María Ariza, CEO of Bolsa Institucional de Valores (BIVA), more than 30 Mexican start-ups procured more than USD 50 million in capital in just 24 months (2017 and 2018).[24]

In 2019, Fondo de Fondos, a specialized investment firm, launched the first impact investment fund in Latin America for funds up to USD $125 million. This fund is designed to invest in Mexican funds that comply with certain social and environmental criteria. CEO Felipe Vilá acknowledges interest from international investors, mainly in Europe, and the lack of other viable alternatives within the sector in Latin America, as the main driving forces for this project.[25]

One of the most important steps toward promoting impact investing in Mexico came in 2020 with the launching of the first sustainable stock index by BIVA (Mexican exchange) and FTSE Russell (a wholly owned subsidiary of the London Stock Exchange Group) called FTSE4Good-BIVA.[26] This index measures the performance of Mexican companies demonstrating strong environmental, social, and governance practices,[27] allowing investors to analyze prices and calculate market performances based on market behavior.[28]

The creation of FTSE4Good-BIVA is especially favorable for impact investment in Mexico, as it gives investors information on how stocks of companies in the sector are behaving in the market. This index provides informational certainty regarding the market and gives up-and-coming investors the tools to begin investing in these companies.

---

23. Alianza por la Inversión de Impacto México (2018). Inversión de Impacto en México. Agenda de un mercado en Crecimiento, http://aiimx.com.mx/.

24. C. Zepeda (2018, Oct. 18), La inversión de impacto: El camino para revertir carencias en México con rentabilidad financiera. El Financiero, https://www.elfinanciero.com.mx/economia/la-inversion-de-impacto-el-camino-para-revertir-carencias-en-mexico-con-rentabilidad-financiera.

25. A. Pineda (2019, May 24), Así será el primer fondo de fondos para inversión de impacto en América Latina. *Expansión*, https://expansion.mx/emprendedores/2019/05/24/asi-sera-el-primer-fondo-de-fondos-para-inversion-de-impacto-de-america-latina.

26. R. Villar (2020, Mar. 3). Inversión de impacto 2020: En el punto de inflexión, https://medium.com/new-ventures-mexico/inversi%C3%B3n-de-impacto-2020-en-el-punto-de-inflexi%C3%B3n-4aa94c6da43d.

27. Biva, https://www.biva.mx/informacion_de_mercado/indices/informacion_general.

28. Índice bursátil, https://capital.com/es/indice-bursatil-definicion.

The Mexican market for impact investment has been growing over the last decade, and today it is not only increasing in size due to its growing popularity but also in quality, as different tools become available to make investments in Mexico easier and more transparent and efficient.

Industry Opportunities

In Mexico, some segments of the public sector can benefit significantly from private sector investment. Education, healthcare, and the environment are examples of areas in which the resources provided by the government have proven to be insufficient. The public sector provides a window of opportunity for successful impact investing from an economic, social, and environmental standpoint in these areas.

Education

In Mexico, education is generally low quality and insufficient. Statistics indicate that 25 percent of elementary and secondary schools have too few teachers; only 62 percent of secondary school graduates continue with high school studies; only four out of ten elementary schools have computers and internet access.[29] According to the Programme for International Student Assessment (PISA) testing, as of 2018, Mexico was in 53rd place in reading, 57th place in science, and 61st place in math, with scores in all categories below the Organisation for Economic Co-operation and Development (OECD) average.[30]

In 2020, the COVID-19 pandemic drastically altered educational paradigms everywhere in the world, forcing schools and students to adapt and migrate to online learning. Many elementary schools in Mexico, lacking access to computers or the internet, had to suspend classes indefinitely because of the pandemic. Impact investment in this sector could help provide internet service and computers to schools in need, augmenting basic public education in Mexico in an important way that would enable lower-income students to keep up with their higher-income counterparts.

29. A.K. García (2018, Dec. 25), Educación en México: Insuficiente, desigual y la calidad es difícil de medir. *El Economista*, https://www.eleconomista.com.mx/politica/Educacion-en-Mexico-insuficiente-desigual-y-la-calidad-es-dificil-de-medir-20181225-0028.html.

30. Pruebas PISA: Qué países tienen la mejor educación del mundo (y qué lugar ocupa América Latina en la clasificación), (2019, Dec. 3), https://www.bbc.com/mundo/noticias-internacional-50643441.

Healthcare

Mexico spends USD 3,992 per capita on general health, which is below the international average. The lack of investment in the healthcare sector directly affects disease prevention and diagnosis, as well as the treatment and rehabilitation of patients.[31]

Impact investment targeting specific problems in this sector, such as the lack of hospitals, equipment, and medication, can improve the Mexican healthcare system, and help it reach more people in a more effective way. A report by the Global Impact Investing Network (GIIN) states that out of 13 impact investment international firms that invested in healthcare, 12 invested directly in primary care (healthcare centers, hospitals, and clinics), nine invested in pharmaceuticals (distributing and manufacturing), and eight invested in medical equipment and supplies, with an overarching goal of expanding access to quality, affordable healthcare for low-to-middle income populations.[32] Historically, Mexico's government has been deficient when it comes to allocating resources to the healthcare sector,[33] which suggests that there is an important investment opportunity in this sector.

Environment

As the NATGAS case demonstrates, investing in cleaner energy sources in Mexico can be both profitable and beneficial for the environment. In accordance with the Paris Agreement,[34] Mexico made a commitment to obtain 35 percent of its energy requirements from clean energy sources by 2024, and that number will increase to 43 percent by 2030.[35] This commitment requires action, including incentives, and opens an opportunity for impact investing in renewable resources in Mexico, making it attractive for investors.

---

31. Estadísticas en salud de México | Actualización de Estadísticas de Salud de la OCDE 2019, (2019, Oct. 3), *Canifarma*, https://codigof.mx/estadisticas-en-salud-de-mexico-actualizacion-de-estadisticas-de-salud-de-la-ocde-2019/.

32. Global Impact Investing Network, G. (2016). *Impact Measurement in the Healthcare Sector* [PDF] at 10.

33. D. Celis (2021, Apr. 21), La Crisis del Sector Salud, https://www.elfinanciero.com.mx/opinion/dario-celis/2021/04/21/la-crisis-del-sector-salud/.

34. https://unfccc.int/process-and-meetings/the-paris-agreement/the-paris-agreement.

35. A. Lobo (2019, Oct. 16). Los compromisos climáticos de México, https://wrimexico.org/news/los-compromisos-clim%C3%A1ticos-de-m%C3%A9xico#:~:text=El%20Acuerdo%20de%20Par%C3%ADs%20implica,ciento%20para%202030%2C%20ser%C3%ADa%20limpia.

Mexico currently has the capacity to produce only approximately 31 percent of its energy from renewable resources such as solar, nuclear, wind, hydroelectric, and geothermal.[36] Strategic impact investing can increase that capacity and help Mexico come closer to the respective goals for 2024 and 2030. Projects in this industry have the potential to help combat climate change and contamination in Mexico, while providing solid financial returns.[37]

Policy Framework and Government Initiatives

Mexico has yet to create a comprehensive body of law that regulates impact investing. However, there are several laws that regulate these types of transactions, especially between the private and public sectors. The most relevant is the Public-Private Associations Law, which is a federal law. Its goal is to regulate the relationship between the private and public sectors for the joint development of infrastructure projects to increase social well-being and investment in the country.[38] This law, however, does not specifically regulate impact investments as a different modality with its own tailored set of rights and obligations for the parties involved.

As the impact investment industry expands in Mexico, lawmakers may focus on tailoring the current legal regime to meet the specific requirements and challenges of that industry, creating more certainty and transparency for investors and investees alike. The best approach may be to focus on two Mexican laws, the Public-Private Associations Law[39] and the Acquisitions, Leases, and Public Sector Services Law,[40] which regulates the involvement of the public sector, as these laws are the most relevant laws in this regard because they cover the most important topics related to this industry.

---

36. Forbes Staff (2020, May 17), México genera del total 31% de energía renovable: Sener, https://www.forbes.com.mx/economia-mexico-energia-renovable-sener/#:~:text=M%C3%A9xico%20cuenta%20con%20capacidad%20instalada,con%20la%20Secretar%C3%ADa%20de%20Energ%C3%ADa.

37. O. Zavaleta (2020, May 20). Las energías renovables, su relevancia en México y en el mundo, https://egade.tec.mx/es/egade-ideas/opinion/las-energias-renovables-su-relevancia-en-mexico-y-en-el-mundo.

38. Public-Private Associations Law (Jan. 16, 2012), https://www.diputados.gob.mx/LeyesBiblio/pdf/LAPP_150618.pdf.

39. *Id.*

40. Acquisitions, Leases, and Public Sector Services Law (January 4, 2000), https://www.diputados.gob.mx/LeyesBiblio/pdf/14_200521.pdf.

Challenges in Impact Investing

The two leading challenges to impact investing in Mexico are the effects of COVID-19 and corruption.

COVID-19

The pandemic has taken the world by surprise; in Mexico it has taken more than 300,000 lives.[41] The economic consequences of the pandemic have resulted in the closing of more than 1.6 million businesses, leaving segments of the population with no jobs or income of any kind.[42] The pandemic is not over, and in the author's experience, the health and livelihoods of many people continue to be affected.

Impact investing can help Mexico revive its economy and help the population with struggles that the COVID-19 pandemic has amplified. Mexico, like many countries around the world, now has two crises: the healthcare crisis and the economic crisis. Impact investments in healthcare and in projects that benefit those who have lost businesses and jobs can help alleviate both of those crises.

Corruption

Corruption is a key obstacle to investment of all kinds in Mexico, including impact investment. In the 2021 Corruption Perceptions Index by Transparency International, Mexico ranked 124 out of 180 countries in corruption, with a score of 31 on a scale of 100 (least corrupt) to 0 (most corrupt).[43]

Impact investment projects in the education, healthcare, and environmental sectors in Mexico require interaction with the government. Corruption could hinder potentially successful projects, or it could result in rewarding certain investors with an unfair or undeserving advantage, or it could discourage investors from entering the market at all.

The fight against corruption was a main pillar of the campaign platform of the current Mexican president, Andrés Manuel López Obrador

41. Conacyt (2022, Jan. 26). Covid-19 Mexico, https://datos.covid-19.conacyt.mx/.

42. EFE (2021, Dec. 21). Cerca de 1,6 millones de negocios cerraron en México por la pandemia. Los Angeles Times, https://www.latimes.com/espanol/mexico/articulo/2021-12-21/cerca-de-1-6-millones-de-negocios-cerraron-en-mexico-por-la-pandemia.

43. Country Data (2021), *Transparency International*, https://www.transparency.org/en/countries/mexico.

(AMLO).[44] However, statistics have instead indicated an increase in corruption over his first two years in office.[45] This means that corruption is still a significant problem in Mexico and, if impact investment projects involve the government, it can become a challenge for all parties involved.

44. Forbes Staff (2018, Dec. 3), Las 45 promesas que realizó AMLO en su toma de posesión, https://www.forbes.com.mx/45-promesas-que-realizo-amlo-en-su-toma-de-posesion/.

45. Forbes Staff (2020, May 22), Actos de corrupción crecieron en el primer año de AMLO: Inegi, https://www.forbes.com.mx/noticias-actos-de-corrupcion-crecieron-en-el-primer-ano-de-amlo-inegi/.

Asia

14

China

Angela M. Gallerizzo[1]

Market Overview and Impact Investing Growth

China has only recently become interested in impact investing. This sector is still in its very early stages and lacks the full necessary human capital, government support, and abundance of high-quality investees to form a fully functioning system.[2] Although China may still be in its early stages, environmental, social, and governance (ESG) factors in the country are evolving and improving at a rapid rate.[3] Almost from scratch, the Chinese asset management industry has begun to embrace sustainable impact investing, and is now actively using ESG factors in its investment decisions.[4] One powerful driver of this change has been demand from international clientele, such as European pension funds, insurers, and sovereign wealth funds. Chinese asset managers have had to build ESG into decisions about their portfolios to meet these demands.[5] The rapid globalization of China's equity markets has led to the importation

1. Attorney licensed in New York, New Jersey, and the District of Columbia.

2. Cissy Chen, *Building an Impact Investing Ecosystem in China*, HARVARD BUSINESS SCHOOL, SOCIAL ENTERPRISE, BLOG IMPACT INSIGHTS (Jan. 10, 2019), https://www.hbs.edu/socialenterprise/blog/building-an-impact-investing-ecosystem-in-china/.

3. *Going Green: The Rise of Sustainability Investing in China*, FUNDS EUROPE, MAGAZINE ISSUES, (Nov. 2020), https://www.funds-europe.com/digital-advertorials/going-green-the-rise-of-sustainability-investing-in-china.

4. Douglas Beal, *China Leapfrogs Its Way Towards Sustainable Investing*, LINKEDIN BLOG (July 8, 2019), https://www.linkedin.com/pulse/china-leapfrogs-its-way-towards-sustainable-investing-douglas-beal.

5. *Id.*

of an ESG mindset to the admitted companies.[6] Issuers in China's growing green bond market have also had to comply with new international ESG standards.[7]

Given China's sheer size, it has the potential to be a game-changer in the area of impact and ESG investing. Key factors already in place include a growing green credit market that is encouraging companies to invest in ESG-related projects, strategic government policies now being enacted to promote sustainability programs, and an increase in companies that are eager to leverage new technology to accelerate the impact.[8]

So far, ESG awareness in China, however, has focused primarily on the environment. Other social aspects, such as gender equality, have been seen as less important.[9]

Growing Sector Opportunities

Some organizations have been created to build an impact investing ecosystem in China. These include the Global Impact Investing Association, established in 2018 by the former CEO of China Merchants Bank, which aims to lead impact investing in China, and CreditEase, which was established to build a microfinance business in China.[10] Additionally, Chinese institutions such as the Narada Foundation, the China Global Philanthropy Institute, and Ehong Capital are fueling growth in this sector in the country.[11]

The Asset Management Association of China (AMAC) and the China Securities Regulatory Commission are starting to discuss sustainable impact investing, and are in the process of issuing guidelines on ESG reporting for Chinese companies.[12] AMAC circulated China's first self-regulation standards for the asset management sector on green

6. Fiona Reynolds, *ESG Investment Starts to Gain a Foothold in China*, Nikkei Asia (Jan. 7, 2020), https://asia.nikkei.com/Opinion/ESG-investment-starts-to-gain-a-foothold-in-China.

7. *Id.*

8. Arthur Lau, Elizabeth Soon & Cynthia Chen, *China's ESG Iceberg: Sustainability in the Age of Technological Disruption*, PineBridge Investments (Sept. 9, 2020), https://www.pinebridge.com/en/insights/chinas-esg-iceberg-sustainability-in-the-age-of-technological-disruption.

9. *Supra* note 6.

10. *Supra* note 2.

11. Mike Muldoon & Caleb Ballou, *Social Impact Investing in China—A Tipping Point*, The Rockefeller Foundation, Blog (Apr. 5, 2019), https://www.rockefellerfoundation.org/blog/social-impact-investing-china-tipping-point/.

12. *Supra* note 4.

investment, which encourages fund managers to focus on sustainable investment.[13] China's Banking and Insurance Regulatory Commission has also begun to launch guidance for China-based banks and non-bank financial institutions to incorporate ESG into their entire credit extension regimes, along with providing other measures to promote sustainable finance.[14] These actions are expected to jumpstart a long-awaited boom in Chinese sustainable investment, positioning the country in the ESG investment space, which has grown to an estimated 40 percent of all professionally managed assets.[15]

The technology industry in China has also been a key driver of change and is now setting the tone on ESG adoption through its use of technology to enable progress toward inclusive economic development, to change behaviors toward more sustainable, socially responsible practices, and to track more ESG measures.[16]

Policy Framework and Government Initiatives

Environmental protection has become a government priority in China, and "part of China's structural shift toward sustainable growth."[17] Key enablers of ESG adoption in China are new government policies in recent years that incentivize companies to comply with stricter environmental standards, and government subsidies and incentives to grow the green financing market.[18] The Chinese president recently announced stronger climate targets for China, and recently addressed the UN General Assembly stating that China would reach carbon neutrality by 2060.[19] This was the first time that the world's largest CO2 emitter had "pledged to end its net contribution to climate change."[20] The Chinese government also announced its plans to stimulate domestic growth by advancing the adoption of green technologies, and upgrading urban infrastructures to become

13. Michael Lai, ESG *Gains Traction in China as Investor Base Expands*, Franklin Templeton, Emerging Markets Blog (July 22, 2020), https://www.franklintempleton.com.au/insights.

14. *China Awakens to the Power of Responsible Investing*, Financial Times, https://www.ft.com/brandsuite/ping-an/china-awakens-to-the-power-of-responsible-investing.html?fbclid=IwAR2oe5W6qGvhw_2IeIJeHGK3IU9tB1d_Uw-Q5xNTTnU7ZvsX0sVrhqeZa-w.

15. *Id.*

16. *Supra* note 8.

17. *Id.*

18. *Id.*

19. *Supra* note 3.

20. *Id.*

more green friendly.[21] Chinese government plans also include budgetary increases for a smart grid, and a renewed focus on usage and storage of renewable energy.[22] China is already the world's largest manufacturer and installer of solar panels, and its mass expansion of solar manufacturing, which was supported by significant government tax breaks and financial incentives, caused prices worldwide to drop by 80 percent.[23]

With regard to ESG disclosures, Chinese regulators are setting goals for mandatory ESG disclosures by domestically listed companies, initially set for the end of 2020, postponed due to delays as a result of the coronavirus pandemic, and now starting to take effect in 2022.[24]

Common Funding Products and Vehicles

Banks in China, the primary source of credit to companies, are increasingly recognizing the financial opportunities associated with green financing products and are actively incorporating these products into their lending activities.[25] The establishment of the "Green Financial System" by the Chinese government has also paved the way for the green bond market.[26] In just four years after its adoption, China became the world's second largest issuer of green bonds after the United States.[27]

Sourcing Opportunities

There are various sourcing opportunities for the growth of impact investing in China. These include green financing products by banks, issuance of green bonds by Chinese corporates, and growing investor interest in ESG-related investments by mutual and private equity funds.[28] There

---

21. *Id.*
22. *Id.*
23. *Id.*
24. Jessica Tan, *A Green Wave of ESG Is Poised to Break over China*, World Economic Forum (Dec. 4, 2020), https://www.weforum.org/agenda/2020/12/green-wave-of-esg-investment-is-breaking-in-china/; Zoey Zhang, *What is ESG Reporting and Why is it Gaining Traction in China?* CHINA BRIEFING, Dezan Shira & Associates, Jan. 13, 2022, https://www.china-briefing.com/news/what-is-esg-reporting-and-why-is-it-gaining-traction-in-china/#:~:text=Regardless%20of%20the%20current%20scope%20of%20practice%2C%20it,Environmental%20Information%20by%20Law%20will%20come%20into%20effect..
25. *Supra* note 8.
26. *Id.*
27. *Id.*
28. *Supra* notes 6 and 8.

have been a growing number of domestic ESG-themed funds being listed as ESG-focused funds, though these ESG standards still differ from standards observed abroad.[29] With the new ESG-focused interest, rich families throughout China and Asia are pouring millions into impact investment funds, and companies are now "turning to Asia to attract new socially conscious investors and as a place to invest."[30] Recently, Chinese philanthropists have also joined together to promote impact investing as the coronavirus pandemic offered a global reminder of the importance of sustainable development.[31]

Challenges in Impact Investing

Challenges to the expansion of impact investing in China exist. While listed corporations must follow certain reporting standards, the quality of that reporting has generally been low. This can, of course, present an obstacle for asset managers seeking ESG information to factor into their investment decisions.[32]

Another challenge has been that ESG standards set by foreign buyers are not always consistent with those set by Chinese companies. What is important in China from an ESG perspective may differ from that in other parts of the world.[33] There are also differences in standards between the different types of companies in China, for instance, private sector companies in China tend to follow stricter ESG standards for governance than do state-owned enterprises.[34]

There is also a lack of data to give local asset owners confidence that their investment "will actually have financial returns that will equal or beat a standard benchmark."[35] Since ESG data is hard to quantify and measure, and can be difficult to collect and analyze, many start-up companies in China are now leveraging new technology in an attempt to address these problems.[36] Still, Chinese companies lag behind their

29. *Supra* note 13.
30. K. Oanh Ha, *Rich Asian Families Are Pouring Millions into Impact Investing*, Bloomberg Businessweek (Feb. 24, 2021), https://www.bloomberg.com/news/articles/2021-02-24/warren-buffett-s-grandson-is-selling-rich-asians-on-impact-investing.
31. Chai Hua, *Chinese Philanthropists Promote Impact Investing in Wake of Pandemic*, China Daily (Mar. 20, 2020), https://www.chinadailyhk.com/article/125073.
32. *Supra* note 4.
33. *Id.*
34. *Supra* note 13.
35. *Supra* note 4.
36. *Supra* note 8.

developed-market peers when it comes to ESG disclosures, and this primarily can be attributed to three factors: lack of a unified set of guidelines on the materiality of information for disclosure, lack of processes in place by companies to collect high-quality data, and market for ESG ratings and data in China still being in its early stages.[37] "Although ESG investing deploys more than $30 trillion worldwide, the vast majority of Chinese companies do not report enough ESG data to show whether they qualify for the funds."[38]

Without enforced ESG disclosure rules from Chinese regulators, most Chinese companies do not believe the benefits of tapping additional funding outweigh the extra work involved, since China's stock markets are "dominated by retail investors who are used to wild swings and typically seek fast returns," and as such, companies have been able to raise funds without publishing ESG information.[39] China's financial authorities have also expressed concerns about the market readiness and ability of domestically listed companies to disclose ESG information, and the costs to Chinese companies associated with mandatory ESG reporting.[40]

A further challenge has been the investment mindset of China's corporate culture. A shift in this mindset to establish that "assets invested according to ESG factors outperform benchmarks in the long run," will ensure that this corporate culture does not become a barrier to progress in this area.[41] Indeed, there has been a growing body of evidence that social and environmental factors are compatible with competitive returns.[42]

Opportunities for a Growing Market (Future of the Market)

There are now several indications that China is well-positioned to assume a leadership role going forward in the area of impact investing.[43] First, the rise of family offices in China has resulted in a flexible pool of business-oriented capital seeking to foster public good."[44] Second, the correspond-

---

37. *Supra* note 24.

38. *Why China Is Missing Out on Trillions in Sustainable Investment*, Bloomberg Green (June 14, 2020), https://www.bloomberg.com/news/articles/2020-06-14/why-china-s-missing-out-on-trillions-in-sustainable-investment.

39. *Id.*

40. *Supra* note 6.

41. *Id.*

42. *Supra* note 14.

43. *Supra* note 8.

44. *Id.*

ing growth of venture capital in China has given rise to "a new generation of Chinese venture philanthropist models and funds" seeking to deploy capital to innovate for public good.[45] Third, a younger generation with strong social values is increasingly controlling private wealth and mobilizing social entrepreneurship activity in the country.[46] Fourth, approximately 65 percent of charitable giving in China is now done through corporations, and their corporate social responsibility activities are growing.[47] And last, the Chinese government is increasing support for impact investing through a recent regulation giving philanthropic organizations more flexibility to engage in charitable for-profit investment activities.[48]

Moreover, there are now 50 Chinese signatories on the UN Principles for Responsible Investment, which clearly reflects a growing change in management mindset toward impact investing and sustainability that is expected to grow in the coming years.[49]

45. *Id.*
46. *Id.*
47. *Id.*
48. *Id.*
49. *Supra* note 3.

15

India

Samiksha Godiyal[1]

Market Overview and Impact Investing Growth

While the term "impact investment" was first coined by the Rockefeller Foundation in New York in 2007,[2] its appearance in India preceded the formal conceptualization. In India, a break in the model of risk and return was noticed as early as 1946 with the foundation of the Amul Dairy Cooperative, a successful business employing low-income dairy farmers to professionally manage a supply chain. The Amul brand is managed by the Gujarat Co-operative Milk Marketing Federation Ltd., which is jointly owned by about three million milk producers. The cooperative structure was conceived as a response to the exploitation of sundry milk producers by agents and traders. The model helped India emerge as the largest milk producer in the world. More than 15 million milk producers contribute milk through 144,500 dairy cooperative societies.[3] The milk is then processed and marketed throughout the country, ensuring a better life for millions at the Base of Pyramid.[4]

Similarly, Fabindia Limited was incorporated in 1976 as a community-based business model to source and sell products that are made from

1. Lawyer based in New Delhi practicing before the Indian Supreme Court and the Delhi High Court.

2. E.T. Jackson and Associates Ltd., *Accelerating Impact: Achievements, Challenges and What's Next in Building the Impact Investing Industry*, The Rockefeller Foundation, New York (July 2012).

3. https://www.ibef.org/industry/agriculture-india/showcase/amul (last visited Jan. 20, 2022).

4. Base of Pyramid refers to the poorest two-thirds of the economic human pyramid living in abject poverty. Seema Tewari, Harjit Singh, Shobhit Wadhwa & Deepak Tandon, *Scaling Impact Investment for Sustainable Development Goals: An Empirical Analysis*, 15(5) Australasian Accounting, Bus. & Fin. J. (2021).

traditional techniques, skills, and hand-based processes in India. The company links more than 55,000 craft-based rural producers to modern urban markets, and creates a profitable base for skilled, sustainable rural employment, while seeking to preserve India's traditional handicrafts. Its founder, John Bissell, described his vision as: "In addition to making profits, our aims are constant development of new products, a fair, equitable and helpful relationship with our producers, and the maintenance of quality on which our reputation rests."[5]

Amul and Fabindia are social enterprises; however, their growth may not be a direct application of the impact investment theory. The establishment of the Aavishkaar Bharat Fund (ABF) in 2001 was perhaps the first formal recognition of impact investment in India. ABF is an Indian venture capital firm focusing on infusing early-stage and expansion capital in entities that aim to solve problems for low-income populations and cater to underserved areas in India. ABF invests in businesses with high social impact in the agricultural, financial services, healthcare, waste management, sanitation, renewable energy, and logistics sectors. Until now, it has made 58 investments across India, Indonesia, Sri Lanka, and Bangladesh. The investments have benefitted almost 70 million persons, of which more than 50 percent are women, and generated around 250,000 jobs.[6]

Moving away from these early examples, impact investments gained momentum after the 2007–2008 global financial crisis.[7] There has been a clear transition of values among the next generation, which is demanding greater accountability and responsibility toward society and the environment in investment decision-making.[8] In India, the impact investment story is centered considerably around the expansion of microfinance industry and financial inclusion since 1970, and its crash in early 2011. Through these years, while private equity investors made high returns on investments, the interest rates charged to the microfinance beneficiaries frequently exceeded 25 percent and the fallout had larger implications for the impact investment market as a whole. In the wake of close to 30 farmer suicides in the southern Indian State of Andhra Pradesh, and a subsequent government ordinance, the success of the microfinance sector

5. https://www.fabindia.com/about-us (last visited Jan. 20, 2022).

6. https://www.cdcgroup.com/en/our-impact/fund/aavishkaar-emerging-india-fund/ (last visited Jan. 20, 2022).

7. Shamika Ravi, Emily Gustafsson-Wright, Prerna Sharma & Izzy Boggild-Jones, *The Promise of Impact Investing in India*, Brookings India (July 2019).

8. Georgette Fernandez Laris, *Philosophical Foundations of Impact Investing* (Sept. 2017), https://sevenpillarsinstitute.org/philosophical-foundations-of-impact-investing/.

in India (with an estimated value of US$6.7 billion and nearly 30 million beneficiaries in 2010–2011) became questionable. The debate regarding priority between the objectives of profitability and sustained development was brought to the forefront.[9]

The introduction of the [Indian] Companies Act of 2013 was another crucial chapter in the Indian impact investment story.[10] The legislation mandated companies above a certain profit threshold to spend 2 percent of their net profits on Corporate Social Responsibility (CSR) activities. Over time, different models have evolved to utilize CSR funds, which in turn have not only increased philanthropic spending but also greatly enhanced total impact investment resources in India.

Another factor that contributed significantly to the ease of impact investment in India is the adoption of the UN Sustainable Development Goals (SDGs) in 2015. According to UN estimates, in order to achieve the SDGs by 2030, developing nations must invest around US$3.9 trillion annually. Private and public sectors are expected to invest only US$1.4 trillion, leaving an investment gap of US$2.5 trillion, which social impact investments are expected to fill.[11]

Accomplishment of these goals for growth and progress has altered the philosophy of development. These goals provide globally accepted objective measures of social impact.[12] Examining the progress of these goals in India through NITI Aayog's[13] SDG India Index facilitates impact measurement, a key driver for impact investment. This has also changed the way investments are generally viewed. Just as the world community has accepted that all future development should be sustainable, so should all investment. Impact investment fits this requirement.[14]

9. Ravi, Gustafsson-Wright, Sharma & Boggild-Jones, *supra* note 7.

10. *Id.*

11. UNCTAD, *World Investment Report, 2014: Investing in the SDGs: An Action Plan.*

12. Tewari, Singh, Wadhwa & Tandon, *supra* note 4.

13. NITI Aayog is the premier policy think tank of the government of India, providing directional and policy inputs. Apart from designing strategic and long-term policies and programs for the government of India, NITI Aayog also provides relevant technical advice to the Centre, States, and Union Territories, https://www.niti.gov.in/ (last visited Jan. 29, 2022).

14. Renita D'souza, *Impact Investments in India: Towards Sustainable Development*, ORF Occasional Paper (June 2020).

Growing Sector Opportunities

India has been described as a "testbed of new impact-investment ideas."[15] In the last ten years, India has raised US$10.8 billion through impact investment in 586 enterprises and 490 million people. The average contribution of impact investors has tripled from US$5 million to US$17 million. Most of this investment has been made by private sector enterprises (including private equity and venture capital funds)[16] and the CSR funds of corporates.[17] Notably, philanthropies, charitable organizations, domestic funds, and the government are relatively smaller contributors to the impact investment sector in India.[18]

India has about two million social enterprises and at least 75 active impact investors. India's impact investors fall into three categories:[19]

- **Fund managers** (such as Aavishkaar,[20] Acumen,[21] and Elevar[22])
- **Development finance institutions** (such as the National Bank for Agriculture and Rural Development and FMO Entrepreneurial Development Bank)
- **Foundations, high-net-worth individuals, and family offices** (such as Omidyar Network India, Michael and Susan Dell Foundation)

Impact investors in India engage with social enterprises at different stages through early-stage capital as well as debt and growth capital.[23] However, a majority prefer seed or early-stage funding. Further, unlike conventional commercial investors, impact investors engage in active investing and are more directly involved in strategy and business development. This is perhaps because impact investments involve a longer

---

15. Vivek Pandit & Toshan Tamhane, *A Closer Look at Impact Investing*, McKinsey Q. (Feb. 28, 2018), https://www.mckinsey.com/industries/private-equity-and-principal-investors/our-insights/a-closer-look-at-impact-investing.

16. *Id.*

17. Sakshi Sharma & Kunjana Malik, *Need to Boost Impact Investing in India* (Oct. 31, 2021), https://www.dailypioneer.com/2021/sunday-edition/need-to-boost-impact-investing-in-india.html.

18. Saahil Kejriwal, *Impact Investing*, India Dev. Rev. (Sept. 2019), https://idronline.org/idr-explains-impact-investing/.

19. D'souza, *supra* note 14.

20. https://aavishkaarcapital.in/ (last visited Jan. 29, 2022).

21. https://acumen.org/ (last visited Jan. 29, 2022).

22. https://elevarequity.com/ (last visited Jan. 29, 2022).

23. D'souza, *supra* note 14; Ravi, Gustafsson-Wright, Sharma & Boggild-Jones, *supra* note 7.

investment duration, and the enterprises they invest in are often smaller, younger, and likely to take longer to mature.[24]

In terms of returns, a majority of impact investors earn above-market returns, defined in the Indian context as beating the Sensex (India's weighted stock market index of 30 companies listed on the Bombay Stock Exchange).[25]

Agriculture, education, and healthcare have seen the highest number of investments and returns, followed by financial services, housing, and skilling sectors. Traditionally, these sectors have lacked infrastructure, particularly in the rural parts of the country. The agricultural sector is the largest employer in India—it accounts for 42.6 percent of the country's total employment.[26] Impact investment has helped to create sustainable business models for farmers to increase their yields, reduce costs, and have better access to markets. The healthcare sector has witnessed increased investments since the COVID-19 pandemic, and this has accelerated the growth of online pharmacy and specialty clinics. Similarly, impact investments have sustained the online mode of education made necessary in the pandemic.[27]

The most recent collated data on impact investment in India is the report prepared by the Impact Investors Council for the year 2020. Overall, in 2020, impact investing in India contributed toward 11 of the 17 SDGs, and focused on enterprises related to gender equality (SDG 5) and industry, innovation, and infrastructure (SDG 9). While the volume of impact investment in India decreased during the pandemic, there was increased interest in early-stage enterprises and technology-based business models.[28]

The general trends in impact investment in India are also corroborated by a study of the Omidyar Network in India. Omidyar Network is a philanthropic investment firm that aims to bring about social impact on a large scale. It funds commercial businesses and nonprofit organizations in multiple geographies.[29] Omidyar made its first direct investment

24. Ramraj Pai, Swasti Saraogi, Shriya Nene & Aman Kalsi, *2020 in Retrospect: India Impact Investment Trends*, Impact Investors Council.

25. D'souza, *supra* note 14; Ravi, Gustafsson-Wright, Sharma & Boggild-Jones, *supra* note 7.

26. https://data.worldbank.org/indicator/SL.AGR.EMPL.ZS?locations=IN (last visited Jan. 20, 2022).

27. Sharma & Malik, *supra* note 17.

28. Pai, Saraogi, Nene & Kalsi, *supra* note 24.

29. Matt Bannick, Paula Goldman, Michael Kubzansky & Yasemin Saltuk, *Across the Returns Continuum*, OMIDYAR NETWORK.

in India in 2008. In 2013, Jayant Sinha, then head of Omidyar in India described India as the global epicenter for impact investing.[30]

Over the years, Omidyar has invested more than US$250 million in India—70 percent in equity investments and 30 percent in grants.[31] Omidyar's investment in India is focused in five sectors: education, emerging technology, governance and citizen engagement, financial inclusion, and property rights. In terms of returns, Omidyar's strategy is clear—investors should accept below-market returns only in certain limited situations where they are intentionally pursuing market-level impact.

Policy Framework and Regulation

There is no distinct legal and regulatory structure for social enterprises and impact investors in India. Social enterprises have been operating as regular commercial businesses or nongovernmental organizations. Impact investment funds have so far been regulated as Alternative Investment Funds or Social Venture Funds under the Securities and Exchange Board of India (Alternative Investment Funds) Regulations, 2012 (AIF Regulations).[32] The Securities and Exchange Board of India (SEBI) is India's capital markets regulator (similar to the U.S. Securities and Exchange Commission) established under statute. One of its key functions is investor protection.

Under AIF Regulations, an AIF is an entity incorporated in India as a trust, or a company, or a limited liability partnership. It is a privately pooled investment vehicle that collects funds from investors, whether Indian or foreign, for investing in accordance with a defined investment policy for the benefit of its investors. AIFs cannot be collective investment schemes or mutual funds.

Alternative Investment Funds are required to be registered with the SEBI and its securities cannot be subscribed by the public. The investment strategy and purpose of the AIF has to be transparent to its contributors. AIFs can raise funds by issuing units, and each scheme of an AIF is required to have a corpus of at least US$200 million. Other than

30. A. Thillai Rajan, Pawan Koserwal and S. Keerthana, *The Global Epicenter of Impact Investing: An Analysis of Social Venture Investments in India*, 17 J. PRIV. EQUITY (Spring 2014).

31. *What We've Learnt about Accelerating Impact in India: 10 Years in India (2008–2018)*, OMIDYAR NETWORK.

32. Meyyappan Nagappan, Rahul Rishi & Anuja Maniar, *Impact Investing Simplified: A Guide to Making and Receiving Impact Investments in India*, NISHITH DESAI ASSOCS. (2019).

its employees or directors, a contributor to an AIF is required to make an investment of at least US$10 million.

Within the AIF Regulations, Social Venture Funds are a special kind of AIF that invest primarily in securities or units of social ventures, and that satisfy social performance norms laid down by the fund. Its investors may agree to receive restricted or muted returns.[33] Social Venture Funds are required to invest at least 75 percent of their investible funds in unlisted securities or partnership interest of social ventures.

Apart from SEBI regulation, the Impact Investors Council[34] is an important informal forum for self-regulation of impact investors in India. It is a member-based industry body with the objective to help strengthen the impact investing ecosystem in the country. The council consists of more than 50 members, including major contributors such as Aavishkaar, Acumen, Omidyar Network, Elevar Equity, MacArthur Foundation, and Tata Capital. Its stated objectives include increasing the flow of private capital to social impact sectors such as financial inclusion, clean energy, education, water and sanitation, and healthcare, and working effectively with the government through advocacy efforts. It also aims to concretize impact measurement and monitoring.

Challenges in Impact Investing

Impact investors in India have benefitted millions at the Base of Pyramid. India has a vast population of people in need that significantly overwhelms its public resources. Also, India still has a large proportion of unmet social needs. The global pandemic that we are currently in the midst of has highlighted the overlooked concerns of migrant workers and disguised unemployment. If social enterprises are nurtured to grow in a conducive legal framework, their impact will scale and will reach a sizeable number of people. The pressing target for the success of impact investment is a steady flow of capital into social impact projects to make sustainable development a reality. In India, this goal has distinctive risks and challenges.

To begin with, the undefined regulatory structure for impact investors in India restricts their ability to realize their desired objectives. Under the AIF Regulations, there is an implicit condition that investments in social ventures will be nonprofit. Most of the entities defined as "social

33. Section 2 of the Securities and Exchange Board of India (Alternative Investment Funds) Regulations, 2012.

34. https://iiic.in/about-impact-investors-council/ (last visited Jan. 20, 2022).

ventures" under the AIF Regulations (like trusts, societies, etc.) are nonprofit entities. This is not consistent with the theory of impact investment. Arguably, the AIF Regulations do not allow investors to earn market-level returns; they are constrained to accept restricted or muted returns. This may be the reason why domestic funds are not eager to participate as impact investors in India. This could also be one of the reasons why there is a lack of capital contribution across the risk-return continuum.[35]

Additionally, trusts, societies, and other nonprofit entities (such as companies incorporated under section 8 of the [Indian] Companies Act 2013) are not only governed by the AIF Regulations but also by other laws that may contradict the AIF Regulations in terms of the possibility of investors making returns. The [Indian] Foreign Contributions Regulation Act 2010 (FCRA) and the [Indian] Income Tax Act 1961 (ITA) also contradict the AIF Regulations on significant aspects. For instance, while the AIF Regulations permit for-profit organizations to receive foreign contributions, the ITA and the FCRA only contemplate foreign grants and donations to be made to nonprofit entities. This has possibly hindered the growth of impact investment and the blending of capital in India, which is the principle behind proliferation of impact investments.[36]

India still has stringent exchange control restrictions in place that limit the convertibility of foreign contributions in monetary terms. Further, in view of the FCRA stipulation that foreign grants and donations are permitted only in nonprofit entities, a foreign investor looking to invest for profit has to adopt the Foreign Direct Investment (FDI) route. FDI in India is facilitated through the Foreign Investment Facilitation Portal under the government of India. Over the years, the FDI process has been liberalized for most sectors, and investors from everywhere are permitted to participate, except territories sharing a land border with India. However, FDI in some relevant sectors, such as print media, broadcasting, and insurance, is still under the control of public authorities, adding yet another regulatory layer to the impact investment process.

Apart from this, industry analysis has revealed three significant challenges in the Indian context:

- Lack of flow of capital across the risk-return continuum
- Lack of suitable exit mechanisms for investors
- Lack of structured impact measurement models

35. D'souza, *supra* note 14.
36. *Id.*

Surprisingly, lack of government support was only conceived as a moderate challenge by a majority of the players.[37]

These challenges call for streamlined remedies. There is a need to assign a distinct legal status to social enterprises and impact investors. Formulation of an entirely new legal regime may be advisable to do away with conflicting statutes governing the field. Setting up a single-window regulatory body and allowing space for industry self-regulation (for instance by recognizing the role of the Impact Investors Council) may also be helpful.

India's taxation system needs to be sensitized to impact assessment models. Tax benefits under the ITA are available to nonprofit enterprises—not businesses operating for profit even where the profit or income generates social impact. A reward in the form of tax concessions may attract more domestic funding in social enterprises.

As far as foreign funding is concerned, the rigid FCRA requirements—that is, an organization becomes eligible to receive foreign donations only three years after its incorporation and after it has obtained the prior permission of the central government—provide significant pushback to the growth of impact investment in India. This needs to be rectified, and the implicit mistrust in entities receiving foreign contributions needs to be sacrificed to be able to achieve the full potential of impact investing in India.

Further, awareness about social enterprises and impact investment is necessary to take the philosophy a step forward and garner investment across the returns' continuum—ranging from fully commercial investments to philanthropic grants. Investment in early-stage and high-risk ventures that can achieve market-level impact through pioneering a new market model, providing industry infrastructure, and influencing policy is also necessary to harness comprehensive social impact in India where community values are otherwise conducive to social gain.[38] Apart from standardizing the legal and regulatory regime, the government can facilitate awareness campaigns in this direction in collaboration with existing social enterprises and impact investors.

In terms of exit options, in the 2019 budget speech, Finance Minister Nirmala Sitharaman proposed to set up the Social Stock Exchange (SSE)—an electronic fund-raising platform for social enterprises to raise

37. *Id.*; https://www.cdcgroup.com/en/our-impact/fund/aavishkaar-emerging-india-fund/ (last visited Jan. 20, 2022).

38. Bannick, Goldman, Kubzansky & Saltuk, *supra* note 29.

funds through equity, debt, and mutual funds.[39] The SSE is yet to be established; once set up, it is likely to provide greater liquidity and profitable exit options to impact investors.

For a structured approach to impact measurement, adopting global trends in addition to monitoring progress in terms of SDGs is important. The introduction of social impact bonds as an investment tool is a step in the right direction.[40] In this structure, the investor makes payments only when pre-agreed social outcomes or outputs are achieved and verified.[41] This makes room for tracking the social progress and ensures transparency for investors. Further, a progressionist measure of impact in India can be examining gender-diverse investments. Studies have reflected that women-led enterprises find it difficult to access traditional forms of financing.[42] Impact investments can be used to noticeably overcome this barrier and reduce gender-based economic inequality.

---

39. Budget 2019–2020, Speech of Nirmala Sitharaman, Minister of Finance (July 5, 2019).

40. https://indianexpress.com/article/cities/pune/undp-and-pcmc-join-hands-for-first-social-impact-bond-7125350/ (Dec. 29, 2020).

41. Ravi, Gustafsson-Wright, Sharma & Boggild-Jones, *supra* note 7.

42. *Id.*

16

Korea

Soo-Young Song and Kimberly Kim[1]

Market Overview and Growth of Impact Investment

The growth of impact investment, that is, investment made to generate a measurable, beneficial, social, or environmental impact alongside gaining a financial return,[2] was initiated by American and European asset managers. In the midst of this trend of impact investment, the COVID-19 outbreak increased interest in sustainability, leading Korean investors to become more involved in environmental, social, and corporate governance (ESG) investment, which weighs financial as well as ESG factors. Such interest is expected to continue in 2022 in Korea's private and public sectors.

Initially, Korea's private sector placed impact investment in the limelight. Impact investment, which primarily focuses on the resulting impact when making investment decisions, can be grouped as:

1. ESG investment;
2. Responsible investment into companies whose management activities fully reflect social and ethical values;
3. Investment that prioritizes social values even at the risk of low financial returns;
4. Investment with a specific theme toward innovative and market-oriented solutions such as applying sustainable production methods, conserving the environment, and forming a sustainable community; and

1. Ms. Song is a partner and Ms. Kim an associate of Shin & Kim LLC, Seoul, Korea.

2. *What Is Impact Investing?*, Global Impact Investing Network, https://thegiin.org/impact-investing/need-to-know/ (last visited Feb. 10, 2021).

5. A combination of the foregoing types.

However, in 2020, Korean investors began to develop a more sophisticated understanding of ESG investment through the emergence of impact investment companies that adhere to the Global Impact Investment Network's (GIIN) definition of impact investment, that is, investment made to generate positive, measurable, social, and environmental impact alongside a financial return. ESG investment, although sharing certain traits with impact investment, thus focuses on obtaining financial gains by considering ESG factors rather than simply emphasizing "impact" above all else. GIIN's definition of impact investment broadens the scope of "impact investment" by including investments in existing companies, including large or mid-size companies, that invest in businesses to achieve social or environmental impact as a type of project. In Korea, such forms of investment have long been viewed as a type of ESG investment.

Korea's interest in impact investment accelerated as the government became more involved. The Moon Jae-in administration tackled issues of social economy through its "social finance activation" program in February 2018 and by exerting continuous efforts to activate the "social economy ecosystem" through the financial sector. The Moon Jae-In administration's endeavors gradually increased awareness for social economy enterprises. Whether the new Yoon Suk-yeol administration will continue such policy remains to be seen.

On top of equity investments, Korea also regards loans and guarantees to social economy enterprises as a form of impact investment. The Social Finance Council (SFC)[3] announced that 2,508 companies received KRW 558.6 billion[4]—surpassing the 2021 target amount of KRW 516.2 billion—in the form of loans, guarantees, and capital investments as of

3. The 20 institutions participating in the Social Finance Council are as follows: Financial Services Commission, Ministry of Economy and Finance, Ministry of SMEs and Startups/Financial Supervisory Service, Korea Federation of Banks, Korea Credit Information Services/Korea Inclusive Finance Agency, Korea SMEs and Startups Agency, Small Enterprise and Market Service, National Credit Union Federation of Korea, MG Community Credit Cooperatives/Korea Credit Guarantee Fund, Korea Technology Finance Corporation, Regional Credit Guarantee Foundation/Korea Growth Investment Corp., Korea Venture Investment Corp./Nonghyup, Suhyup, Korea Social Enterprise Promotion Agency, Korea Social Value, and Solidarity Foundation.

4. Closed at USD 1 = KRW 1084.48 on Dec. 7, 2020, *South Korean Won*, WALL ST. J. Section on Markets, https://www.wsj.com/market-data/quotes/fx/USDKRW/historical-prices (last visited Feb. 8, 2021).

October 2021. The SFC aims to provide more than KRW 569.6 billion in 2022, an increase of more than 10 percent.[5] While the proportion of loans and guarantees is still large, the extent of equity investment in impact investment is also increasing (see Table 14.1).

Table 14.1 Increasing Impact Investment Amount by Private and Public Sectors (Unit: KRW billion)

Type	Provider	Target for 2021	Amount Provided in 2021 (Number of Companies)	Target for 2022
Loan	Korea Inclusive Finance Agency	10	6.4 (103)	10
	Korea SMEs and Startups Agency	80	99.9 (445)	80
	Small Enterprise and Market Service	35	10.4 (252)	15
	National Credit Union Federation of Korea	30	34.4 (243)	35
	MG Community Credit Cooperatives	15	15.5 (65)	20
	Subtotal	170	166.6 (1,108)	160
Guarantee	Korea Credit Guarantee Fund	100	158.9 (712)	120
	Regional Credit Guarantee Foundation	15	15.2 (310)	15
	Korea Technology Finance Corporation	135	136.9 (292)	150
	Subtotal	250	311 (1,314)	285
Investment	Korea Growth Investment Corp.	30	33.2 (23)	50
	Korea Venture Investment Corp.	66.2	47.8 (63)	74.6
	Subtotal	96.2	81 (86)	124.6
Total		516.2	558.6 (2,508)	569.6

5. Park Sung-Jin, Financial Services Commission, Section on Press Release, Holding of the 3rd (Written Meeting) of the Social Finance Council in 2021 (Dec. 16, 2021), https://fsc.go.kr/no010101/77077?srchCtgry=&curPage=&srchKey=sj&srchText=%EC%82%AC%ED%9A%8C%EC%A0%81%EA%B8%88%EC%9C%B5%ED%98%91%EC%9D%98%ED%9A%8C&srchBeginDt=&srchEndDt=.

Characteristics of Organizations and Enterprises Receiving Impact Investment

Organizations and enterprises that are subject to impact investment include the following:

- **Cooperative.** A "business organization that intends to enhance its partners' rights and interests, thereby contributing to local communities by being engaged in the cooperative purchasing, production, sale, and provision of goods or services" under article 2(1) of the Framework Act on Cooperatives.
- **Social enterprise.** "Pursues a social objective aimed at enhancing the quality of life of community residents by providing vulnerable social groups with social services or job opportunities or by contributing to the communities while conducting its business activities, such as the manufacture or sale of goods or services" under articles 2(1) and 7(1) of the Social Enterprise Promotion Act.
- **Village enterprise.** A village-level enterprise that effectively realizes the local community's interests by solving common local problems through profit-making businesses that use various local resources, and by creating incomes and job opportunities, under the Ministry of the Interior and Safety's Ministerial Implementation Guidelines to Promote Village Enterprises.
- **Self-sufficient.** An enterprise where two or more welfare recipients or those of low income organize a cooperative or joint venture to operate a business with the aim to rise from poverty under article 18 of the National Basic Living Security Act.
- **Social venture.** A business that is established by a social entrepreneur to commercialize innovative technologies or business models that would solve social problems.

As the interests of venture capitalists and the government in impact investment increased, organizations and enterprises subject to receiving impact investment attracted attention. Of particular interest were social ventures, whose goal is to solve social problems through commercializing innovative technologies or business models, and social enterprises, whose goal is to help vulnerable social groups or contribute to the community to enhance the quality of the lives of community residents. Of the two, social ventures attract investment funds more easily than social enterprises as a result of the Social Enterprise Promotion Act, which obliges the latter to use at least two-thirds of its distributable profits for social purposes. Comparatively, under the Act on Special Measures for the Promotion of

Venture Businesses, social ventures mainly receive equity investments through funds, including those managed by Korea Venture Investment Corp. and by Korea Growth Investment Corp. The Korean government is trying to make the investment process easier by announcing a "Guideline for Distinguishing Social Ventures" and proposing to amend the Act on Special Measures for the Promotion of Venture Businesses to provide a legal basis for social ventures.

Major Industries Subject to Impact Investment and Future Prospects

Practical information about social ventures that have become subject to major impact investment can be gained in various ways. One such method includes analyzing information provided by impact investment companies, including Yellowdog, Sopoong, HG Initiative (HGI), D3 Jubilee (D3), and Crevisse Partners (Crevisse).

The common investment focus of these companies includes educational technology, food technology, healthcare, and childcare. Yellowdog invested intensively in sustainable urban solutions covering areas of quality education, environmental solutions, wellness and healthcare, and gender equality.[6] Sopoong's investment focus areas include lifestyle and agri-food, education opportunities, and sustainable environment,[7] while HGI focuses on childcare, education, healthcare, and sustainable production.[8] D3's major investment focus industries are health, education, environment, and social infrastructure,[9] whereas Crevisse emphasizes sustainable cities and communities, climate change countermeasures, clean energy, quality education, inclusive welfare, high-quality jobs, and economic growth.[10]

Although many impact investors claimed their investment focus incorporates the environment, little was invested in companies that directly deal with environmental issues. Rather, the extent of environment-related investments is limited to companies that approach carbon emission issues indirectly, such as food technology.

---

6. Yellowdog, Section on Investment Theme, http://www.yellowdog.kr/en/investment-theme/ (last visited Feb. 5, 2021).

7. Sopoong Ventures, Section on Investment Theme, https://sopoong.net/ (last visited Feb. 5, 2021).

8. HG Initiative, http://www.hginitiative.com/?lang=en (last visited Feb. 5, 2021).

9. D3 Jubilee Partners, https://d3jubilee.com/ (last visited Feb. 5, 2021).

10. Crevisse Ventures, http://ventures.crevisse.com/ (last visited Feb. 5, 2021).

This deficiency may soon change as global and societal interest toward the environment is growing, particularly through investments in climate technology to actively promote the transition to net-zero emissions.[11] All 195 member countries of the Paris Climate Change Accord must meet their greenhouse gas emission reduction targets, with more than 100 countries declaring a goal to achieve net-zero emission by 2050. Accordingly, many countries are expected to implement policies such as carbon pricing, gradual closure of carbon-emitting business activities, and investments in green infrastructure. Thus, dramatic and significant changes will speedily occur, specifically within the next ten years, to fight the rise of global average temperature through rapid decarbonization.

Impact Investment-Related Issues: Case Analysis

Despite Korea's significant strides in impact investment, issues still remain when defining impact investment as "investments made to generate positive, measurable social and environmental impact alongside a financial return." These issues include distinguishing impact investment from other investment types and measuring impact.

Impact investment companies provide some guidance on distinguishing impact investment from other investment forms. For instance, Yellowdog first defines the social problem it plans to solve through investment, and then conducts due diligence on target companies that operate within that field. Specifically, Yellowdog:

1. Assesses whether the subject company's business meets at least one of 17 UN Sustainable Development Goals (SDGs).
2. Assesses:
   - Whether the company expressed willingness to solve the selected social problem, whether its business model contributes to solving the problem, and whether the company's investors can exert positive influences to create an impact.
   - Whether the company defines a theory of change that effectuates actual impact.
   - Whether the company designs a methodology to quantify, assess, and evaluate the value of impact based on its theory.

11. Samil PwC, *PwC Climate Technology Report—Climate Tech, Next Destination for Venture Capital* (2021), https://www.pwc.com/kr/ko/publications/research-insights/samilpwc_the-state-of-climate-tech.pdf.

3. Ensures that the impact is ingrained in the company's management and organizational culture, and supports decision-making consistent with the company's mission.
4. Examines the impact's sustainability and the company's efforts to preserve the impact by reflecting the values in its organizational culture or articles of incorporation.[12]

Sopoong also uses UN SDGs to determine social value, that is, value contributing to public interest and community development that cannot be measured by accounting methods. Sopoong further considers financial performance when determining impact as it believes a start-up social venture must be able to respond to increased demand. To measure growth, Sopoong considers sales growth rate or increase rate of its enterprise value, rather than the absolute sales amount. Sopoong finds the company's growth rate to be a meaningful indicator of potential recognition that helps the social venture and investors alike.

While foreign standards such as the Social Return on Investment, the B Impact Assessment, and the ISO 26000 exist to measure impact, Korea developed independent standards that are more attuned to fitting its needs. For instance, the Ministry of Employment and Labor and the Korea Social Enterprise Promotion Agency developed the Social Value Index (SVI) to assess social performance created by organizations including social enterprises that pursue social value. SVI is based on a scale of 100 points allocated among three categories, which are further divided into 11 quantitative and three qualitative specific measurement indicators:

- **Social performance** considers social mission management, main business activities' social value, efforts to establish social economy ecosystem, profit reinvestment for social purposes, democracy in operation, and worker involvement.
- **Economic performance** considers job creation, financial performance, and labor performance.
- **Innovative performance** considers innovation in corporate activities.

Although the objective factors for identifying impact investment have been seemingly established, the measurement of those factors is not as clear. For instance, GIIN's 2020 survey showed that impact investors use

12. Yellowdog Impact Report 2020, YELLOWDOG (2020), http://www.yellowdog.kr/wp-content/uploads/2020/04/YellowdogImpactReport2020.pdf.

a wide variety of industry frameworks, tools, and systems.[13] Investors commonly use a combination of SDGs, the IRIS Catalog of Metrics, and IRIS+ Core Metrics Sets to help them understand, measure, and manage impact. The vast majority used at least one external resource, but, on average, three tools, systems, or frameworks were used. Only 11 percent of respondents used no external resources, some stating that they used proprietary rather than external frameworks.

According to GIIN's report, comparing impact results with market performance is the most significant challenge that impact investors face within their organizations. While objective numbers like sales increase or the number of intellectual property rights owned may estimate performance, impact performance, such as "solving social problems" or "proposing alternatives," is quite difficult to measure. This is especially true for companies that solve age-old social problems by suggesting innovative ways or newly appearing problems due to changes in social structure.

Yet, the industry as a whole is making progress by developing infrastructure to strengthen the market's approach to both impact verification and comparison. Ultimately, coalescing around more standardized approaches in Korea can facilitate the analysis of impact performance and lead to smarter investment decisions.

Conclusion

ESG investment is a new form of the corporate social responsibility movement, a trend that started 20 years ago when it was simply considered a fad. However, now, with a new generation of decision-makers in charge, ESG is developing to be much more, as impact investment that emphasizes generating positive, measurable, social, and environmental impact is gaining increased attention. With considerable development in the area and anticipated growth resulting from global and societal needs toward sustainability and the environment, impact investment in Korea will continue to gain importance.

13. Global Impact Investing Network, 2020 Annual Impact Investor Survey, June 11, 2020, https://thegiin.org/assets/GIIN%20Annual%20Impact%20Investor%20Survey%202020.pdf.

Europe

17

Europe

Roberto Randazzo[1] *and Fabio Gallo Perozzi*[2]

Market Overview and Impact Investing Growth

Impact investing in Europe has long stimulated a debate among investors, legislators, policy makers, and the public over what it should and could accomplish. Today, this debate revolves around environmental, social, and governance (ESG) factors, which recently led to the adoption of a framework by the European legislature within the more general context of sustainable finance.[3] Notably, the environmental ("E") dimension is currently the most robust, while social ("S") profiles are already being integrated.

Despite the adoption of a European framework for sustainable finance, impact investing does not yet have an official, shared, and regulated definition. It has been called many names and defined in many ways.

- The European Sustainable Investment Forum (EUROSIF)[4] refers to it as "venture capital for sustainability."[5]

---

1. Partner, Legance, Milan, Italy; former president, esela—The legal network for social impact (transitioned to Global Alliance of Impact Lawyer—(GAIL)).

2. Junior Associate, Legance, Milan, Italy.

3. *See* the combined provisions of Regulation (EU) 2019/2088 "on sustainability-related disclosures in the financial services sector" and Regulation (EU) 2020/852 "on the establishment of a framework to facilitate sustainable investment, and amending Regulation (EU) 2019/2088," both further analyzed in the paragraph on the Regulatory Framework.

4. *See* Eurosif, *Venture Capital for Sustainability* (2007).

5. To give another example, the World Economic Forum has referred to impact investing as "blended value investing" (Samans, *Blended Value Investing: Capital Opportunities for Social and Environmental Impact*, World Econ. Forum, 2006).

- The European Union (EU) Parliament defined "social impact investing" as the "use of private investment capital to finance activities that generate a social benefit as well as a financial return" adding that "social impact investment typically differs from more traditional types of investment in providing greater flexibility in repayment terms, lower interest rates, and the acceptance of greater risk than commercial lenders would normally consider."[6] This definition has been more recently confirmed by the EU Parliament itself, in its briefing around the European framework for sustainable finance.[7]
- As generally acknowledged,[8] this official—but not regulated—European definition shares the main characteristic features of the definitions given in the global context, for instance, by the Global Impact Investing Network (GIIN). According to GIIN, impact investments are investments made into companies, organizations, and funds with the intention to generate a measurable, beneficial social or environmental impact alongside a financial return.[9]

In the academic field, a definition is being built around the following core elements:[10]

- **Intentionality.** Impacts should be targeted intentionally, and investment should achieve a positive benefit for society. This requires an explicit before-the-event statement and an investment strategy that proactively pursues economic, social, or environmental goals.

---

6. *See* European Parliament, *Social Impact Bonds: Private Finance that Generates Social Returns* (2014), https://www.europarl.europa.eu/EPRS/538223-Social-impactbonds-FINAL.pdf. The European Parliament stressed also that social impact investments are "sometimes referred to as 'social enterprise financing' or 'social finance' but also—confusingly—sometimes called simply 'social investment.'"

7. *See* European Parliament, *Sustainable Finance—EU Taxonomy, A framework to facilitate Sustainable Investment* (2020).

8. *See* Maduro, Pasi & Misuraca, *Social Impact Investment in the EU. Financing Strategies and Outcome-Oriented Approaches for Social Policy Innovation: Narratives, Experiences, and Recommendations*, Publ'ns Office of EU (2018).

9. Adapted from the Global Impact Investing Network (GIIN), https://thegiin.org/impact-investing/need-to-know/#what-isimpact-investing.

10. *See* Nicholls, Paton & Emerson, Social Finance (2015); TIRESIA—Politecnico di Milano, *Tiresia Impact Outlook* (2019).

- **Measurability.** Impacts should be measured quantitatively and qualitatively, ideally by independent third parties, to maximize trustworthiness and credibility.
- **Additionality.** Investment must be made in undercapitalized areas, and consider whether the impact outcome would have occurred without the investment.

Market figures vary widely, since the definition has not yet been uniformly established. According to EUROSIF, impact investing assets under management equaled €108 billion ($128 billion) in 2017 and a positive CAGR at 5 percent.[11] This suggests that today the value of the impact investing in Europe might exceed €130 billion. Based on a different definition of impact investing, the European Venture Philanthropy Association (EVPA) reported impact investors had funded social purpose organizations with €6.2 billion ($6.5 billion) in 2019.[12]

The European Union's impact investing market has grown rapidly in depth and sophistication and is among the fastest growing markets around the globe.[13] In 2017, the social impact investing market was calculated as 12 times larger, in nominal terms, than in 2011, with the most rapid growth between 2014 and 2015.[14] Looking at the bigger picture, as reported by Morningstar, the total value of investments in 3,432 "sustainable" funds exceeded $1 trillion worldwide at the end of June 2020. Europe remained the leading market, with a total stock of $870 billion and 2,703 funds (82 percent of the total).[15]

Uncertainty surrounding the COVID-19 pandemic did not reduce funding, which globally reached a record high in Q2 2020 (+72 percent on Q1).[16] Asset managers continued "greening" their offerings, by converting traditional funds into sustainable funds, with repurposed funds now accounting for 21 percent of the European sustainable fund universe.[17] Recent data shows that most of the resources are invested in water, sanitation, and hygiene sectors.[18]

---

11. *See* Eurosif, *European SRI Study 2018* (2018).
12. *See* EVPA, *The 2020 Investing for Impact Survey* (2021).
13. *See* GIIN, *2020 Annual Impact Investor Survey* (2020).
14. *See* Mackevičiūtė et al., *European Parliament, Social Impact Investment—Best Practices and Recommendations for the Next Generation* (2020).
15. *See* Morningstar, *Global Sustainable Funds Flows* (2020).
16. *See id.*
17. *Id.*
18. *See* GIIN, *supra* note 13.

Nonetheless, the maturity level of the EU impact investing market remains low in most (80 percent) Member States, especially among Central and Eastern Europe (CEE) countries. A high maturity level is usually recognized in Germany, France, Portugal, Italy, and, although no longer a European member, the United Kingdom.[19]

Several factors are driving this growth, including expanding demand by institutions and the public sector that private capital meet social and environmental challenges under the Sustainable Development Goals (SDGs)[20] and Paris Climate Agreement.[21] Most importantly, impact investing growth has been leveraged by public funding, with the European Commission urging Member States to "explore and develop innovative ways of securing additional private financing for social investment, for instance through public private partnerships."[22] Moreover, emergence of common standards and sustainable finance taxonomy, on both the supply and demand sides of impact investing, facilitating cross-border impact investments, are having a positive impact.

The public sector and private–public investing mechanisms have been crucial to the growth of the European impact investing market, as evident from the first initiatives. For example, Europe's largest impact fund was launched in 2012 by the British government, with £600 million. In 2010, the UK was also the first to issue Social Impact Bonds (SIB),[23] followed by Finnish SIB supporting migrants' integration, a project co-financed by EFSI and Epiqus, the private fund manager.[24] Portugal has also introduced SIB incentives. Such investments can be recorded as expenditures for tax purposes, and the amount invested can be marked up 130 percent.

19. Mackevičiūtė et al., *supra* note 14.

20. *See* UN Division for Sustainable Development Goals, Department of Economic and Social Affairs.

21. *See* Paris Agreement to the United Nations Framework Convention on Climate Change, T.I.A.S. No. 16-1104 (Dec. 12, 2015).

22. *See* the communication to the European Parliament, the Council, the European Economic and Social Committee, and the Committee of the Regions by the European Commission, *Towards Social Investment for Growth and Cohesion—Including Implementing the European Social Fund 2014–2020* (2013).

23. For a definition of SIBs under a European perspective, see European Parliament, *Social Impact Bonds. Private Finance that Generates Social Returns, Briefing*, 2014, according to which "with a social impact bond, typically a private investor funds a social service provider to implement a social programme in return for a promise ('bond') from the public sector to reimburse the initial investment and pay a rate of return if the programme achieves predefined social outcomes."

24. Fifty organizations from the public Finnish sector are currently estimated to be using SIB funds.

In addition, investors can have their investment refunded and registered as revenue in the same year if the social impact is achieved.

The Global Steering Group for Impact Investment (GSG) plays a key role in many European impact investing initiatives.[25] As an example, in 2014, the Portuguese GSG's National Advisory Board (NAB) supported the creation, with the Portuguese government, of Portugal Inovação Social (EMPIS), a €150 million public-driven initiative, making use of the European Social Fund to fund social innovation and social entrepreneurship to promote collaborative networks among public, private, and social economy players, and to stimulate the country's impact ecosystem.

Policy Framework and Government Initiatives

The European orientation toward impact investing has its roots in the Treaty on European Union.[26] This was highlighted and reinforced in the European Pillar of Social Rights, proclaimed by the European Parliament, the European Council, and the European Commission. According to it,

> Pursuant to Article 3 of the Treaty, the aims of the European Union are inter alia to promote the well-being of its peoples and to work for the sustainable development of Europe based on a highly competitive social market economy, aiming at full employment and social progress. The Union shall combat social exclusion and discrimination, promote social justice and protection, equality between women and men, solidarity between generations and protection of the rights of the child.[27]

Policy Framework

Institutions in Europe play a vital role in the development of the impact investing market through the definition of parameters and providing public funding.

25. The Global Steering Group for Impact Investment (GSG) was established in 2015 as successor to the Social Impact Investment Taskforce announced in 2013, following the G8 Social Impact Investment Forum. The GSG currently represents 33 countries (seven European Member States) through National Advisory Boards (NABs).

26. *See* European Union, *Treaty on European Union* (1992). It is also known as "Treaty of Maastricht."

27. *See* European Parliament, European Council, European Commission, *Interinstitutional Proclamation on the European Pillar of Social Rights* (2017).

The European Union's recognition of the strategic importance of impact investing can be traced back to the Dutch presidency in 1997. However, from a regulatory and policy perspective, there has been a surge since 2010, starting with "Europe 2020 Flagship Initiative Innovation Union" (2010).[28] This initiative has encouraged the market to adopt social innovation solutions as a resource for growth and jobs, mobilizing private investors as well.

Thereafter, the Social Business Initiative (SBI),[29] in 2011, played a key role in supporting European social enterprises, social innovation, social entrepreneurs, and other key stakeholders of the social economy. It did so through 11 primary measures on issues such as access to funding (through an initiative on the European social entrepreneurship and venture capital funds), increasing the visibility of impact investing players (through the Social Innovation Europe platform and SME Forum[30]), and creating a favorable legal environment.

On a similar base, the EU Programme for Employment and Social Innovation (EaSI), was launched in 2013. It is managed directly by the European Commission, with a total budget for 2014–2020 of €919 million.[31]

In 2014, the European Fund for Strategic Investments (EFSI), also known as the Juncker Plan, combined private and public investments with a focus on a wide range of social infrastructures and projects in the fields of education, university, healthcare, and social housing. It supported social enterprises through investment mechanisms mediated by social incubators/accelerators and payment-by-results tools. Unfortunately, "the full potential of EFSI was not used for the impact investing market: EFSI was used for EaSI, but not for the Social Impact Accelerator (SIA) managed by the European Investment Fund (EIF)."[32]

28. *See* European Commission, Directorate-General for Research and Innovation, *Europe 2020 flagship initiative Innovation Union*, SEC(2010) 1161, communication from the Commission to the European Parliament, the Council, the European Economic and Social Committee and the Committee of the Regions, Publications Office (2011), https://data.europa.eu/doi/10.2777/47750.

29. *See* European Commission. *Social Business Initiative, Creating a Favourable Climate for Social Enterprises, Key Stakeholders in the Social Economy and Innovation* (2011).

30. *See id.*

31. In 2018, the "EaSI Capacity Building Investments Window" was built up in support of selected financial intermediaries that had not yet reached sustainability.

32. Mackevičiūtė et al., *supra* note 14.

Coming to the Social Impact Accelerator (SIA), this initiative was established in 2015, as the first pan-European public–private partnership supporting social enterprises with equity finance. Managed by the European Investment Fund, this fund-of-funds directly invests in social impact funds across all of Europe.[33]

More recently, in 2018, the European Union adopted the Action Plan on Financing Sustainable Growth,[34] covering sectors beyond finance, with sustainability a priority for the growth of all European Member States. This strategy was reconfirmed by the new Von der Leyen European Commission and in the European Green Deal.[35]

The Platform on Sustainable Finance plays a key role in the development of European financial policies. As an advisory body of the European Commission, the Platform draws on the work of the European Technical Expert Group on sustainable finance (2018–2020) to promote:

---

33. Its first investment, in late 2013, was in the "Social Venture Fund," a German social venture capital fund with more than €16 million in funding.

34. *See* European Commission, *Action Plan: Financing Sustainable Growth* (2018).

35. *See* European Commission, *Communication from the Commission—The European Green Deal* (2019). In the framework of the European Green Deal, the Commission announced a renewed sustainable finance strategy, which aims to provide the policy tools to ensure that financial system genuinely supports the transition of businesses toward sustainability in a context of recovery from the impact of the COVID-19 outbreak. *See also* Commissioner McGuinness' opening remarks at the ECON Committee Structured Dialogue, January 25, 2021:

> "We will present a Renewed Sustainable Finance Strategy, review the non-financial reporting directive, and present an EU Green Bond Standard. We are also actively working on the next steps for the EU Taxonomy. We received over 46,000 replies to the public consultation on the first delegated act for the taxonomy, on climate mitigation and adaptation. I think it would be helpful to take a step back and look at what the taxonomy is, and what it is not. It is a classification system that identifies sustainable activities—providing clarity and preventing greenwashing. It is not a mandatory list of activities that investors must invest in but a guide. [. . .] The Taxonomy goes further in some cases than existing legislation and policy because it is necessary to do so. Because the EU is committed to climate neutrality by 2050, and the Taxonomy is a science-based guide to achieving that target. [. . .] Many sectors need to transition towards sustainability and the taxonomy provides a guide to that end. It will allow business to set out clear plans and commit financing to meet thresholds. Investments will be taxonomy-aligned where they meet thresholds—or where there are clear plans to get there. The Commission will consider recalibrating the technical screening criteria where serious concerns are raised, but we do not want to break the link with science or the alignment with Green Deal targets."

- European classification system, based on the so-called European taxonomy, already entered into force, to determine whether economic activity is sustainable;
- European Green Bond Standards;
- Methodologies for European climate benchmarks and disclosures for benchmarks; and
- Guidance to improve corporate disclosure of climate-related information.

Regulatory Framework

Alongside policy development, the European Union has focused on defining common rules and regulatory parameters to drive the impact investing market. Based on strong social commitment to European core principles, this approach has led to the adoption of several legislative acts that guide sustainable finance sector, with a focus also on the corporate segment covering both ESG factors and impact investing dynamics.

The following laws are the foundations of this regulatory framework:

- Regulation (EU) 2019/2088 on sustainability-related disclosures in the financial services sector (SFDR Regulation)
- Regulation (EU) 2020/852 on the establishment of a framework to facilitate sustainable investment, and amending Regulation (EU) 2019/2088 (Taxonomy Regulation)
- Regulation (EU) 2017/1991, amending Regulation (EU) 345/2013 on European venture capital funds, and Regulation (EU) 346/2013 on European social entrepreneurship funds
- Regulation (EU) 346/2013 on European social entrepreneurship funds

Because of their importance, we discuss the first two and other relevant legislation in more detail.

SFDR Regulation (EU) 2019/2088. This regulation, also called the SFDR Regulation, requires financial market participants, including institutional investors, financial intermediaries, and financial advisors, to comply with several transparency policies regarding sustainability risks and factors. Most importantly, it envisages a definition of sustainable investment as:

- "[I]nvestment in an economic activity that contributes to an environmental objective, as measured, for example, by key resource efficiency indicators on the use of energy, renewable energy, raw materials, water and land, on the production of waste, and greenhouse gas emissions, or on its impact on biodiversity and the circular economy; or

- [I]nvestment in an economic activity that contributes to a social objective, in particular an investment that contributes to tackling inequality or that fosters social cohesion, social integration and labour relations, or an investment in human capital or economically or socially disadvantaged communities."[36]

As a further condition, sustainable investment cannot significantly harm any of the environmental objectives mentioned by the Regulation, and the investee companies must follow good governance practices, particularly sound management structures, employee relations, remuneration of staff, and tax compliance (this is the so-called principle of doing no significant harm). In the absence of specific legislation by the European legislator on impact investing, it should however be noted that through the definition of sustainable investment, the SFDR Regulation expressly refers to two of the key principles of impact investing, namely, intentionality (evident in the determination, ex ante, of specific environmental or social objectives) and measurability (through the use of indicators). Accordingly, impact investment funds are positioning themselves precisely within the scope of article 9 of the SFDR Regulation, thus distinguishing themselves from investments which, although promoting environmental or social characteristics—as expressly provided for in article 8 of the SFDR Regulation—do not pursue a sustainable investment objective.

The SFDR Regulation also defines "sustainability risk" as "an environmental, social or governance event or condition that, if it occurs, could cause an actual or a potential material negative impact on the value of the investment."[37] Similarly, sustainability factors are referred to as "environmental, social and employee matters, respect for human rights, anti-corruption and anti-bribery matters."[38]

The SFDR Regulation for the first time outlined a precise parameter within which financial market participants must move to be compliant and contribute to the sustainable growth objectives valued by the European Union.

Furthermore, the SFDR Regulation combines two typical approaches of sustainable finance. On the one hand, starting from the definition of sustainability risks and adverse sustainability impacts, the SFDR Regulation imposes transparency obligations on sustainability (articles 3

36. *See* art. 2, par. 17, of the SFDR Regulation.
37. *See* art. art. 2, par. 22, of the SFDR Regulation.
38. *See* art. 2, par. 24, of the SFDR Regulation.

through 7) following the typical "negative" ESG approach. On the other hand, through the definition of sustainable investments, it endorses and regulates (articles 8 through 11) the "positive" approach typical of impact investors.

Finally, on April 6, 2022, the European Commission adopted through a Delegated Regulation the Regulatory Technical Standards (RTS) to be used to disclose sustainability-related information in the field of financial services, in accordance with the SFDR Regulation.[39] This delegated regulation is scheduled to come into effect on the 1st of January 2023, but as communicated through a Supervisory Statement by the European Supervisory Authorities (ESAs), "national competent authorities are encouraged to refer financial market participants and financial advisers to the requirements set out in the draft RTS [and] to use the interim period until 1 January 2023 to prepare for the application of the RTS."[40]

Taxonomy Regulation (EU) 2020/852. This regulation partly amended SFDR Regulation by defining which economic activities are environmentally sustainable. It also set a common language for sustainability based on technical criteria and a classification system (article 3) under which an activity is considered sustainable if it:

- Makes a substantial contribution to one of the six listed environmental objectives; and
- Does not significantly harm the other objectives.[41]

Taxonomy is a common term in the European legal system. For readers practicing in jurisdictions where it is less common, it refers to a system of classification.[42] To that end, the Taxonomy Regulation:

---

39. *See* Commission Delegated Regulation (EU) . . ./. . . of 6.4.2022 supplementing Regulation (EU) 2019/2088 of the European Parliament and of the Council with regard to regulatory technical standards specifying the details of the content and presentation of the information in relation to the principle of "do no significant harm," specifying the content, methodologies, and presentation of information in relation to sustainability indicators and adverse sustainability impacts, and the content and presentation of the information in relation to the promotion of environmental or social characteristics and sustainable investment objectives in pre-contractual documents, on websites, and in periodic reports, Document C(2022) 1931 final (2022).

40. *See* Updated Joint ESA Supervisory Statement on the application of the Sustainable Finance Disclosure Regulation (2022).

41. In particular, the activity must also be conducted in compliance with the minimum safeguards laid down in art. 18 of the Taxonomy Regulation.

42. https://www.google.com/search?q=taxonomy+definition&rlz=1C1CHBD_enUS882US882&oq=taxonomy&aqs=chrome.1.69i57j0i433i512l2j0i512j0i457i512j0i512l5.2737j0j15&sourceid=chrome&ie=UTF-8.

- Defines the main criteria for environmentally sustainable economic activities;
- Adds further transparency obligations to financial market participants;
- Provides similar obligations for undertakings subject to nonfinancial reporting (pursuant to article 19(a) or article 29(a) of Directive 2013/34/EU); and
- Mandates that the European Commission extend the scope of current regulatory framework beyond environmentally sustainable economic activities to include other sustainability objectives, such as social objectives.

This integration of "social" objectives is critically important, considering the COVID-19 pandemic and its effects. Specifically, the European Commission, according to article 26 of the Taxonomy Regulation had to publish, by December 2021, a report describing the provisions required to extend the taxonomy's scope beyond environmentally sustainable economic activities to cover social objectives. Accordingly, the Commission mandated the EU Platform for Sustainable Finance to edit a Draft Report on a Social Taxonomy, published on July 12, 2021 (the Platform's advice fed into the final Commission report).[43] Following public feedback on the draft report and a postponement by the Commission with respect to the adoption of the report describing the provisions required to extend the taxonomy's scope, the Platform edited "Final Report on Social Taxonomy—Platform on Sustainable Finance," published in February 2022.[44]

Under the Taxonomy Regulation, the Commission had to define, through delegated acts, technical screening criteria to identify environmentally sustainable activities for each of the six environmental objectives.[45] A first delegated act on sustainable activities for climate change adaptation and mitigation objectives was formally adopted on June 4, 2021, while in February 2022, the Commission approved a Complementary Climate Delegated Act, including, under strict conditions, specific

43. *See* Draft Report by Subgroup 4: Social Taxonomy, July 2021.

44. *Platform on Sustainable Finance*, https://ec.europa.eu/info/business-economy-euro/banking-and-finance/sustainable-finance/overview-sustainable-finance/platform-sustainable-finance_en.

45. The Taxonomy Regulation establishes the following six environmental objectives: climate change mitigation; climate change adaptation; the sustainable use and protection of water and marine resources; the transition to a circular economy; pollution prevention and control; the protection and restoration of biodiversity and ecosystems.

nuclear and gas energy activities in the list of economic activities covered by the EU taxonomy.[46] Another delegated act for the remaining objectives will be published in 2022.

Lastly, on July 6, 2021, the Delegated Act supplementing article 8 of the Taxonomy Regulation was adopted by the Commission, to specify the content, methodology, and presentation of information to be disclosed by large financial and nonfinancial companies on the share of their business, investments, or lending activities that are aligned with the EU Taxonomy.[47]

Other relevant legislation. Directive (EU) 2016/2341 on the activities and supervision of institutions for occupational retirement provisions (IORPs) required regulated pension funds to consider ESG issues. The directive provided that "the system of governance shall include consideration of environmental, social and governance factors related to investment assets in investment decisions and shall be subject to regular internal review."[48]

Regulation (EU) 346/2013 on European "social entrepreneurship funds" provides the label can only be used by funds with a qualifying portfolio that provides services or goods generating a social return and "the achievement of measurable, positive social impact as its primary objective in accordance with its articles of association, statutes or any other rules or instruments of incorporation establishing the business." Such a regulation explicitly mandates a duty to measure and publicize the impact outcome pursued through the investment portfolio.

Finally, the European Commission, building on technical advice from European supervisory authorities, has been drafting amendments

46. *See* Commission Delegated Regulation supplementing Regulation (EU) 2020/852 of the European Parliament and of the Council by establishing the technical screening criteria for determining the conditions under which an economic activity qualifies as contributing substantially to climate change mitigation or climate change adaptation and for determining whether that economic activity causes no significant harm to any of the other environmental objectives, Document C/2021/2800 final, 2021. *See* Commission Delegated Regulation amending Delegated Regulation (EU) 2021/2139 as regards economic activities in certain energy sectors and Delegated Regulation (EU) 2021/2178 as regards specific public disclosures for those economic activities, Document C(2022)631 Final, 2022.

47. *See* Commission Delegated Regulation Supplementing Regulation (EU) 2020/852 by specifying the content and presentation of information to be disclosed by undertakings subject to Article 19a or 29a of Directive 2013/34/EU concerning environmentally sustainable economic activities, and specifying the methodology to comply with that disclosure obligation, Document C(2021)4987 final, 2021.

48. *See* art. 21 of Directive (EU) 2016/2341.

to the UCITS Directive, Solvency II, AIFM Directive, MiFID II, and the Insurance Distribution Directive to require consideration of sustainability factors and risks when applying prudent person principle, governance, and risk management.

In addition to the European regulatory profile, there are government initiatives developed by each European Member State. As an example, the French Solidarity Investment Fund regulation is a key standard for impact investments and may become a model for other Members. It provides for the creation of "90/10 funds," which invest 10 percent of their assets in solidarity-based organizations, a form of European social enterprise, and 90 percent toward socially responsible investment strategies, thus channeling billions of euros to impact investment funds.

Looking forward, proposed regulatory developments must be considered. For instance, the European Parliament has made recommendations to the European Commission on corporate due diligence and corporate accountability regarding ESG, value chain, and Business Human Rights due diligence.[49] In addition, a proposal for a Directive on Corporate Sustainability Due Diligence (CSDD), was adopted on February 23, 2022, at the conclusion of the consultation process of the EU Commission on the subject of sustainable corporate governance.[50] The proposed due diligence obligation is defined as an obligation of means and concerns actual and potential negative impacts on human rights and the environment, with respect to the entity's operations, those of its subsidiaries and those entities in the value chain with which the company has an established direct or indirect business relationship. Lastly, on April 21, 2021, the EU Commission adopted a proposal for a Corporate Sustainability Reporting Directive (CSRD), which would amend the existing reporting requirements of the Directive 2014/95/EU—also called the Non-Financial Reporting Directive (NFRD).[51] Most importantly, the CSRD proposal aims to require to report according to mandatory EU sustainability reporting standards to be developed by the European Financial Reporting

49. *See* European Parliament, *Corporate Due Diligence and Corporate Accountability—European Parliament Resolution of 10 March 2021 with Recommendations to the Commission on Corporate Due Diligence and Corporate Accountability* (2021).

50. *See* European Commission, *Proposal for a Directive of the European Parliament and of the Council on Corporate Sustainability Due Diligence and Amending Directive (EU) 2019/1937*, Document COM/2022/71 final, 2022.

51. *See* Proposal for a Directive of the European Parliament and of the Council Amending Directive 2013/34/EU, Directive 2004/109/EC, Directive 2006/43/EC, and Regulation (EU) No 537/2014, as regards corporate sustainability reporting, Document COM/2021/189 final, 2021.

Advisory Group (EFRAG) by October 2022, providing investors and stakeholders with homogeneous and comparable information, on the basis of a common methodology in line with the regulatory framework and, in particular, with the SFDR and the Taxonomy Regulation. In planning the green transition and recovery from the COVID-19 pandemic, the European Union is relying on policies and legislative initiatives on impact investing. As a result, evaluation, measurement, transparency, and reporting of nonfinancial parameters, linked to the social and environmental impact of an economic activity, are becoming mainstream. They are also becoming a part of the strategic character and value of a company, or a fund, in the long term.

Challenges in Impact Investing

The continuing growth of impact investing is linked to several challenges. First, there is still a need to further define its operational scope, balancing the demand for legal certainty with the need for flexibility. This means proceeding with the policies and regulations already in place, at a taxonomy level for example, but without going into excessive bureaucratization, which could be avoided, for instance, by developing rules and taxonomies around core principles and involving market actors.

The "social" dimension, a constituent pillar of the European Union, still needs to be developed and fully integrated into the sustainable finance framework. What has been described so far in terms of eco-sustainability can be the starting point for evaluating the social impact of economic activities based on the principles of impact measurement and management.

Regarding impact measurement, which is at the heart of impact investing, it will be necessary to continue the ongoing effort to achieve a univocal and standardized approach that facilitates the comparison of achieved outcomes. Regulatory changes, including the establishment of a European taxonomy, have certainly been a step forward, but the market is still fragmented in this respect.

A more harmonized system of impact measurement could also have a positive effect on another factor already mentioned. The impact investing market varies from country to country in Europe, with reliable statistical data still lacking. This results in the use of rough estimates. European institutions, policy makers, and legislators could benefit from bringing greater uniformity to impact measurement.

Furthermore, the level of institutional experience, skills, and external assistance to support impact investors can be significantly increased, for instance, by leveraging public and private partnerships, and by engaging networks of experts and practitioners.

Another challenge concerns suitable exit opportunities for impact investors, as pointed out by the European Fund and Asset Management Association (EFAMA). It noted that exit opportunities must be balanced with a long-term investment horizon since social and environmental impact can often only be done over the long term.[52]

Finally, there is still insufficient integration of social and environmental impact profiles regarding tax incentives and public procurement. If done correctly, they could be more actively mobilized to foster impact investing.

Opportunities for a Growing Market

Alongside public funding, regulatory and policy development has been the most crucial factor in the growth of Europe's impact investing market. The impetus comes from the combination of public funds and the creation of common rules.

As noted, legislative acts such as Taxonomy and SFDR Regulations have significant implications by creating common rules on transparency, science-based measurement, and reporting risk and positive impact of economic and financial activities.

The growth of a purpose-oriented corporate sector parallels European growth of sustainable and impact investment markets. The former represents the convergence of for-profit entities toward social and environmental dimensions, as well as a tension of nonprofit entities toward entrepreneurial dynamics. This is an ongoing process taking its cue from Europe's strong social entrepreneurship tradition. Looking at European social economy figures, a recent study showed that in Europe there are two million social economy entities (10 percent of all businesses), with 6 percent of European employees (11 million people) working for social economy entities, and up to 160 million people in Europe being members of social economy entities.[53]

The social economic ecosystem in Europe relies on corporate models characterized by strong social and environmental dimensions, and the capacity to combine profit and business activities with the pursuit of common benefits. This combination makes them attractive targets

52. EFAMA, *Report on Responsible Investment* (2016).

53. *See* Maduro, Pasi & Misuraca, *supra* note 8. *See also* https://ec.europa.eu/growth/sectors/social-economy_en.

for investments, such as impact investments, seeking not only financial returns but also positive social and environmental impacts. They represent an intersection of impact and investibility. Anglo-American experience of the so-called fourth sector is similarly "comprised of organizations that pursue social purposes while engaging in business activities."[54]

The following European entities can be characterized as "hybrids," in the sense they operate outside the traditional legal categories of non-profit and for-profit organizations. They have "a social purpose and a business method."[55]

Social enterprises are a first cluster of such hybrid models, which include for instance, the "Impresa sociale" (Italy, Legislative Decree 112/2017), the "Société d'impact societal" (Luxemburg, Law 12 December 2016), the Community interest company (United Kingdom, the Companies Act 2006, Part 1, Section 6), the "Entreprise de l'économie sociale et solidaire," and the "Enterprise solidaire d'utilité sociale" (France, Law 2014-856). These are companies whose primary social mission overlaps with entrepreneurial, trading, or commercial activities. Despite some differences, they share common traits, namely:

- There is at least a partial profit lock, with dividends able to be distributed to shareholders according to caps established by each jurisdiction;
- Activities primarily carried on for a social aim or a common benefit purpose must be among those listed by law or approved by a specific regulatory authority.

In the European Parliament 2018 recommendation to the European Commission for adoption of a "Statute for Social and Solidarity-based Enterprises," other common elements of these entities are:

- Private law entity independent from the State and public authorities;
- Pursuit of general interest or public utility purpose;
- Conduct socially useful and solidarity-based activity (i.e., support vulnerable groups; combat social exclusion, inequality, and

54. *See* Sabeti, *The Emerging Fourth Sector: A New Sector of Organizations at Intersection of the Public, Private and Social Sectors* (2009). On the semantic debate around the term Fourth Sector, see Rask, Puustinen & Raisio, *Toward a Theory of Fourth Sector Involvement*, ECPR Conference (2018).

55. *See* Rask, Puustinen & Raisio, *supra* note 54, at 3, where reference is made to Sabeti, *supra* note 54.

violations of fundamental rights; protect the environment; and support biodiversity);

- Have at least a partial profit block and other constraints on allocation of profits/assets, including at dissolution, with the majority of profits reinvested for a social purpose; and
- Have a democratic governance involving employees, customers, and stakeholders affected by its activities, with members' power and weight in decision-making not necessarily based on the capital held.

Another entity is a Profit-with-Purpose company set up to run a business and distribute dividends to shareholders. They have full capacity for profit distribution with specific rules concerning aims of "common benefit," and the measuring, evaluation, and reporting of impact generated.

B Corps are fitting examples of Profit-with-Purpose companies. B Corps originated in the United States in 2006 and have gone global, including Europe.[56] Among the best-known examples, Danone is now a certified B Corp, with multiple subsidiaries certified as B Corps. The B Corp mark, once registered with the non-profit organization B Lab, becomes evidence of the value (environmental, social, cultural, etc.) generated by the company and that it has established measurement processes. To receive the certificate, organizations must pass a complex assessment—the B Impact Assessment (BIA)—that considers impacts in the areas of governance, community, workers, customers, and environment.

The B Corp phenomenon inspired Benefit Corporations, for-profit entities governed by specific regulations concerning both the aims of "common benefit" and the assessment of the impacts generated. Italy was the first country, outside the United States, to introduce the model, which it called the "Società benefit." It includes rules, for example, for measuring and reporting the impact pursued.[57] On a similar basis, the French mission-driven company (or *Société à mission*) was adopted in 2019 and requires the mission-driven company to add a "purpose" (*raison d'être*) related to specific social and/or environmental objectives into its bylaws.[58]

---

56. *See* Honeyman, Jana & Marcario, *The B Corp Handbook: How You Can Use Business as a Force for Good* (2019).

57. *See* Law 208/2015, art. 1, paras. 376–384, and in particular, regarding measurement, annexes 4 and 5, on the External Assessment Standard and Assessment Areas, respectively.

58. *See Code de commerce*, art. L210-10.

In addition to the preceding two models, there are also traditional for-profit businesses that pursue social needs on a purely voluntary basis and not according to a specific legal form, status, certification, or constituent document. This is the biggest group in the impact entrepreneurship ecosystem.

Finally, Europe has a strong tradition around cooperatives, who vary from one jurisdiction to another. Such entities are commonly established in the traditional legal forms of companies (joint-stock company, limited liability company, etc.), but with some peculiarities:

- They conduct entrepreneurial, trading, or commercial activities pursuing both profit (dividends distribution allowed within certain limits) and a "mutual" purpose (e.g., shareholders' common interest to jointly benefit from better working conditions, more advantageous prices, or lower costs for raw materials and services).
- Democratic governance defines them [evident in principle of "one head one vote" (voting right assigned equally to each shareholder, not in proportion to shareholding value) and principle of "open door" (directors required, for instance, to encourage new shareholders).

The result is that Europe has an ecosystem of hybrid companies that integrate, by law or voluntarily, impact measurement and management principles into their business, thus gaining an advantage over companies in other countries. Impact investors are increasingly turning to these hybrid business models expressly recognized and regulated by the legislature, as well as with a legal capacity for dividend distribution.

Much work remains in Europe on this ecosystem. Ten out of 27 European Member States have not yet introduced specific organizational legislation to recognize and regulate social enterprise activity.[59]

Future of the Market

With the recent green transition and the definition of a well-defined policy and regulatory parameters, the European Union has demonstrated its commitment to sustainability, inclusion, and resilience for growth of the European impact investment market over the next decade and beyond.

Among key elements of this sustainable growth model are impact measurement, common reporting rules and standards, transparency,

59. *See* Mackevičiūtė et al., *supra* note 14.

disclosure, and due diligence (particularly regarding value chain and business human rights principles).

The Taxonomy Regulation is a step forward, providing market clarity on what is "sustainable" and attracting more cross-national impact investments. Similarly, the SFDR Regulation clarifies the duties of investors to achieve a more sustainable financial system. The two Regulations combined, as well as a European standard for Green Bonds, will improve disclosure by financial institutions and companies on how sustainability is factored into their decision-making, thus fostering a sustainable, inclusive, and resilient growth. Impact investors can now more easily and reliably find opportunities for investments that fit their impact ambitions, potentially increasing the amount of money flowing into the cause.

Networks play a significant role in the development, at policy and regulatory levels, of the parameters of impact investing. By bringing together policy makers, legislators, and practitioners, they exchange data, case studies, best practices, and other elements useful to reaching a definition of impact investing and drawing its boundaries. Among these networks of experts are the European Venture Philanthropy Association (EVPA); esela, the legal network for social impact (transitioned to Global Alliance of Impact Lawyer—GAIL); National Advisory Boards (NABs) of the Global Steering Group for Impact Investment (GSG); and the Expert group on social economy and social enterprises (GECES).

Finally, opportunities for a growing market come from the European Commission budget for the European Union, which makes social and environmental impact a core priority. The European's multiannual financial framework (MFF) for 2021–2027 provides for a long-term European budget of €1,074 billion.[60] Together with the Next Generation European recovery instrument of €750 billion (in the European Recovery Plan), it will allow the European Union to provide an unprecedented €1.8 trillion over the coming years. Among the tools envisaged by the next investment plan is the so-called InvestEU, which builds on the experience of previous Juncker Plans. It brings together a range of existing European financial instruments to counteract fragmented markets and policies; facilitates access to finance and guarantees for those with risk profiles; and promotes investments in competitive, sustainable growth, social resilience, and inclusion. Resources will be allocated to finance

60. *See* Council Regulation (EU, Euratom) 2020/2093 "laying down the multiannual financial framework for the years 2021 to 2027." *See also* Press Release, Multiannual Financial Framework for 2021–2027 Adopted, Dec. 17, 2020.

sustainable infrastructure (€11.5 billion) and social investments and skills (€4 billion) targeting social enterprises and microfinance.[61]

Impact investing in Europe has gone beyond a national scope, which seems the only path ahead to meet major challenges like the climate crisis and SDGs that ignore geographic borders. European current legislations and policies on sustainable finance, ESG market, and impact investing have the potential to differentiate genuine initiatives from opportunistic behavior (e.g., "greenwashing"), thus making these sectors mainstream. The road has been traced, including next necessary steps such as inclusion of social profiles. It is up to the European Union to set an international standard for sustainable growth and start down the road.

61. *See* European Commission, *The InvestEU Programme: Questions and Answers*, Fact Sheet (2018).

18

France

Marc Weitz[1]

Legal Overview and Impact Investing Growth

Since 2001, France has been at the forefront of impact investing starting with its Law on New Economic Regulations (NRE Act), which required listed companies to disclose information in their annual reports about measures taken to account for the environmental and social impacts of their activities. Around 30 topics were identified in a subsequent 2002 decree. The law was designed mainly to create security transparency for shareholders, and marked a significant change by empowering shareholders and other stakeholders (including rating agencies) to better assess the overall performance of companies.[2]

In 2007, a nationwide multi-stakeholder dialogue on sustainable development, called the "Grenelle for environment," was launched in France. It concluded by setting goals for sustainable development and led to the adoption of two new laws: the Grenelle I Act (August 3, 2009) and the Grenelle II Act (July 12, 2010). During this process, in which business organizations, trade unions, environmental and consumer nongovernmental organizations (NGOs), and academics participated, agreement was reached regarding the positive effects of the NRE Act, but also its limits. Building on the NRE mechanism, section 225 of the Grenelle II Act, the new rule required companies to provide details in their annual reports "on how they take into account the social and environmental consequences of [their] activity and [their] social commitments in favor

1. Attorney, The Law Office of Marc Weitz, Los Angeles, California.

2. *Mandatory Reporting Built on Consensus in France*, Ministère des Affaires Etrangères—France (Dec. 2012), https://www.diplomatie.gouv.fr/IMG/pdf/Mandatory_reporting_built_on_consensus_in_France.pdf.

of sustainable development."[3] It also increased the number of reporting companies to those with more than 500 employees, and broadened the covered topics to 40 categories. This was followed by Article 173 in 2015, which was a "comply-or-explain requirement for [investment managers] to report on their portfolios' ESG [environmental, social, and governance] integration, greenhouse gas emissions risks and contribution to a low carbon economy."[4]

Labeling

Several bodies label and certify funds meeting ESG criteria. Unfortunately, criteria and standards for ESG vary and lack a common consensus. This is at a time when ESG "green" enterprises have trouble finding traditional financing while a large demand exists for ESG-qualified investments.[5]

The Autorité des marches financiers (AMF) in France and the Autoriteit Financiële Markten (AFM) in the Netherlands have proposed a European regulatory framework for providers of sustainability-related services. The standards are aimed at preventing misallocation of investments, greenwashing, and ensuring investor protection.[6]

France implemented ESG labeling rules in 2015 with the Socially Responsible Investing (SRI, or ISR in French) Label for ESG funds and the Greenfin Label for Green Funds.[7]

3. The implementation decree was published on April 26, 2012, and amended section 225-102-1 of the Commercial Code.

4. Vibeka Mair, *ESG Country Snapshot: France: 173 Reasons to Be Cheerful*, Responsible Investor, (Sept. 12, 2018), https://www.responsible-investor.com/articles/esg-country-snapshot-france.

5. Camille Guézennec & Guillaume Malochet, *Impact Investing: A Way to Finance the Social and Solidarity Economy? An International Comparison*, Commissariat Général à la stratégie, et à la prospective (June 2013), https://www.strategie.gouv.fr/sites/strategie.gouv.fr/files/atoms/files/dt_-_impact_investing_-_vu_hm_final_le_21-06vcg9h00.pdf.

6. Laura Van Geest & Robert Ophèle, Position Paper: *Call for a European Regulation for the Provision of ESG Data, Ratings, and Related Services*, Autorité des marches financiers (Dec. 15, 2020), https://www.amf-france.org/sites/default/files/private/2020-12/amf-afm-position-paper-call-for-a-european-regulation-for-providers-of-esg-data-ratings-and-related-services.pdf.

7. Dominique Blanc, *France Strengthens Sustainable Funds Management Monitoring Tools*, Natixis (Sept. 24, 2020), https://gsh.cib.natixis.com/our-center-of-expertise/articles/france-strengthens-sustainable-funds-management-monitoring-tools.

- **Greenfin Label.** Created by the French Ministry of Ecological Transition, the goal of the label "Greenfin" is to guaranty that funds meet the criteria of Green Investment.[8] These are funds that invest in the fight against climate change in the areas of energy, construction, waste control, industry, clean transportation, information technology, agriculture and forest, and adaption to climate change. Nuclear energy and companies that explore and produce fossil-fuel energy are excluded, while distributors, transportation companies, producers of equipment, and services are limited to fossil-fuel use of 33 percent of revenue. Companies that get more than 33 percent of their revenue from activities considered wasteful, such as those that are not fuel efficient or exploit the forests, are excluded from the label. As of February 2021, 55 funds carry the Greenfin Label worth €17 billion.
- **Investissement Socialement Responsible (ISR in French, or SRI in English) Label.** This is a specific label created by the French Ministry of Economy and Finance in 2016 to designate funds investing in a socially responsible manner based on its indicators. Three external organizations are licensed by its Comité Français d'Accréditation (Cofrac) to measure and issue the SRI label: Afnor Certification, Ernst & Young France, and Deloitte. Funds must follow six pillars to quantify their ESG activity: defined objectives, analytical methodology, portfolio construction and management, engagement with invested companies about their philosophy, strategy presentation to investors, and measurement of the impact of ESG strategy in each investment.[9]
- **Relance Label.** Due to the COVID-19 economic crisis, the French government, in October 2020, created a program to designate with the label "relance" investment funds supporting small- to mid-sized businesses.[10] Beyond the requirement of investing at least 30 percent in French companies, all the stocks

8. *Le label Greenfin*, Ministère de la transition écologique (Feb. 12, 2021), https://www.ecologie.gouv.fr/label-greenfin.

9. *Les critères d'atrribution du label, ministère de l'Économie et des finances et de la relance*, https://www.lelabelisr.fr/label-isr/criteres-attribution/ (last visited Feb. 10, 2021).

10. Aurélie Blondel, *Les fonds "relance" une aubaine pour les* épargnants*?*, Le Monde (Jan. 29, 2021), https://www.lemonde.fr/argent/article/2021/01/29/les-fonds-relance-une-aubaine-pour-les-epargnants_6068010_1657007.html.

in the fund must meet ESG requirements and not invest in stocks active in carbon.

Government Support

In 2001, France launched *fonds solidaires*—saving plans where up to 10 percent of assets allocated to employee saving funds are invested in social projects. Six years later, France issued its first "green bonds" to finance green projects, issuing $32.1 billion in new bonds in 2020.[11] It also has an Impact Initiative.

- **Green Bonds.** Like many countries, France found success in issuing Green Bonds. These bonds support public and private ESG projects, such as those focusing on renewable energy, energy efficiency, clean transportation, waste management, and climate change adaptation.[12] This could include a French village looking to improve its bus system, sewage system, or energy needs but lacking the means. Other beneficiaries could be small projects considered too risky, lacking sufficient returns, or too small for investors. Investing in Green Bonds can be done directly or by investing in Green Bond funds. Between 2016 and 2018, the top-five-performing funds, according to Morning Star, returned between 1.59 percent and 3.68 percent. The drop in interest rates has pushed this return higher, especially in the last year. One of the goals of the Green Bonds is to encourage ESG investing and phase out tax incentives.
- **Targeted Impact Investing.** The Ministry of Environment and Solidarity controls the French Impact Initiative, whose goal is scaling up social businesses through a €50-million seed fund and a €1-billion accelerator fund for "engaging different areas and local ecosystems in social innovation."[13] Projects apply directly to the government for support. BNP has issued six social impact contracts (CIS) that provide a vehicle for private investors to support experimental new initiatives from social organizations.

11. Nina Chestney, *Global Green Bond Issuance Hit New Record High Last Year*, Reuters (Jan. 24, 2021), https://www.reuters.com/article/us-greenbonds-issuance/global-green-bond-issuance-hit-new-record-high-last-year-idINKBN29U013.

12. Romain Thomas, *S'y retrouver dans la jungle des fonds d'obligations vertes*, Le Monde (Jan. 6, 2020), https://www.lemonde.fr/argent/article/2020/01/06/s-y-retrouver-dans-la-jungle-des-fonds-d-obligations-vertes_6024887_1657007.html.

13. *Id.*

They come with the guarantee that the French government will reward investments with a premium if agreed measured social outcomes are met.

Pension Funds

Additional support for impact investing comes from two government pension funds, ERAFP and FRR.

The public sector additional pension scheme (RAFP) is a mandatory, points-based scheme created for fully qualified and trainee civil servants working in the French central government (civilians and military), local and regional authorities and the public hospitals sector, as well as members of the judiciary. The French Public Service Additional Pension Scheme (ERAFP) is the public-sector administrative entity that manages this pension scheme. ERAFP has €39 billion under management for France's 4.6 million civil servants.[14] It has applied SRI/ESG principles since 2005.[15] ERAFP has a 100 percent SRI policy based on a charter of five investment values. Because several trade union leaders sit on its board, three of those values cover human rights, social progress, and employee democracy. The other two are the environment and good governance and transparency.[16]

Fond de réserve des retraites (FRR) receives its funding from four main sources: private social security funds, privatization resources, mobile phone licenses, and stock market transaction tax. It covers 17 million French in a pay-as-you-go system. The FRR began its SRI investment in 2003.[17] It also votes proxies in accordance with SRI principles.

Case Studies

Mirova is a French asset manager that developed a calculator in 2016 to determine the carbon footprint of its investment portfolio.[18] By 2018, it

14. Susanna Rust, *ERAFP Retenders €475m in Domestic Equity Mandates*, IPE MAGAZINE (Feb. 17, 2021), https://www.ipe.com/news/erafp-retenders-475m-in-domestic-equity-mandates/10050747.article.

15. Nina Rohrbein, *France: Showing the Way on ESG*, IPE MAGAZINE (May 2010), https://www.ipe.com/france-showing-the-way-on-esg/34802.article.

16. SRI at ERAFP, *Retraite additionelle de la function publique*, https://www.rafp.fr/en/article/sri-erafp (last visited Feb. 11, 2021).

17. *SRI Strategy of the FRR* (Feb. 2021), http://www.fondsdereserve.fr/en/socially-responsible-investment.

18. *Mirova Selected for PRI Leaders Group 2020 by the UN Principles for Responsible Investing*, BUSINESSWIRE (Oct. 8, 2020), https://www.businesswire.com/

was able to put its portfolio in line with the two-degree Celsius limit set by the Paris Agreements.[19] All its funds are 100 percent SRI-labeled with €19.6 billion in assets under management.[20] Its carbon impact analysis (CIA) focuses on three factors. The first is the life cycle approach considering not just emissions produced directly by a company but also its suppliers and distributors. Second, they subtract carbon emissions saved by the implementation of carbon-reduction solutions. Third, Mirova calculates the impact of future research and development.

Caisse des dépôts et consignations (CDC)[21] has applied ESG standards to real estate, infrastructure investing, and development within the French territory. In addition, it invests in stocks and bonds of companies engaged in ESG-positive businesses. Its primarily focus, however, is investment in real estate that is energy efficient, both newly constructed and renovated to environmentally sustainable material. Each infrastructure investment is done with an analysis of its public utility, energy use, CO2 output, impact on biodiversity, water, and greenhouse gasses. CDC works with the state to develop urban and territorial areas in a sustainable manner.

Since each fund has its own investment methodology, it becomes more difficult when adding a layer of sustainability to the investment process. *La Financière Responsable* addresses the absence of a concrete definition of SRI by following principles it calls "the Compass of the SRI Market,"[22] which uses a broad-to-narrow approach, beginning with the full range of euro stocks, in the European Union.[23] Next is a macroeconomic analysis to anticipate risky sectors and those that are potentially profitable. Step three is where it deviates from normal SRI analysis by excluding companies with direct negative environmental impacts: the arms industry, those involved in human rights controversies, those who have had mass layoffs in the last three years, and those lacking

news/home/20201008005940/en/Mirova-Selected-for-PRI-Leaders-Group-2020-by-the-UN-Principles-for-Responsible-Investing.

19. https://unfccc.int/process-and-meetings/the-paris-agreement/the-paris-agreement, (last visited Feb. 11, 2021).

20. Mirova Website, Chiffres Cles (Feb. 2021), https://www.mirova.com/fr.

21. https://www.caissedesdepots.fr/sites/default/files/2020-04/charte_investissement_responsable_cdc_avril_2014.pdf (last visited Feb. 11, 2021).

22. *La boussole du marché de l'ISR*, La Financière Responsable, https://www.la-financiere-responsable.fr/la-boussole-du-marche-de-isr/ (last visited Feb. 11, 2021).

23. *Gestion Intégrale IVA: processus d'investissement*, La Financière Responsable, https://www.la-financiere-responsable.fr/gestion-integrale-iva-processus-dinvestissement/ (last visited Feb. 11, 2021).

transparency. Next, they seek investments that have models of sustainable growth around a coherent strategy. The last step follows up with a regular review of the 30 stocks in the portfolio to verify their investments' continued commitment to their SRI criteria along with their performance. They try to avoid turnover with an eye toward the long term.

Opportunities and Conclusion

Those seeking to invest in French ESG funds should begin with the labels just described. Each of the entities certifying those labels offers a list of funds meeting their criteria. French ESG investing has been supportive of both traditional and small green investments. The labeling initiatives are aimed at identifying funds that invest in stocks and bonds meeting definable ESG criteria. A good start is to visit the France Invest ESG site.[24] Here one can find downloadable publications, including an ESG Investing Guide in both English and French.

Beyond that, France looks to support smaller green investment, for example, by supporting projects in small French villages, as described earlier. Investment in France's Green Bonds is a way to support this kind of development. France's impact investments, such as the BNP CIS contracts, described earlier, are another opportunity for investment in French ESG.

Being part of the EU, the French aim to coordinate their ESG investment criteria, regulation, and support with the European Union. Thus, any review of ESG investing is always studied with an eye toward the European whole. Transparency and measurement are problems not unique to France, but France has been addressing these issues for more than 20 years. Look for continued leadership from France in solving the problems of "greenwashing" and innovation in investment vehicles and transparency.

24. https://www.diplomatie.gouv.fr/IMG/pdf/Mandatory_reporting_built_on_consensus_in_France.pdf (last visited July 7, 2022).

19

Germany

Jörg Rehder[1]

Market Overview and Impact Investing Growth

Attention to environmental, social, and governance (ESG) issues in Germany can be traced back to 1713 when the German father of sustainable forestry, Hans Carl von Carlowitz, realized that cutting down more trees than could grow back would destroy the environment. The German explorer and scientist, Alexander von Humboldt, reached a similar conclusion in 1800 when, during an expedition to South America, he realized that Lake Valencia in Venezuela was drying up because of the surrounding deforestation to create farmland.

During the next centuries, progress was made to ensure that current generations could meet their needs without destroying the environment and ensuring the needs of future generations were not compromised. The Agenda 2030,[2] adopted by the United Nations in 2015, sets forth 17 Sustainable Development Goals (SDGs); this is a major effort on a global level to combat poverty and to protect the planet. The 2015 Paris Climate Agreement,[3] the first ever international treaty on climate change, is

1. Partner, Schiedermair Rechtsanwälte, Frankfurt, Germany.

2. https://sustainabledevelopment.un.org/content/documents/21252030%20Agenda%20for%20Sustainable%20Development%20web.pdf. The United Nations subsequently issued *The Sustainable Development Goals Report 2021* (https://unstats.un.org/sdgs/report/2021/The-Sustainable-Development-Goals-Report-2021.pdf) and concluded that "years, or even decades of progress have been halted or reversed" due to the COVID-19 pandemic" *Id.* at 3. The report added that "without adequate [health, social and economic] data, the most vulnerable populations who need help the most remain invisible" *Id.* at 62. On a more positive note, according to the report the COVID-19 pandemic made clear that societies need to put greater effort on compiling data to ensure that progress is made on combatting poverty.

3. https://unfccc.int/sites/default/files/english_paris_agreement.pdf.

another effort to mitigate adverse climate change and to focus on environmental sustainability.

On the global level, the focus on ESG of late has been on environmental sustainability, that is, the "E." The "S" and the "G" have not garnered as much attention. In this context, the European Union issued Regulation 2020/852 (Taxonomy Regulation)[4] on June 18, 2020, which provides for an environmentally sustainable investment framework. As a regulation, it is directly applicable in Germany. The Taxonomy Regulation, an example of emphasizing environmental sustainability, establishes criteria as to what financial products and services will qualify as being environmentally sustainable.

In terms of an investment approach, Germany has traditionally stayed away from the "short termism" criticized by the European Commission in its Study on Directors' Duties and Sustainable Corporate Governance of July 2020.[5] Its approach has been called "Rhine capitalism"[6] with German corporations focusing not only on the short-term interests of their shareholders but also on the well-being of their employees, creditors, suppliers, and local communities. Germany's longer-term approach to investment and growth is reflected in its long-standing socially-just labor and employment laws, two-tier corporate board structure, shareholder democracy, viable *Mittelstand*, and strong business ethics—each an "S" or a "G" factor.

Policy Framework and Government Initiatives

Germany has supported impact investment as both a policy and regulatory framework. As discussed next, one of the leaders in Germany in pursuing and supporting impact investing is the Kreditanstalt für Wiederaufbau (KfW),[7] a state-owned development bank that was established in Frankfurt, Germany, shortly after World War II as part of the Marshall Plan.

---

4. Regulation 2020/852 of the European Parliament and of the Council of June 2020 on the establishment of a framework to facilitate sustainable investment and amending Regulation 2019/2088.

5. *Study on Directors' Duties and Sustainable Corporate Governance*, Final Report (July 2020), https://op.europa.eu/en/publication-detail/-/publication/e47928a2-d20b-11ea-adf7-01aa75ed71a1/language-en.

6. Also referred to as socialist capitalism; a middle ground between laissez-fair capitalism and true socialism.

7. The German federal government is an 80 percent shareholder of the *Kreditanstalt* für *Wiederaufbau* (Reconstruction Credit Institute). The German states hold the remaining 20 percent.

Policy Framework

Germany's engagement with impact investment includes Green Bonds, sustainability stock index, and the efforts of the KfW.

Government and Corporate Bonds

The Federal Republic of Germany issued its first Green Bond in September 2020.[8] The Green Bond market, however, is not limited to government bonds. A number of German juggernauts have been at the forefront of issuing corporate green bonds since 2020, including Deutsche Bank issuing green bonds for €500 million in June 2020,[9] Volkswagen (VW) issuing its first green bond for €2 billion in September 2020,[10] and Schaeffler AG, a supplier to the automobile industry, issuing green bonds for €350 million, also in 2020.[11] While VW will use the proceeds for research and development for e-cars and associated components, Schaeffler will use the funds to refinance a portfolio of sustainability projects.

Sustainability Stock Index

The Deutsche Börse AG introduced in March 2020 the DAX50 ESG stock index.[12] The DAX50 ESG lists 50 German companies that the Deutsche Börse deems pursue and support sustainability.[13] To be eligible

---

8. German Federal Ministry of Finance Press Release of August 24, 2020, https://www.bundesfinanzministerium.de/Content/EN/Pressemitteilungen/2020/2020-08-24-Germany-to-issue-Green-German-Federal-Securities-from-2020.html.

9. *Deutsche Bank begibt erste grüne Anleihe* (Deutsche Bank Issues First Green Bond), Frankfurter Allgemeine Zeitung of June 2, 2020, https://www.faz.net/aktuell/finanzen/deutsche-bank-begibt-erste-gruene-anleihe-16797074.html; *see also Deutsche Bank sammelt mit Öko-Anleihe halbe Milliarde ein* (Deutsche Bank Collects Half a Billion with Eco-Bonds), Handelsblatt of June 2, 2020, https://www.handelsblatt.com/finanzen/maerkte/anleihen/nachhaltiges-investment-deutsche-bank-sammelt-mit-oeko-anleihe-halbe-milliarde-ein/25880796.html?ticket=ST-11285494-ZNq2HbtIPHTac1bMyOhw-ap4.

10. *Volkswagen platziert erfolgreich erste Green Bonds mit 2 Milliarden Euro Volumen* (Volkswagen Successfully Issues First Green Bonds with a Volume of 2 Billion Euros), Press Release of Volkswagen of September 16, 2020, https://www.volkswagenag.com/de/news/2020/09/Volkswagen_Green_Bonds.html#.

11. *Schaeffler begibt erstmals (grünen) Schuldschein* (Schaeffler Issues for the First Time a (Green) Bond), Finance Magazine of April 9, 2020, https://www.finance-magazin.de/finanzierungen/schuldscheine/schaeffler-begibt-erstmals-gruenen-schuldschein-41098/.

12. This is comparable in many respects to the U.S. Dow Jones Sustainability Indices (DJSI) or the UK's FTSE4Good Index.

13. *Deutsche Börse stellt neuen Nachhaltigkeitsindex vor* (Deutsche Börse Introduces New Sustainability Stock Index), published in the Handelsblatt on March 4,

for the DAX50 ESG, a company must be listed on one of Germany's three primary stock indices—DAX, MDax or TecDax—and have ESG filters in place based on the Global Compact Screening of Sustainalytics.[14] The DAX50 ESG is not without its critics; they point out that a number of companies (e.g., cement, chemical, and natural gas producers) are, but should not be, included in such a sustainability index.

Case Study: Kreditanstalt für Wiederaufbau

KfW has a number of purposes, including providing financing for infrastructure projects, environmental projects, and education programs, as well as to loans, grants, and subsidies to small- and medium-sized enterprises (SMEs) and start-ups. KfW emphasizes integrating the UN's 17 SDG's into its financing; in 2019, KfW provided funding of €77.3 billion, of which 38 percent alone was used for climate and environmental protection.[15] More specifically, as part of its liquidity portfolio, KfW uses a "best in class" approach, meaning it invests in bonds and issuers only if the sustainability is in the top half of the respective sector. Just as importantly, KfW applies "exclusionary" criteria by investing only in bonds and issuers that do not engage in excluded activities (e.g., forced labor or child labor, pesticides or herbicides subject to international bans, commercial logging operations in primarily tropical forests, radioactive material, tobacco goods, online betting, or pornography).[16]

Regulatory Framework

Turning to its legislative framework, Germany has recently added to its statutory framework features promoting ESG—in particular, as to "S" and "G." As noted, the German economy has traditionally not focused on short-term investing; instead, both Germany's public and private sectors generally take a relatively long-term approach to growth and investment.

The German legislature got an early start on improving corporate governance in Germany when it enacted the Act on Control and Transparency in the Corporate Sector in 1998. Under this statute, management

2020, https://www.handelsblatt.com/finanzen/banken-versicherungen/banken/dax-50-esg-deutsche-boerse-stellt-neuen-nachhaltigkeitsindex-vor/25608862.htmlrates.

14. Sustainalytics is a Netherlands-based company that rates companies on their ESG performance (*see* www.sustainalytics.com).

15. KfW at a Glance—Facts and Figures, https://www.kfw.de/KfW-Group/.

16. Exclusion Criteria for KfW's Liquidity Portfolio, https://www.kfw.de/nachhaltigkeit/KfW-Group/Sustainability/Sustainable-Banking-Operations/Sustainable-Investment/KfWs-Sustainable-Investment-Approach/Exclusion-Criteria/.

boards[17] of stock corporations were required to implement early warning systems so that they receive timely warnings of issues that could affect a company's financial viability. Failure to heed this requirement may lead to personal liability. On April 11, 2017, Germany enacted the Act to Strengthen the Non-Financial Reporting by Companies in their Management and Group Management Reports, which resulted in section 289b et seq. being added to Germany's Commercial Code.[18] Under German Commercial Code section 289b et seq., certain corporations (including those with net revenues in excess of €40 million, those that are "capital markets oriented," or those with more than 500 employees, as well as credit institutions and insurance companies) must disclose, as part of their annual reports, nonfinancial information regarding the company's performance on environmental, social, and employee matters as well as on human rights, anti-corruption, and bribery. It is estimated that this statute impacts between 500 and 600 large German entities.

In December 2019, Germany enacted the Act to Implement the Second Shareholders' Directive.[19] Two provisions of the act are especially notable in terms of improved corporate governance of publicly held entities. First, the act gives shareholders of publicly held entities the right to have a more significant "say on pay" of management board member's compensation if the supervisory board makes significant changes to their compensation.[20] Shareholders may also reduce the maximum amount of management board compensation as set by the supervisory board.[21] These provisions were added because of recent discussions concerning the heightened disconnect between executive's salaries and average salaries of employees. Additionally, to increase transparency on executive

17. Unlike in the United States, Germany subscribes to a two-tier board system. Large German companies, that is, those with more than 2,000 employees, must have, in addition to a management board (*Vorstand*), a supervisory board (*Aufsichtsrat*), of which half of the members represent the interests of the employees. The purpose of the supervisory board, as the name would indicate, is to supervise the affairs of the management board; in essence to serve as a check and balance. The practical impact is that, unlike in the United States, German employees of large companies have direct representation on a board responsible for a corporation's long-term strategy.

18. Section 289b German Commercial Code was enacted to implement Directive 2014/95 of the European Parliament and of the Council as regards disclosure of non-financial and diversity information by certain large undertakings and groups.

19. Federal Law Gazette I, at 2637 (2019); this statute was enacted to implement Directive 2017/828 amending Directive 2007/36 as regards the encouragement of long-term shareholder engagement.

20. Section 120a(1) German Stock Corporation Act.

21. Section 87(4) German Stock Corporation Act.

compensation, the act requires each publicly held entity to prepare a separate annual Compensation Report on compensation earned by each management board and supervisory board member (including, for example, bonuses and stock options).[22] This Compensation Report must be made available on the company's website.

As for diversity and inclusion, Germany also implemented a quota system for women to become members of supervisory boards.[23] Under Germany's Stock Corporation Act, since 2016, publicly held entities with more than 2,000 employees must have at least 30 percent women (and 30 percent men) on their supervisory boards.[24] This has made a difference in that of 188 publicly held companies recently studied, 32.2 percent of the supervisory board members were female.[25] The provision concerns only supervisory boards, it does *not* apply to management boards. The same study found only 10.7 percent of management board members were female.

Pursuant to section 111(5) of Germany's Stock Corporation Act, the supervisory boards of publicly held companies, and certain other large companies, not subject to the afore-referenced statutory 30 percent thresholds must disclose their "goals" in terms of percentage of women who will be members of their supervisory board and management board. Not impressively, as of 2017, more than 78 percent of companies either failed to report their goal or set their goal as having "zero" female management board members.[26]

This may change. On January 6, 2021, then-Chancellor Merkel's cabinet passed a bill that would require publicly held entities with more than 2,000 employees and that have more than three management members to have at least one female and one male management board member.[27] This would impact about 70 German companies, of which 30 do not

22. Section 162 German Stock Corporation Act.

23. Unlike in the United States, quotas are permissible under German law and may be used to promote diversity and inclusion.

24. Section 96(2) German Stock Corporation Act.

25. Report by *Frauen in die Aufsichtsräte e.V.* (Women on Supervisory Boards Association) and German Federal Ministry of Families, Senior Citizens, Women and Youth of April 30, 2020, https://www.fidar.de/wob-indizes-studien/wob-index-185/uebersicht.html.

26. German Ministry for Families, Senior Citizens, Women, and Youth Report of February 19, 2021, https://www.bmfsfj.de/bmfsfj/themen/gleichstellung/frauen-und-arbeitswelt/quote-privatwitschaft/quote-fuer-mehr-frauen-in-fuehrungspositionen-privatwirtschaft-78562.

27. Draft Leadership Position Act, German Bundestag Printed Matter 19/26689, https://dip21.bundestag.de/dip21/btd/19/266/1926689.pdf.

currently have a female management board member. Also under the draft Leadership Position Act, companies that set a goal of zero management board members would be required to explain why they do not seek to have female management board members.

Finally, Germany's Act on Corporate Duty of Care to Avoid Human Rights Violations in the Supply Chain ("Supply Chain Act") will enter into force on January 1, 2023.[28] The essence of this act is to ensure that suppliers of German entities meet minimum human rights standards in terms of child labor, discrimination, exploitation, and fair employment laws. Failure to observe the act's provisions may, depending on the size of the company and the type of violation, subject a company to a fine ranging from €100,000 to 2 percent of the company's annual revenue. The act will be effective in 2023 for companies with at least 3,000 employees; this threshold is reduced to 1,000 employees in 2024 (currently only approximately 2,900 companies in Germany meet this threshold). The essence of the statute is that corporations are required to implement a risk-management system for the purpose of combatting human rights violations and environmental risks within the corporation's supply chain. The statute also requires corporations to essentially introduce a whistleblower system—traditionally a touchy issue in Germany.[29]

Corporate Governance Code

Germany issued a Corporate Governance Code in 2002. The code is not statutory law, but instead a code of best practices for publicly held entities. The Code Commission reworked the code in its entirety in 2020.[30] It includes principles, recommendations, and suggestions. The principles are essentially what is set forth by statute. Publicly held entities are encouraged to follow the recommendations and, if they do not, to explain the nonobservance ("comply or explain").[31] Corporations should also observe the suggestions, but this is left within their discretion. Nonpublic entities are to use the code as soft law guidance.

In addition to reworking the code, the Code Commission also added some significant provisions. To begin, the code provides guidance as to what constitutes an "independent" supervisory board member as a

28. Federal Law Gazette I, at 2959 (2021).

29. Section 8 Supply Chain Act.

30. Federal Gazette, Federal Ministry of Justice and Consumer Protection of March 20, 2020, https://www.bundesanzeiger.de/pub/publication/5JK04En2np4amYCKabv;wwwsid=CC5F8A33F3E5CD0189BFD42E2062B186.web05-pub?0.

31. Section 161 German Stock Corporation Act.

shareholder representative, including requiring that such an individual (or a close family member) not have been a member of the company's management board two years prior to becoming a supervisory board member[32] nor having served on the supervisory board for more than 12 years. The revised code also requires supervisory board members to conduct a self-assessment and provide information to management how they performed the assessment (e.g., by engaging external advisors). Finally, as to the variable compensation of management board members, the code states that supervisory boards are to prepare performance criteria for management board members regarding the corporation's long-term strategy.

Sustainability seals providing uniformity to ESG standards have become popular in Europe and elsewhere. A number of Member States have authorized such seals, which confirm ESG compliance. The European Union is paving the way for a pan-European ecolabel for financial products; this, however, has not yet been implemented.

In the meantime, the German-speaking European countries (Germany, Austria, Switzerland, and Liechtenstein) have introduced the FNG Seal of Sustainability for Investment Funds (FNG),[33] a seal that confirms an investment fund qualifies as sustainable, as defined by a Berlin-based association of banks, financial investors and advisors, funds, and entrepreneurs. Though the FNG seal does not enjoy widespread recognition outside German-speaking countries, approximately 170 investment funds received the seal in 2021. Using the seal subjects the fund to an annual audit that the fund does not engage in greenwashing. The seal's purpose is to provide investors with comfort that the fund meets certain minimum criteria with respect to human rights, employees' rights, environmental protection, and combatting corruption and bribery. Though the FNG seal is certainly a step in the right direction, generating uniform standards or sustainability seals for use throughout the European Union remains a hot topic.

---

32. Unlike in the United States where an individual may serve as an officer and director of a U.S. corporation simultaneously, an individual may not simultaneously serve on the management board and the supervisory board of a German corporation.

33. *Forum Nachhaltige Geldanlagen e.V.* (Forum for Sustainable Financial Investments Association).

Challenges in Impact Investing

Lack of Uniform Binding Standards

A common theme in all the country chapters of this book is that the lack of uniform binding standards and impact measurements—not only in Germany, but globally—remain the primary hurdle for quicker growth of ESG-based investing. Most corporate ESG reporting remains voluntary. ESG-based investing will benefit from continued legislation from the European Union and Germany. One significant step in this direction, at least in the financial services sector, will be the regulatory technical standards (RTS) concerning sustainability-related disclosures as called for in Regulation 2019/88.[34] These will heighten protection for investors by improving ESG disclosures to end-investors and, thereby, reduce the risk of greenwashing. The European Supervisory Authorities' goal is that RTS are to apply as of January 1, 2023.

ESG versus Antitrust Law

Another aspect of ESG that has not garnered much attention (yet) is whether antitrust laws may hamper an ESG investment or financing strategy. For example, does the cutting off of capital resources to an energy sector that does not pass ESG muster constitute illegal collusion?[35] Germany's Federal Cartel Agency issued a report on October 1, 2020,[36] discussing to what extent pursuing public interest sustainable goals in tandem may actually be a violation of antitrust laws. Without coming to a definitive conclusion, Germany's Federal Cartel Office contemplated whether it should continue to review competition issues primarily through a regulatory balancing test lens, or should it consider also other issues, for example, the environment, the public good, and so on.

---

34. Final Report on Draft Technical Standards as published by the European Supervisory Authorities on February 2, 2021, https://www.esma.europa.eu/sites/default/files/library/jc_2021_03_joint_esas_final_report_on_rts_under_sfdr.pdf.

35. Banks' Energy Boycott is an Antitrust Problem, Wall St. J. July 14, 2020, https://www.wsj.com/articles/banks-energy-boycott-is-an-antitrust-problem-11594746486 (a number of large commercial banks have, in parallel, decided against providing financing for oil drilling in the Arctic and for coal mining).

36. Öffene *Märkte und nachhaltiges Wirtschaften—Gemeinwohlziele als Herausforderung* für die *Kartellrechtspraxis* (Open Markets und Sustainable Business—Public Interest Goals as a Challenge for the Antitrust Practice), published by the German Federal Cartel Office on October 1, 2020, https://www.bundeskartellamt.de/SharedDocs/Publikation/DE/Diskussions_Hintergrundpapier/AK_Kartellrecht_2020_Hintergrundpapier.pdf;jsessionid=C298594FFC846339AF9E9BBADB65EC25.2_cid371?__blob=publicationFile&v=2.

Conclusion

Though initially not at the forefront of ESG investing, Germany's diverse institutional investment playing field, including asset managers, investment and pension funds, insurers, churches, and foundations, has caused Germany to quickly become a leader in impact investing. This stems not only from increased attention being given to ESG, but also to an increased awareness and acceptance that investors are demanding a commitment to sustainability.

Just like any other country, Germany has not been immune from corporate corruption, negative headlines for corporate malfeasance, and corporate crises, causing impact investing to become a sort of corporate "safe haven." Though the German corporate arena has never focused on quarterly short-termism, German managers have nevertheless quickly realized that going beyond the minimum requirements currently set forth by ESG hard law, and implementing sustainability measures, is not only of value vis-à-vis stakeholders, suppliers, employees, and local communities, but it is also beneficial in terms of a long-term financial strategy.

20

Italy

Roberto Randazzo[1] *and Fabio Gallo Perozzi*[2]

Market Overview and Impact Investing Growth

As a key premise, the third sector is an important part of Italian society. It covers a range of different organizations that belong neither to the public sector (i.e., the state) nor to the traditionally market-driven private sector (profit-making private enterprise).

Leading third sector organizations include:

- Charities, as associations and foundations,
- Voluntary and community organizations,
- Social enterprises, and
- Think tanks and private research institutes (excluding universities and colleges).

The role of the third sector in Italy is confirmed by the Italian Constitution, notably article 118, which embraces the principle of subsidiarity, according to which activities of general interest—typically performed by the State—must be carried out first and foremost at the level closest to citizens, for example by involving private individuals and associations.

The Italian Constitution also recognizes core characteristics of the impact economy, such as social and environmental aspects of economic activity plus balancing economic and nonfinancial interests. Indeed, article 2 of the Italian Constitution endorses social solidarity, while other provisions provide economic initiative cannot conflict with social purpose, and private property must be directed toward a purpose ensuring

1. Partner, Legance, Milan, Italy; former president, esela—The legal network for social impact (transitioned to Global Alliance of Impact Lawyer—GAIL).

2. Junior Associate, Legance, Milan, Italy.

its social function.[3] In addition, on February 8, 2022, the amendments to articles 9 and 41 of the Italian Constitution were approved, introducing the protection of the environment, biodiversity, and animals among the fundamental principles. This is the first amendment since 1948 made to one of the articles of the Italian Constitution, containing the so-called Fundamental Principles of the constitutional order (articles 1–12).

From these premises, principles appear that have guided and inspired Italian legislators over the years: development of a consolidated welfare state, widespread third sector, and, more recently, a growing social economy and impact market.

As in many other countries, the 2008 financial crisis followed by the COVID-19 pandemic, brought to the surface more societal and environmental challenges. They also increased the importance of involving and directing the private sector toward positive (and measurable) social and environmental impact objectives. In addition to aiding economic recovery, these objectives support Sustainable Development Goals (SDGs)[4] and undertakings such those under the Paris Climate Agreement.[5]

The Italian impact-investment market has grown considerably over the past decade in terms of players, diversification of tools, and development of regulations and policies. It is generally recognized that Italy has a relatively high maturity level in this market and could serve as a model for many other markets.[6]

Estimates of the impact investment market vary according to the definitions adopted. One source is TIRESIA—Technology, Innovation and Research for Social Impact—the international research center promoted by the School of Management of Politecnico di Milano,[7] whose surveys

---

3. Regarding the mentioned provisions on economic initiative and property, see arts. 2, 41, and 42 of the Constitution of the Italian Republic.

4. *See* Malcolm Farley, *Four Things You Should Know about the Sustainable Development Goals*, UNICEF, https://www.unicefusa.org/stories/four-things-you-should-know-about-sustainable-development-goals/34503?gclid=Cj0KCQiAq7COBhC2ARIsANsPATHMXvU7AldrLrDqrxHa7p_7mJUrWUPmyK2I4P33DuF-yPjQ-Nz5vDQaAv0IEALw_wcB (last visited Dec. 29, 2021).

5. *See What's in the Paris Climate Agreement?*, Economist (October 29, 2021), https://www.economist.com/interactive/paris-climate-agreement-annotated/?gclid=Cj0KCQiAq7COBhC2ARIsANsPATGXE7UxPuevyOs7An6E8o77wmLLAZpxt-wDQI6FSTrUamnNoZy5eCJYaAhvGEALw_wcB&gclsrc=aw.ds.

6. *See* Mackevičiūtė et al., European Parliament, *Social Impact Investment—Best Practices and Recommendations for the Next Generation* (2020).

7. MIP Politecnico di Milano has become the first B Corp business school in Europe (see https://www.bcorporation.net/en-us/find-a-b-corp/company/gsom-polimi-it).

rely on the principles of intentionality, measurability, and additionality (as described in the European chapter, Chapter 15, of this book). According to the 2019 TIRESIA impact outlook, the Italian impact investing market, from 2006 to 2019, rose to around €8 billion (mostly in the form of credit, and only partly, around 15 percent, through venture capital investments).[8] Similarly, between 2014 and 2018, green bonds were issued in Italy for a total amount of €5.1 billion, involving nine issuers in 12 deals mainly in the energy sector (77 percent), while according to a more recent survey Italy ranked 9th globally in terms of green bonds issued.[9] By looking at market figures, it is also relevant noting that 2021 has seen a decisive growth that has led to assets invested in funds classified as articles 8 or 9 of the SFDR Regulation (see Chapter 15) weighing in total almost 30 percent of the total assets invested in funds in Italy, with around 40 percent managed by Italian entities.[10]

Turning to the supply side of impact capital, foundations, especially banking foundations, are the main players in the Italian market. This is not surprising since by law they must invest part of their revenues in support of third sector projects.[11] An example is the 2019 creation by Fondazione CRT of the Fondazione Sviluppo e Crescita CRT, which is committed to impact investments and has an endowment of $53 million.[12] Fondazione Social Venture Giordano dell'Amore is another foundation that is very active in the field.[13]

Alongside these forms of grants, Italy has recently seen an increase in the private impact investment market. Sì-Social Impact fund (SEFEA impact) and SocialFare Seed are leaders in third sector

8. *See* TIRESIA—Politecnico di Milano, *Tiresia Impact Outlook* (2019). TIRESIA ensures that investments classified as impact investing demonstrate intentionality, additionality, and a commitment to impact measurement. On this ground, the report disaggregated its estimates of market size into three grades of impact investment: strictly impact, impact, and almost impact. The mentioned €8 billion size comprehends all the three grades.

9. *See* Climate Bonds Initiative, *The Green Bond Market in Europe* (2018). *See also* Climate Bonds Initiative, *Global Green Bond State of the Market 2019* (2020).

10. *See* Forum per la Finanza Sostenibile, *Gli investimenti sostenibili in Italia -Tendenze e prospettive di mercato* (2021). This is data extrapolated from an earlier report by Assogestioni (June 2021), which in detail identified 1208 and 139 funds under art. 8 and 9 SFDR regulation, respectively.

11. A total of 88 Italian banking foundations control assets of around US$45 billion (see the Country profile on Italy in Global Steering Group for Impact Investment, *Transition to Impact Economies—A Global Overview*, 2019).

12. *See* https://www.sviluppoecrescitacrt.it/.

13. *See* https://www.fondazionesocialventuregda.it/.

projects, while OPES-LCEF and Oltre Venture are oriented toward the mainstream market.[14]

A recent project is the "Ospedal Grando Impact Investing"[15] for the modernization of Treviso's hospital using impact investing funds to finance large infrastructure projects. Similarly, the public–private initiative "Programma 2121"[16] for inclusion of prisoners in working opportunities was led by the Italian Ministry of Justice and the multinational developer Lendlease. The program is expected to have "a positive socio-economic impact on the life of the inmate and on society as a whole, offering professional learning opportunities and post-detention employment perspectives to the inmate, while reducing the likelihood of reoffending due to social and economic exclusion."[17]

Policy Framework and Government Initiatives

Although growing rapidly, the Italian impact ecosystem is still relatively young. Its policies and regulatory parameters remain fundamental. At the same time, Italy is being strongly influenced by the European approach, as described in an earlier chapter.

Policy Framework

In 2018, the Italian government announced a €21 million outcomes fund, Fondo Innovazione Sociale. Over three years, it strengthened the ability of public administrations, working with private sector actors, to implement social innovation action aimed at generating new solutions, models, and approaches.

Universities and research centers are also contributing to Italy's impact ecosystem, remaining at the forefront of developing skills for impact investment managers. The Ministry of Education, Universities and Research, for instance, launched a $1.1 million program to support ten Italian universities in the development of impact investing and measurement knowledge.[18]

---

14. *See* https://sefeaimpact.it/; https://socialfare.org/en/socialfare-seed/; http://www.opesfund.eu/; https://www.oltreimpact.com/.

15. *See* https://ospedalgrando.com/social-impact/?msID=9b4d67e6-2e84-4985-bca1-eaef37e22e65.

16. *See* https://www.plusvalue.cloud/programma-2121/?msID=2950ac57-fe9c-4935-b021-2e694f05340e.

17. *See* note 16.

18. *See* Global Steering Group for Impact Investment, *supra* note 11.

Importantly, impact investing, including social impact bonds, was among the tools envisaged in the Report for the President of the Council of Ministers "Initiatives for Recovery, Italy 2020–2022,"[19] the Italian post-pandemic economic and social recovery plan. Under it, impact investing will be used to attract private capital for art and culture, as well as for social infrastructure.

Significant support was also provided by the Social Impact Agenda per l'Italia (SIA) and the Italian National Advisory Board (NAB) of the Global Steering Group for Impact Investing (GSG), which involve players in the Italian impact market, from policy makers to investors, entrepreneurs, and practitioners. At the request of the 12th Parliamentary Commission on Social Affairs, SIA recommended strengthening and adjusting national social policies, outlining fundamental steps to foster national impact ecosystem, and using funds from the European Recovery Plan.[20]

Impact measurement has become important for the Italian government in allocating European resources under both the European's multiannual financial framework (MFF) for 2021–2027 (with €1.074 billion budget) and the Next Generation European recovery instrument (with €750 billion budget under the European Recovery Plan).[21]

Regulatory Framework

Since European regulations apply automatically and uniformly, with some exceptions, to all European countries, including Italy, European regulatory framework on sustainable finance has a large impact on the Italian impact market. As discussed in the European chapter, Chapter 15, in this book, Italy's social impact investing market mainly operates under Regulation (EU) 2019/2088 on sustainability-related disclosures in the financial services sector (SFDR Regulation) and Regulation (EU) 2020/852 on the establishment of a framework to facilitate sustainable investment, and amending Regulation (EU) 2019/2088 (Taxonomy Regulation), as well as Regulations (EU) 346/2013 on European social entrepreneurship funds (EuSEF Regulation) and (EU) 345/2013 on European venture capital funds (EuVECA Regulation).

19. *See* Iniziative per il rilancio "Italia 2020–2022," Rapporto per il Presidente del Consiglio dei Ministri, https://www.governo.it/sites/new.governo.it/files/comitato_rapporto.pdf.

20. *See* Commissione XII—Affari Sociali della Camera, *Memoria per audizione documento xxvii, n. 18* (2021).

21. *See* Chapter 15.

As to environmental, social, and governance (ESG) disclosure, fund managers must include in their annual report and communications to investors whether and to what extent environmental, ethic, and social criteria are used in managing assets.[22] Similarly, the Italian public authority responsible for regulating securities markets (CONSOB) required[23] asset managers and insurance companies offering products and services labeled as "ethical" or "socially responsible" to disclose how those qualifications affected their investment decisions.

Given the preceding and 2021 fulfilments under the SFDR Regulation for financial operators, sustainability is clearly impacting the entire financial market. At the same time, it is necessary to consider these tools not in isolation but rather in the broader context of European policies (i.e., the European Green Deal),[24] the aforementioned financial strategy plans, and regulatory developments in the corporate sector.[25]

Indeed, impact investing is one dimension of the impact economy that also promotes a paradigm shift toward corporate sustainable and inclusive models. Indeed, there are for-profit hybrid entities that, as a core business strategy, balance profit distribution with the pursuit of positive social and environmental impact. Italy has special legal forms and statuses for such hybrid companies.[26]

First is the Società Benefit.[27] In 2016, Italy became the first country outside the United States to authorize this type of benefit corporation. The Italian version distributes profits, while pursuing positive impact to be measured, evaluated, and reported. With the ability to distribute profits, it represents a combination of impact and investibility.

---

22. Legislative Decree 252/2005 already made such disclosures mandatory for pension funds.

23. *See* Decision n. 15691.

24. *See* European Commission, *Communication from the Commission—The European Green Deal* (2019).

25. Regarding regulatory developments in the corporate sector, without going into detail here, it shall be considered, for example, the innovative scope and implications of the two legal initiatives already mentioned in the European Chapter, Chapter 15; *see* European Parliament, *Corporate Due Diligence and Corporate Accountability—European Parliament Resolution of 10 March 2021 with Recommendations to the Commission on Corporate Due Diligence and Corporate Accountability* (2021); as well as European Commission, *Proposal for a Directive of the European Parliament and of the Council on Corporate Sustainability Due Diligence and Amending Directive (EU) 2019/1937*, Document COM/2022/71 final (2022).

26. *See* Randazzo, Gallo Perozzi & Longo, *ESG and Impact Investing Italy*, LEXOLOGY (2022).

27. *See* Law 208/2015.

Next is Innovative Start-ups with Social Vocation (SIAVS),[28] which must carry out activities in certain sectors and are subject to temporary bans on profit distribution (for a maximum period of 60 months). They benefit from specific fiscal advantages for equity investors.

Third is the Impresa Sociale,[29] a specific kind of social enterprise. If established as a company, it can distribute profits within designated limits.[30] As with SIAVS, Impresa Sociale is restricted to specific sectors established by law.[31] The Minister of Labor and Social Policy issued guidelines on mandatory impact evaluation and measurement by Impresa Sociale.

Fourth is the Social Cooperative,[32] a formalization of the cooperative model. The Social Cooperative pursues a defined social purpose and operates in specific sectors, or employs disadvantaged people in agricultural, industrial, commercial, or service sectors.

Finally, Legislative Decree 124/2019 introduced a new reward criterion in public procurement tenders for companies that measure their social or environmental impact. Under the decree, bidders using the assessment method recognized by the Società Benefit law will be given higher tender scores.

Challenges in Impact Investing

Despite growth of the Italian impact investment market, challenges remain. First, it will be necessary to follow (or, better yet, anticipate) global and European paths on green economy, business human rights, social innovation, and sustainable corporate governance. This means making those aspects integral parts of Italy's mainstream market, through measurement systems, taxonomies, regulatory filters, public procurement, and funds to attract private capital.

---

28. *See* Decree Law 179/2012.

29. *See* Legislative Decree 112/2017.

30. According to art. 3 of Legislative Decree 112/2017, the "Impresa Sociale" can distribute profits at the following conditions:

- Companies are allowed to allocate a maximum 50 percent of their annual profits and operating surpluses to its shareholders (by a free increase in share capital or a distribution of dividends);
- In any case, the amount to be distributed shall not exceed the maximum interest rate for interest-bearing postal bonds, increased by two and a half points compared to the capital paid in.

31. *See* art. 2 of Legislative Decree 112/2017.

32. *See* Law 381/1991. Based on the most recent data (ISTAT, 2017), there were 15.764 social cooperatives in Italy in 2017.

This transition toward an impact economy must involve not only investments (as in areas affected by societal challenges) but also the entrepreneurial ecosystem. In Italy, the ecosystem is mainly small- and medium-sized enterprises (SMEs) with solid connections to their territory, short and sustainable supply chains, and engagement with workers and stakeholders. It will be necessary to encourage large market players to integrate SMEs into their supply chains while stressing impact measurement, business human rights, and ESG due diligence.

In addition, private–public partnerships, and innovative impact finance instruments (such as Social Impact Bonds and pay-by-result programs) must receive more attention.

Finally, the different speeds at which impact investing and the impact economy are developing at regional levels must be considered. A national plan and policy coordination must bring greater consistency among the regions by supporting synergies and cross-learning opportunities.

In conclusion, the public financial sector, steeped in sustainability and inclusion principles, and dominating impact economy,[33] must influence and direct the sustainable transition of other market players.

Growing Sector Opportunities and Future of Market

Demand for impact capital has grown steadily, with areas most affected by the 2008 financial crisis and the COVID-19 pandemic becoming major impact investment targets. As a result, sectors such as healthcare, education, and social housing are very attractive to impact investors. A useful indicator of this is the SDG Dashboard created by the Social Impact Agenda, which shows the areas and related SDGs most in need of impact investment in Italy: industry, innovation, and infrastructure (SDG 9); responsible consumption and production (SDG 12); climate action (SDG 13); and finally, life below water (SDG 14).[34]

Megatrends are also shaping the Italian impact market. For instance, its aging population is among the highest globally.[35] It needs investments in social infrastructures to increase heathcare access and strengthen welfare structures. Similarly, increasing social challenges, such as social inclusion and gender equality, require targeted impact investments. As

33. *See* Business Roundtable *Business Roundtable Redefines the Purpose of a Corporation to Promote "An Economy That Serves All Americans"* (2019); *see also* World Economic Forum, *Davos Manifesto 2020: The Universal Purpose of a Company in the Fourth Industrial Revolution* (2019).

34. *See* Global Steering Group for Impact Investment, *supra* note 11.

35. *See* United Nations, *World Population Prospects: the 2017 Revision* (2017).

an example, the Italian statistical institute (ISTAT), in December 2020, reported the number of employed persons decreased by 101,000, of which 99,000 were women while just 2,000 were men.[36]

An opportunity for growth in the impact sector can come from combining public and private resources. Cassa Depositi e Prestiti (CDP), which manages public funds, played a key role in promoting and expanding the Italian impact ecosystem. Together with the European Investment Fund, CDP launched the Social Impact Italia project to provide guarantees for Italian inclusive financial markets and social entrepreneurship. Italy could push the market toward a sustainable transition by attracting private investment through the lever of public funds, especially in view of upcoming funds for Italy's recovery from the pandemic.

Networks and supporting organizations could become critical players in this regard. For instance, companies and organizations periodically gather in the Forum for Sustainable Finance (FFS) as part of the Eurosif network. Through events, training activities, and guidelines, the Forum plays a key role in promoting impact economy and finance. Similarly, Assobenefit, the national association for "Società Benefit," by statute "contributes to the affirmation of a new economic model of sustainable development in Italy," as well as globally.[37]

Looking at the road ahead, the driving force for Italy's impact market evolution could be the growth of private investment support for-profit organizations uniting entrepreneurial dynamics with social and environmental dimensions. Such cooperation is more likely to generate a high social and environmental impact that will complement (and, increasingly, replace) public resources.

Making all this possible will be legislators who support impact investment by developing appropriate tools for impact measurement, standards, definitions, rules of corporate governance, tax incentives, public procurement, and specific impact investing instruments.

36. *See* ISTAT, Press Release, Employment and Unemployment (Provisional Estimates) (2021).

37. *See* https://assobenefit.org/.

21

Switzerland

Julie Wynne[1]

Market Overview and Impact Investing Developments

Switzerland has become a leading location for sustainable financial services based on its being an international financial center and having a long private banking tradition. Swiss authorities, the financial sector, and civil society are all committed to maintaining this leadership role by developing private and public sustainable initiatives.

Sustainability can even be found in the Swiss Constitution, which states the Confederation shall "promote the common welfare, sustainable development, internal cohesion and cultural diversity of the country."[2] More specifically it also provides that "the Confederation and the Cantons shall endeavor to achieve a balanced and sustainable relationship between nature and its capacity to renew itself and the demands placed on it by the population."[3]

Since 2016, sustainable finance has been an integral part of the Swiss Federal Council's financial market policy. Swiss policy encourages a bottom-up approach, market incentives and corporate responsibility, open dialogue between government authorities and industry, and collaboration through a growing sustainability network.

At the market level, since the early 2000s, Swiss players such as BlueOrchard, responsAbility, Symbiotics, and Fundo were among the first players in the field of sustainable finance. Switzerland also became

1. Partner, MLL Legal, Geneva, Switzerland.
2. Preamble, https://www.fedlex.admin.ch/eli/cc/1999/404/en.
3. Art. 2, https://www.fedlex.admin.ch/eli/cc/1999/404/en.

a market leader in microfinance, with Switzerland now managing around 41 percent of global microfinance funds (US$6.8 billion).

In 2018, assets in Switzerland worth around CHF (Swiss Francs) 720 billion were managed according to environmental, social, and governance (ESG) criteria, equivalent to around 21 percent of total assets under management in Switzerland. These figures highlight the leading role and expertise of Swiss institutions, given that the global average for sustainable investments stands at 11 percent.[4]

In 2020, the market for sustainable investments (SI) in Switzerland continued its double-digit growth. The volume increased to CHF 1,520.2 billion. This figure covers SI funds, sustainable mandates, and sustainable assets of asset owners.[5]

On the level of sustainable funds, volumes increased to CHF 694.5 billion and now represent 52 percent of the overall Swiss fund market (compared to 38 percent in 2019). As such, funds adopting sustainable investment approaches now exceed conventional investment funds for the first time. The amount of SI reported by asset owners (CHF 555.9 billion) corresponds to approximately 33 percent of the total assets managed by Swiss pension funds and insurance companies.[6] All these numbers show the progressive mainstreaming of sustainable investments and their success in Switzerland.

Organizations such as Swiss Sustainable Finance (SSF) and Sustainable Finance Geneva (SFG) bring together various types of players, including banks, external assets managers, lawyers, trust companies, and family offices, who are keys to developing synergies and empowering the sector. As an example, Building Bridges conference, held for the second time in December 2021, was for financial stakeholders, the United Nations, nongovernmental organization (NGOs), academia, and government to work on a common vision of advancing sustainable finance. The Swiss financial center sees sustainability as an opportunity and benefits from the support of the government to establish the necessary framework conditions.

Developments at the legal and regulatory levels focus on transparency for investors through dedicated reporting and framework conditions that enable the pricing of relevant risks. Such measures help to reduce information asymmetries and enable the market to function in a more effective manner that takes long-term effects into account.

4. Swiss Sustainable Finance, Swiss Sustainable Investment Market Study, 2019.
5. Swiss Sustainable Finance, Swiss Sustainable Investment Market Study, 2021.
6. *Id.*

Policy Framework and Government Initiatives

Contrary to the European Union's legislative approach to sustainability, in Switzerland, there is no general legal or regulatory framework regarding sustainability in general or impact investing in particular. The absence of such a coherent framework is because the Swiss Federal Council, the government, wants to rely on existing legal and regulatory frameworks based on the subordination of government to private action. Notwithstanding, the Federal Council recognizes sustainable finance as a key factor for competitiveness of Swiss financial sector as well as a meaningful way for financial sector to effectively contribute to the UN's 2030 agenda.[7]

The following overview gives the reader a better understanding of the fragmented statutory landscape and ongoing legal developments, and market-based solutions favored by the Federal Council, that is, the self-regulatory and industry initiatives, as well as the main stakeholders in the field.

Statutory Landscape

Swiss statutory landscape in the field of sustainable finance is fragmented, as reflected in the most important statutory developments over the last several years.

From an international perspective, Switzerland is a party to numerous treaties (e.g., United Nations Framework Convention on Climate Change (UNFCCC), Kyoto Protocol, Paris Agreement) as well as signatory to many private and public initiatives (e.g., EU International Platform on Sustainable Finance, and Network for Greening Financial Systems (NGFS)). In 2011, Switzerland implemented the Kyoto Protocol by enacting the Federal Act on the Reduction of CO2 Emissions of 2011 (CO2

7. Federal Council Report: Sustainability in Switzerland's Financial Sector, Situation Analysis and Positioning with a Focus on Environmental Aspects, Berne (June 24, 2020), Executive Summary in English: https://www.newsd.admin.ch/newsd/message/attachments/61905.pdf. Full report in French https://www.newsd.admin.ch/newsd/message/attachments/61903.pdf Relevant Swiss Action Plans of the government include:

- October 2019: Adaptation to Climate Changes in Switzerland—Action Plan 2020–2025 by Federal Office for the Environment (FOEN);
- January 2020: Publication of Action Plan on Corporate Social Responsibility (CSR) and on Business and Human Rights by the Federal Council;
- August 2020: Federal Council adoption of FOEN action plan on the implementation of the adaptation strategy in the period 2020–2025.

Act),[8] which was subsequently revised in October 2017 to implement the Paris Agreement. Another revision of the CO2 Act is likely to enter into force soon, including a duty for the Swiss National Bank and the Swiss Financial Market Supervisory Authority (FINMA) to review and consider climate among financial risks. More generally, the revised CO2 Act will explicitly include the financial sector as a stakeholder in reducing Switzerland's greenhouse gas emissions. It aims at aligning investment flows with the goal of making investment and financing activities compatible with low greenhouse gas emissions and establishing a climate-resilient development profile.

Among the different approaches identified for the integration of ESG/sustainability aspects, the Federal Act on War Materials[9] prohibits financing of and investing in companies that produce, trade, and/or store controversial weapons. This negative screening/exclusion approach is commonly considered a minimum standard for sustainably managed assets.

In November 2020, Switzerland rejected a Responsible Business Initiative (*Konzernverantwortungsinitiative*), inspired by the French Duty of Vigilance law, aiming at holding businesses liable for their activities abroad. Instead, new rules, based on the parliamentarian alternative, entered into force on January 1, 2022, and are less far-reaching but include a transparency obligation to report on ESG issues as well as a duty of diligence for mining companies and activities prone to using child labor. The law grants companies one year to adjust to the new obligations. This initiative is only one of many sustainability-related topics that have been adopted by the Swiss parliament. The CO2 Act, the Responsible Business Initiative, as well as other theme-driven pieces of legislation confirm sustainability considerations are of increasing interest to Swiss legislators.[10]

The Financial Market Supervisory Authority (FINMA) considers climate-related financial risks within the traditional risk categories of credit, market, insurance, or operational risks. Put differently, they are accelerators for other risks instead of being a new risk category. This regulatory interpretation allows Swiss financial institutions to incorporate them into their existing risk management framework. The supervisory authority recently revised two of its circulars for banks and insurance companies to

8. Federal Act of 23 December 2011 on the Reduction of CO2 Emissions (CO2 Act), SR 641.71.

9. Federal Act on War Material (War Material Act, WMA), SR 514.51.

10. Swiss Sustainable Finance, *Swiss Sustainable Investment Market Study* (2020), at 49.

explicitly include climate risks in their transparency duties.[11] On November 3, 2021, FINMA published its guidance 05/2021 on preventing and combating greenwashing, wherein FINMA sets forth principles as well as its practice pertaining to the management of sustainability-related collective investment schemes at fund and institutional levels.[12]

The recently enacted Federal Act on Financial Services (FinSA)[13] contains a duty to inform clients about risks related to financial instruments, as well as a duty to assess the appropriateness and/or suitability for portfolio advisory and discretionary asset management.[14] A majority of legal commentators and practitioners are of the view that ESG/sustainability risks and opportunities are to be identified, assessed, managed, and disclosed at the level of each product or investment strategy and in the relevant internal directives. Banks, insurance companies, asset managers, and pension funds should thus consider material climate-related risks as part of their fiduciary duty toward clients. However, there are no legal duties to take into account adverse climate impacts on an investment, or disclose such impact in a transparent manner unless this has been requested by the investor specifically or the product has been labeled to that effect.[15] Even though there are no legal duties to monitor the impact of an investment, some service providers go beyond the mere risk-approach suggested by FINMA and adopt as best practice the assessment not only of ESG/sustainability preferences of their clients but also of the adverse impact of their services/products.

---

11. *Transparency Obligations for Climate Risks—FINMA Opens a Consultation* (Nov. 10, 2020), Proposals to amend Circulars 2019/1 ("Disclosure—banks") and 2016/2 ("Disclosure—insurers"), https://www.finma.ch/en/news/2020/11/20201110-mm-transparenzpflichten-klimarisiken/.

12. *FINMA Publishes Guidance on Preventing and Combating Greenwashing* (Nov. 3, 2021), https://www.finma.ch/en/news/2021/11/20211103-finma-aufsichtsmitteilung-05-21/.

13. Federal Act on Financial Services (FinSA), SR 950.1; Art. 8 and 12 FinSA, art. 398 (2) Swiss Code of Obligations.

14. In discretionary and advisory mandates sustainability risks are part of the financial institution's obligation to clarify the client's risk profile as well as to inform the client about sustainability risks associated with investment objectives and strategy. While providing discretionary services, such risks must be considered when executing orders in accordance with the client's risk profile. As opposed to such mandates, for bank deposits obligations are limited to the conscientious handling of the customers' instructions.

15. Legal Opinion on the incorporation of climate risks and impacts in the financial market (*Rechtliches Gutachten «Berücksichtigung von Klimarisiken und-wirkungen auf dem Finanzmarkt*), Dr. Mirjam Eggen & Dr. Cornelia Stengel, https://www.bafu.admin.ch/bafu/de/home/themen/klima/recht/rechtsgutachten.html.

Self-Regulation and Industry Initiatives

Pursuant to the SIX Directive on Information relating to Corporate Governance,[16] companies listed on the SIX Swiss Exchange Ltd. may voluntarily opt to produce a sustainability report in accordance with internationally recognized standards. SIX Swiss Exchange Ltd. publishes a list of international standards to this effect. In the future, a legal obligation for all public-interest companies, including companies and financial institutions, will replace this voluntary-based opt-in approach. Similar to the Non-Financial Reporting Directive of the European Union,[17] large companies must report annually on nonfinancial matters, including their concepts and monitoring of environmental issues (particularly CO2 targets), social and labor issues, respect for human rights, and fight against corruption.[18] Large companies are defined as those on an aggregate group basis with (1) annual average of at least 500 full-time employees (FTEs) and (2) either total assets exceeding CHF 20 million or revenues of CHF 40 million. They must also report based on the principle of comply or explain, as well as disclose their reporting standards. Moreover, Swiss companies that (1) import or process minerals or metals from conflict or high-risk areas as defined by the Swiss Federal Council, or (2) offer products or services where there is a suspicion of child labor, are subject to special due diligence and related reporting obligations with respect to their supply chain.[19]

In June 2020, the Swiss Bankers Association published a guideline for the integration of ESG considerations into the advisory process for private clients.[20] The guideline concludes that sustainability considerations are fitted into the existing regulatory framework under FinSA. It requires banks, as part of their discretionary portfolio management, not only to outline the range of ESG investments available but also to build investment solutions aligned with their clients' expectations. Without adding

---

16. Directive on Information Relating to Corporate Governance (DCG) (Jan. 2, 2020), https://www.ser-ag.com/dam/downloads/regulation/listing/directives/DCG-en.pdf.

17. Directive 2014/95/EU of the European Parliament and of the Council of 22 October 2014 amending Directive 2013/34/EU as regards disclosure of non-financial and diversity information by certain large undertakings and groups, Official Journal of the European Union, L 330 (Nov. 15, 2014).

18. Revised art. 964bis *et seq.*, Swiss Code of Obligations (CO).

19. *Id.*

20. Guideline for the integration of ESG considerations into the advisory process for private clients (June 2020), https://www.swissbanking.org/en/services/library/guidelines.

an additional binding regulatory burden on banks, the guideline sets the standard of explicitly integrating ESG preferences into the investment process and providing the client with adequate information. As a consequence, the guideline urges banks to give their client advisors appropriate training regarding ESG considerations and investment solutions in order for them to be able to match characteristics of ESG investment solutions with client expectations. It also requires them to document their advice as well as any deviation from the client's ESG preferences, for example, should an ESG alternative meeting suitability test under FinSA not be available.

Swiss Sustainable Finance (SSF), an association organized to strengthen the position of Switzerland as a leader for sustainable finance, issued in summer 2021 Reporting Recommendations on Portfolio ESG Transparency[21] with the goal of creating more comparability and credibility through recommendations for portfolio ESG transparency for both asset owners and asset managers. In addition, SSF launched on December 1, 2021, an ambitious Roadmap with recommended actions for the Swiss financial services industry.[22] It includes concrete measures targeted at various financial market players such as banks, asset managers, insurance companies, and institutional investors.

Along with the Swiss Asset Management Association (AMAS), on June 16, 2020, SSF published nonbinding Recommendations on Sustainable Asset Management[23] on the integration of sustainability considerations into asset management. It was directed at companies in the early stage of ESG implementation. As a follow-up to these recommendations, on November 26, 2021, AMAS and SSF published their Recommendations on Minimum Requirements and Transparency for Sustainable Investment Products.[24] The recommendations are focused on sustainable products developed by the fund and asset management industry and sold to investors by financial service providers. Their three main aims are

21. 2021_06_22_SSF_Reporting_Recommendations_on_Portfolio_ESG_Transparency_full_report_EN_FINAL.pdf (sustainablefinance.ch).

22. https://www.sustainablefinance.ch/upload/cms/user/SSF_Roadmap_for_SwissFinancial_Market_Players_Dec_2021.pdf.

23. *Sustainable Asset Management: Key Messages and Recommendations of SFAMA and SFF* (June 16, 2020), https://www.sustainablefinance.ch/upload/cms/user/EN_2020_06_16_SFAMA_SSF_key_messages_and_recommendations_final.pdf.

24. *Recommendations on Minimum Requirements and Transparency for Sustainable Investment Products* (Dec. 2021), https://www.sustainablefinance.ch/upload/cms/user/RecommendationsforSustainableInvestmentProducts_AMAS_SSF.pdf.

to (1) define the various sustainable investment approaches more precisely and set minimum requirements for implementing each of them; (2) set minimum requirements for informing investors about the various investment approaches and instruments; and (3) explain which sustainable investment approaches are best suited to meeting investors' different objectives.

Common Funding Products and Vehicles

Impact-oriented investments are on the rise in Switzerland. However, while impact investing has been growing rapidly, it only makes up for about 4 percent of all sustainable investments. Institutional investors drive the impact investment market, operating with a strong focus on listed equity.[25]

A total of 41 green bonds, one sustainability bond, and one sustainability-linked bond were listed on SIX Swiss Exchange Ltd. in 2021.[26] Even though the term "green bond" is not defined under Swiss law, issuers in practice rely on the terminology adopted in the Guidelines of the International Capital Market Association (ICMA). To be flagged by SIX Swiss Exchange Ltd. as "green bond," the bonds must be certified under the Climate Bonds Standard set out by the Climate Bonds Initiative (CBI) and aligned with the nonbinding international standards such as the Green Bond Principles, the Social Bond Principles of ICMA. Sustainability bonds on the other hand are certified under the CBI Climate Bonds Standard and aligned with the ICMA Sustainability Bond Guidelines.[27]

In sum, so far, green and sustainability bonds are still a niche investment in Switzerland.

25. Swiss Sustainable Finance, *Swiss Sustainable Investment Market Study* (2020), at 27.

26. Sustainable Bonds, SIX Swiss Exchange Ltd., https://www.six-group.com/en/products-services/the-swiss-stock-exchange/market-data/bonds/green-bonds.html (last visited May 2, 2022).

27. https://finance.swiss/en/sustainable-finance; the ICMA principles are available under https://www.icmagroup.org/sustainable-finance/resource-centre/ (last visited May 2, 2022).

Sourcing Opportunities

Swiss leaders in impact investing rely on global expertise, including the resources of the Global Impact Investing Network (GIIN), and follow international recommendations on sourcing and deal due diligence.[28]

There are different dedicated financial institutions, such as banks and investment managers, active in the field of impact investment. They cover a wide range of asset classes, including Swiss collective investment schemes, equity, debt, public, and private, as well as listed and private assets with underlying companies in many countries.

There are also various public–private partnerships and initiatives aiming at promoting sustainable finance, including impact investing. One of the initiatives is the previously discussed Building Bridges Summit. As noted, it is a unique landmark summit, held for the first time in Geneva in 2019, with the aim of bringing together the finance industry, public leaders, and international organizations to accelerate the achievement of the 2030 UN Agenda as well as of the implementation of the UN Sustainable Development Goals (SDGs) by redirecting financial flows toward sustainable investments.[29]

Challenges and Opportunities for a Growing Sustainable Finance Sector in Switzerland

While there are still some challenges, such as the difficulty in measuring impact and therefore having a common grammar for market players, insufficient investment-ready opportunities, and lack of highly specialized employees, Switzerland with its sustainability ethos appears committed to excelling in sustainable finance and to contribute to sustainable development globally. To succeed even further and strengthen its leadership position, the Swiss financial sector will have to continue mobilizing and increasing its high-level endorsement, leadership, and decisive action by all the major players in the Swiss financial sector.

Synergies have developed between the players who now take decisive actions. In the spirit of consensus, which has long existed, the financial sector and the authorities are likely to develop further by supporting resources and by developing and keeping a flexible framework so the market can freely evolve and innovate.

28. *The Global Impact Investing Network GIIN, A Guide for Impact Investment Fund Managers, Deal Sourcing and Selection*, https://thegiin.org/deal-sourcing-and-selection (last visited May 2, 2022).

29. https://www.buildingbridgesweek.ch/.

22

United Kingdom

Jonathan McGowan[1]

Market Overview and Impact Investing Growth

The roots of impact investing in the United Kingdom (UK) can be found in a 2000 HM Treasury taskforce that analyzed how entrepreneurship could combine financial and social returns.[2] That taskforce led to a number of new initiatives, eventually culminating in the creation of Big Society Capital, a social investment institution, in 2012.[3] A year later, Prime Minister David Cameron used his term as president of the G8 to create the Social Impact Investment Task Force, which was superseded in 2014 by the Global Social Impact Investment Steering Group (GSG).[4]

Despite being an early leader in impact investing, the UK has fallen behind the curve in its development and utilization.[5] Since 2016, the government has commissioned multiple studies and independent agencies

1. Attorney, The McGowan Law Firm, Jacksonville, Florida, USA. Jonathan McGowan practices business law and international legal development in Jacksonville Beach, Florida, USA. He is an elected Fellow at the European Law Institute, Vienna, Austria.

2. HM Treasury, also referred to as Her Majesty's Treasury or the Exchequer, is the treasury department of the government of the United Kingdom. *See generally HM Treasury, A Report to the Chancellor of the Exchequer from the Social Investment Task Force* (2000), https://static1.squarespace.com/static/5a6f0b584c0dbf370367c95a/t/5b27ccd803ce643d6e7ccb10/1529335005229/SITF_Oct_2000.pdf.

3. *Growing a Culture of Social Impact Investing in the United Kingdom* (2017), https://assets.publishing.service.gov.uk/government/uploads/system/uploads/attachment_data/file/664321/Full_Report_Growing_a_Culture_of_Social_Impact_Investing_in_the_UK.pdf.

4. https://www.gov.uk/government/groups/social-impact-investment-taskforce.

5. *Growing a Culture*, *supra* note 3.

focused on stimulating growth in this sector. It remains to be seen if this renewed focus will bring the UK back into a leadership role in this area.

The biggest issue facing impact investing in the UK is not a lack of interest. According to a study by the Scottish Widows Fund, 56 percent of UK investors would be interested in sustainable investments even if it meant a reduction in returns.[6] The problem is a lack of clarity: lack of clarity as to how funds are used, availability of investments, and, most significantly, what exactly is impact investing. Multiple terms and concepts overlap, even in official government studies and reports. The terms environmental, social, and governance investing (ESG); impact investing; social impact investing; social investing; and sustainable investing are conflated depending on the author. For instance, there is a general lack of clarity as to whether ESG investing is a subsidiary of impact investing or if it is a stand-alone form of investment.

In 2016, the UK government commissioned a Government Advisory Group on Impact Investing, chaired by Dame Elizabeth Corley, to further study impact investing and make recommendations for what actions needed to be taken by the government.[7] In 2017, the group released 50 suggestions in a report titled "Growing a Culture of Social Impact Investing in the UK." The first issue identified by the group was the lack of a clear definition of impact investing, or as they referred to it, social impact investing. For the purpose of the study, they defined it as "investment in the shares or loan capital of companies and enterprises that not only measure and report their wider impact on society—but also hold themselves accountable for delivering and increasing positive impact."

The study drew a hard line between ESG investing and social impact investing, distinguishing the two based on intent. They defined ESG investing as investing in institutions that incorporate social principles into their existing business practices, while social impact investing was investing in institutions whose primary or secondary purpose is to effect social change. Common examples of ESG investments in the UK include companies with policies limiting the impact of their business on the environment, human rights policies, and inclusionary hiring practices, based on the United Nations 17 Sustainable Development Goals (SDG).[8] In

6. Scottish Widows, *ESG—What Resonates with Pension Investors* (June 2020), https://adviser.scottishwidows.co.uk/assets/literature/docs/60242.pdf.

7. *Growing a Culture*, *supra* note 3.

8. The 17 Goals are frequently referred to by their number, with some funds utilizing the number and a symbol designated by the UN. They are (1) No poverty; (2) Zero hunger; (3) Good health and well-being; (4) Quality education; (5) Gender Equality; (6) Clean water and sanitation; (7) Affordable and clean energy; (8) Decent

comparison, social impact investing in the UK includes charitable organizations or companies that provide public housing to low-income families, renewable energy, and helping at-risk youth.[9]

With that distinction in place, the study group found that ESG investing had grown significantly, while impact investing still lagged. Based on those findings, the government set a goal of putting social impact investing on the same trajectory as ESG investing. Signs of success are beginning to show, with Big Society Investing reporting social impact investing increased from £830 million in 2011 to £5.1 billion in 2019, with 20 percent of that increase coming in 2019.[10]

However, it should be noted that this distinction is still developing both within the United Kingdom and in other countries that are leaders in this field. Many countries, including those highlighted in this book, will treat ESG and social impact investing as a single concept. This chapter will adopt the distinction used by the Government Advisory Group on Impact Investing and focus narrowly on social impact investing as a stand-alone form of investment.

Growing Sector Opportunities

The fastest growing market in impact investing is social property funds, which are established to fund affordable and keyworker housing needs. Nonexistent prior to 2012, social property funds have since skyrocketed to 42 percent of the market.[11] In 2016, only £356,000 (approximately 17 percent) of the £2 million put into impact investing was invested in social property funds. By 2019, they accounted for £2.1 billion of the £5.1 billion total, becoming the largest segment, at 71.5 percent of the total increase in impact investing, since 2016. The Cheyne Capital Social Impact Fund, which works alongside Big Society Capital, boasts £100 million in investments, developing and managing more than 1,000 new

work and economic growth; (9) Industry, innovation, and infrastructure; (10) Reduce inequalities; (11) Sustainable cities and communities; (12) Responsible consumption and production; (13) Climate action; (14) Life below water; (15) Life on land; (16) Peace, justice, and strong institutions; (17) Partnerships for the goals. https://sdgs.un.org/goals.

9. *See* https://bigsocietycapital.com/impact-stories/.

10. *See* https://bigsocietycapital.com/latest/uk-social-impact-investment-market-now-worth-more-than-5-billion/.

11. https://public.tableau.com/profile/big.society.capital#!/vizhome/2019MarketSizing/2019MarketSizing.

affordable housing units.[12] Cheyne Capital further announced in 2020 they would add a second fund to their portfolio.[13]

Even with the recent surge in investing, only a small portion of the market has been utilized. Resonance Impact Investment Limited estimates that the market to address England's homeless is £20 billion.[14] A November 2020 study by the ESG Social Housing Working Group, found that nearly eight million in the UK are being impacted by the 2020 housing crisis by living in substandard or overcrowded conditions, with more than one million individuals and families on local housing authority wait lists.[15]

One rapidly emerging field is the introduction of green bonds by the UK government. The Impact Investment Institute along with the Green Finance Institute, London School of Economics, and Grantham Research Institute on Climate Change and the Environment released a proposal in October 2020 for the government to introduce a "Green+ Gilt."[16] A Green+ Gilt is a government bond that acts like an impact investment in that the funds are dedicated for clean infrastructure, energy efficiency/green buildings, climate adaptation/natural capital, green jobs, and green development finance. It is expected that these green bonds will allow investors and funds to add stability to their portfolios, while satisfying their need to impact environmental change. In March 2021, Prime Minister Boris Johnson announced that the government-backed savings scheme, National Savings & Investments, will begin offering green bonds.[17] Supporters of this initiative believe that it will not only provide funding for the government's green initiatives, but will also set the standard for social impact investing and open up the market.[18] In June 2021, HM Treasury released the UK Government Green Financing Framework, with the first Green+Gilt issued in September 2021.[19]

---

12. https://bigsocietycapital.com/portfolio/cheyne-capital-social-impact-fund/.

13. https://www.propertyfundsworld.com/2020/04/22/284918/cheyne-launches-second-impact-real-estate-fund.

14. https://resonance.ltd.uk/news/news/are-pension-funds-missing-out-on-the-20-billion-social-impact-property-mark.

15. https://www.impactinvest.org.uk/wp-content/uploads/2020/11/Sustainability-Reporting-Standard-for-Social-Housing-Nov-2020_Final-1.pdf.

16. https://www.lse.ac.uk/granthaminstitute/wp-content/uploads/2020/10/Green_Gilt_Proposal_October_2020.pdf.

17. https://www.ft.com/content/09587e4f-16c3-41bb-8df8-bcb8100fda94 .

18. https://www.lse.ac.uk/granthaminstitute/wp-content/uploads/2020/10/Green_Gilt_Proposal_October_2020.pdf.

19. *See* Jonathan McGowan, *The United Kingdom's Green+ Gilt*, 56 ABA/ILS YIR (2022).

Policy Framework and Government Initiatives

In recent years, the UK government has focused on social investing, through both initiatives and studies, such as the Big Society Capital (BSC), Government's Taskforce for Growing a Culture of Social Impact Investing, and pension funding.

The most notable initiative was the previously noted founding of BSC. It was created through a joint venture of the government and High Street banks under the Dormant Bank and Building Society Act of 2008 as an independent institution.[20] BSC acts as a "social investment wholesaler," investing in fund managers rather than directly into projects. BSC serves as an intermediary between managers, experts, and investors. Since its creation, BSC has established itself as the largest social impact investing firm.

Following the report of the Government Advisory Group on Impact Investing, the government's Taskforce for Growing a Culture of Social Impact Investing in the UK was formed to implement the recommended changes. In 2019, the taskforce was merged with the UK National Advisory Board on Impact Investing to form the Impact Investing Institute. The Impact Investing Institute operates as an independent nonprofit to promote social impact investing in the UK and globally. It has successfully advocated within the UK in many key areas for the development of impact investing.[21] Its projects include the Green+Gilt initiative, Pensions with Impact, and developing the Sustainability Reporting Standard for Social Housing.[22]

The most heavily and noticeably regulated aspect of impact investing relates to pension funds. The regulation of pension funds falls under the Financial Conduct Authority, an independent authority created under the Financial Services and Markets Act 2000 (FSMA). In 2017, the Law Commission, an independent body commissioned by the UK government to review and recommend changes to the laws of the UK and Wales, conducted an intensive study on the regulations of pension funds as they

20. High Street banks is the common term used in the United Kingdom to refer to major retail banking institutions with multiple branches. Barclays, HSBC, Lloyds Banking Group, and Natwest Group are shareholders in BSC. Under the Dormant Bank and Building Society Act of 2008, funds are designated as dormant after 15 years and held in an account established by the Co-operative Banking Group (CBG), https://bigsocietycapital.com/about-us/.

21. https://www.impactinvest.org.uk/about-us/.

22. https://www.impactinvest.org.uk/projects/.

relate to social investing.[23] Despite operating within a heavily regulated field, the study found there is a general lack of regulations looking specifically at the fiduciary duty of funds relating to impact investing and other social investing.

Common Funding Products and Vehicles

The most common funding products and vehicles for impact investing in the UK are property bonds, traditional bank lending, green bonds, and other products.

- **Property bonds.** As of 2019, the largest share of the funding products for impact investing are property bonds, issued through asset managers like Cheyne Capital, PfP Capital, ReSI Capital Management Limited, and Triple Point Social Housing REIT plc.[24] Property bonds allow developers to raise capital for a project through a loan. The loans are secured through a legal charge against the land or development registered with the Land Registry Office, which records all ownership of land and property in England and Wales. To be considered a social impact investment, the development must serve a social purpose, typically providing housing to low-income families. These property bonds accounted for 42 percent of the market in 2019.
- **Traditional bank lending.** Accounting for one-third of the market in 2019, such lending is predominantly through the Charity Aid Foundation, Charity Bank, Royal Bank of Scotland Social and Community Capital, and Unity Trust Bank. These banks are either specifically established to provide traditional loans to charities and corporations focused on social impact, or they are a special department of a larger lending institution with the same focus.
- **Green bonds.** As noted earlier, this is an emerging market used by governments to raise funds dedicated to clean infrastructure, energy efficiency/green buildings, climate adaptation/natural capital, green jobs, and green development finance. This issuance of green bonds is based on the Green Bond Principals released in 2014. While the UK government is developing its Green+Gilt, cities and corporations have issued green bonds since 2014. The market, however, is still underutilized.

---

23. https://s3-eu-west-2.amazonaws.com/lawcom-prod-storage-11jsxou24uy7q/uploads/2017/06/Final-report-Pension-funds-and-socia....pdf.

24. https://public.tableau.com/profile/big.society.capital#!/vizhome/2019MarketSizing/2019MarketSizing.

- **Other products.** The balance of the investment, under 17 percent of the market, is divided among venture capital firms and non-bank lending institutions.

Sourcing Opportunities

The sourcing of funding opportunities relies heavily on corporations, community organizations, or social charities to apply for funding through the various investment providers. In order to make the process more accessible, Access—The Foundation for Social Investment, Big Society Capital, and Inclusive Economy Unit in the Department for Digital, Culture, Media and Sport (DCMS), formed Good Finance in 2016.[25] The Good Finance project offers guidance and resources to social enterprises and charities, including linking them with more than 70 national funds and regional investors.[26] Each fund uses a different approach for financing applications. Big Society Capital solicits proposals through their Ideas for Impact program, an annual call for submissions.[27] The 2021 program offered up to £30,000 in development funding to fund managers, social enterprises, and charities with ideas that could make an impact.[28] Big Issue Invest has a rolling call for submissions, offering the ability to loan between £20,000 and £3 million to social enterprises and charities in the UK.[29]

Challenges in Impact Investing

Practically speaking, the biggest challenge to impact investing in the UK is the lack of clarity and information. The Law Commission, in its report, found "the barriers to social investment by pension funds that we identified were, in most cases, structural and behavioural rather than legal or regulatory." To increase transparency, the Law Commission made five recommendations to the government, including recommendations specifically directed to the Financial Conduct Authority (FCA). The recommendations centered on the funds' lack of transparency in communicating ESG policies, stewardship, and risks to investments in the long-term arising from ESG factors. This lack of standardization by fund managers leads to confusion and hesitancy by fund managers to consider

25. https://www.goodfinance.org.uk/about-project.
26. https://www.goodfinance.org.uk/investors-advisors.
27. https://bigsocietycapital.com/how-we-work/creating-new-ideas/ideas-impact/.
28. https://bigsocietycapital.com/latest/big-society-capital-launches-call-innovative-social-impact-investment-ideas/.
29. https://bigissueinvest.com/seeking-investment/.

social impact in their investment strategies. Some managers still believe the practice conflicts with their fiduciary duty. In a 2018 response, the UK government and FCA agreed with the need for better regulatory guidance in the rights and responsibilities of fund managers and declared an intent to improve regulations.

This lack of standardization was noted in a January 2021 study by the INDIGO technical and learning project of Big Issue Investing and the Government Outcomes Lab (GO Lab) at the University of Oxford's Blavatnik School of Government on impact investing and proposals for standardization of process and reporting.[30] The study found inconsistency of reporting standards made it difficult for fund managers to compare and rate outcomes.[31] The Impact Investing Institute also found lack of standardization in recordkeeping in their first report.[32]

This inconsistency leads to a lack of willingness by fund managers to share investment opportunities, which has led to a low level of awareness of the availability of these products.[33] While ESG investing has seen growth over the past decade, impact investing is still limited due to this lack of information.

Opportunities for a Growing Market (Future of the Market)

The renewed push for social investing and impact investing by the UK government and interested parties offers an optimistic view of the market's future. The issue of lack of clear information as well as uncertainty are currenting being addressed. As organizations such as the Impact Investing Institute continues to establish their presence in the market and drive the conversation, the issue of clarity will become moot. Actions by the government to standardize reporting standards and to incentivize investment will further this development. Once the marketplace becomes comfortable with impact investing, it is likely to continue increasing its share of the marketplace.

30. https://images.bigissueinvest.com/2021/01/ExploringSocialInvestment.pdf.
31. *Id.*
32. https://www.impactinvest.org.uk/wp-content/uploads/2021/02/Impact-Report_Jan.-2020.pdf.
33. https://assets.publishing.service.gov.uk/government/uploads/system/uploads/attachment_data/file/664321/Full_Report_Growing_a_Culture_of_Social_Impact_Investing_in_the_UK.pdf.

Africa

23

Ghana

Joyce Williams[1] and Ellen Bannerman-Quist[2]

Market Overview and Impact Investing Growth

Ghana lies on the shores of the Atlantic Ocean in West Africa. Though it is considered one of the Least Developed Countries (LDCs) in the world, it has one of the fastest-growing economies in Africa.[3] According to World Bank data, Ghana's gross domestic product (GDP) was worth US$72.35 billion in 2020.[4] Ghana is one of the few countries in Africa on track to meet the UN's Sustainable Development Goals (SDGs) of 7 percent annual gross domestic product growth by 2030.[5]

Ghana gained "Lower Middle Income" status from the World Bank in 2011 when it started oil production. The production, however, resulted in a decrease in traditional donor grants, which led to demand for other forms of capital to support Ghana's fast-growing economy. The demand for other forms of capital resulted in increased private capital, including impact investments, to meet the country's developmental needs and SDGs.

1. Founder of Armooh-Williams, PLLC a global boutique law firm based in Alexandria, Virginia.

2. Independent International Arbitrator and the Managing Partner of Bannerman-Quist Legal Consult & Notary in Accra, Ghana.

3. https://nationalinterest.org/blog/buzz/wolf-warrior-diplomacy-why-beijing's-aggression-bhutan-working-181954 (last visited Feb. 2, 2022).

4. https://tradingeconomics.com/ghana/gdp#:~:text=GDP%20in%20Ghana%20averaged%2014.67,1.22%20USD%20Billion%20in%201960 (last visited Feb. 4, 2022).

5. 2015 Sustainable Development Goals, World Bank sds.un.org, https://www.intellecap.com/wp-content/uploads/2020/01/GHANA-IMPACT-INVESTMENT-REPORT_jan_2020.pdf (last visited Feb. 2, 2022).

Policy Framework and Government Initiatives

Ghana has created an impact investment framework to foster an enabling environment to attract Foreign Direct Investments (FDIs).[6]

- The Ghana Investment Promotion Centre Act 2013 (Act 865)[7] was enacted to create incentives for investors such as automatic immigrant quotas based on the investment threshold; exemption from payment of import duties on core machinery, equipment, or project-related investment; tax rebates; tax holidays depending on the business activity; and other locational incentives.[8] The act also sets out criteria for investments supported by the Ghana Investment Promotion Centre (GIPC). Act 865 sets out a flexible minimum foreign capital investment based on equity participation by Ghanaian citizens or employment of Ghanaian citizens in the enterprise. Act 865 also eliminates minimum foreign participation in portfolio investment, export trading, and manufacturing enterprises where the investor is a foreign spouse of a Ghanaian citizen.
- Public–Private Partnership Act 2020 (Act 1039) sets out criteria for transparency in the initiation, development, and funding of public–private partnerships for infrastructure and other developmental goals.[9]
- Companies Act 2019 (Act 992) overhauled the 1963 Companies Code to align setting up companies and corporate governance in Ghana with current global trends.[10]
- Labor Act 2003 (Act 651) established workers' rights in all forms of employment, including entities set up by investors.[11]

---

6. https://www.state.gov/reports/2019-investment-climate-statements/ghana/ (last accessed May 9, 2022).

7. https://gipc.gov.gh/wp-content/uploads/2015/04/GHANA-INVESTMENT PROMOTION-CENTRE-GIPC-ACT-865.pdf (last visited Feb. 2, 2022).

8. https://gipc.gov.gh/incentives-and-guarantees/ (last visited Feb. 6, 2022).

9. https://mofep.gov.gh/sites/default/files/acts/PPP-ACT-1039.pdf (last visited Feb. 5, 2022).

10. https://rgd.gov.gh/docs/Act%20992.pdf (last visited Feb. 5, 2022).

11. https://www.ilo.org/legacy/english/inwork/cb-policy-guide/ghanalabouract2003section109.pdf (last visited Feb. 5, 2022).

- Environmental Protection Agency Act 1994 (Act 490) regulates activities, including business investment, with potential environmental impact.[12]

The government of Ghana introduced Ghana's Beyond Aid reforms to propel Ghana's route to economic development. Furthermore, through the Ministry of Trade and Industry, the government of Ghana is supporting SDGs by promoting the social enterprise sector. Ghana's policy is "to support the achievement of SDGs through the growth of strong, innovative and financially sustainable social enterprise sub-sector that drives measurable social impact in prioritized areas of social need, provides jobs, and supports economic transformation, especially for the urban and rural poor."[13]

The Ministry of Trade and Industry adopted "the Ghana Social Enterprise Policy" (GSEP)[14] to complement Ghana's "Second Medium-Term Private Sector Development Strategy" and other development programs. The goal of GSEP is to support the achievement of SDGs through the growth of a strong, innovative, and financially sustainable social enterprise sector. This would drive measurable social impact in the following areas prioritized by Ghana: social need, jobs, and economic transformation for the urban and rural poor. The Ministry of Trade and Industry has formed a partnership with Social Enterprise Ghana,[15] the British Council,[16] Star Ghana Foundation,[17] and the West Africa Civil Society

12. https://www.ilo.org/dyn/natlex/docs/ELECTRONIC/39863/101264/F1742544814/GHA39863.pdf (last visited Feb. 6, 2022).

13. Draft Social Enterprise Policy, Ghana, February 2017, https://www.intellecap.com/wp-content/uploads/2020/01/GHANA-IMPACT-INVESTMENT-REPORT_jan_2020.pdf (last visited May 9, 2022).

14. https://www.icr-facility.eu/social-enterprise-ghana-business-environment-reform-for-social-enterprises (last visited Feb. 8, 2022).

15. https://seghana.net/; A high-impact network of social entrepreneurs in Ghana working together to strengthen Ghana's social enterprise environment (last visited Feb. 6, 2022).

16. https://www.britishcouncil.org.gh/-A; UK organization in Ghana building connections, understanding, and trust between people in the UK and other countries through culture, education, and the English language (last visited Feb. 6, 2022).

17. https://www.star-ghana.org/; A national foundation with the purpose of increasing active citizenship and philanthropy (last visited Feb. 6, 2022).

Institute[18] to review the GSEP.[19] The GSEP is currently being discussed at the cabinet level.

Beyond impact investment, the Ghanaian government's policies toward improving the business environment have yielded an overall positive working environment for businesses and investors. One of the successes of Ghana's policy initiatives was captured in the World Bank's Ease of Doing Business ranking. In 2018, Ghana ranked 114, a six-point jump from its prior ranking of 120.[20] Over the last two decades, the country has witnessed relative political stability and improved macroeconomic conditions, positioning Ghana as an attractive investment destination.

Furthermore, GIPC, the government agency mandated to promote investments in Ghana, has created a transparent, predictable, and facilitative environment that encourages investments in Ghana. GIPC facilitates support local and foreign investors.[21] It acts as a liaison between businesses, government, and investors by ensuring that the interests of all parties are met and benefits of investments trickle down to the local population. It also guarantees full repatriation of dividends and net profits earned from foreign investment in Ghana by foreign investors.

Global Steering Group

Ghana is a member of the Global Steering Group (GSG). The GSG comprises 33 countries working through 28 national and regional advisory boards to increase impact investment in their respective markets.[22] Each country seeking to become a GSG member must demonstrate national leadership and commitment by forming a national advisory board or an equivalent body. In December 2018, Ghana organized a national impact dialogue, after which a national task force was set up to establish the Ghana National Advisory Board (NAB).[23] In 2019, the task force launched a new entity known as Impact Investing Ghana (IIGH) to promote impact investing in the country and perform the functions of the Ghana NAB.

18. https://wacsi.org/; An institute with the purpose of reinforcing the capacities of civil society in the Ecowas sub-region (last visited Feb. 6, 2022).

19. https://citinewsroom.com/2021/03/stakeholders-meet-to-review-ghanas-draft-social-enterprise-policy/ (last visited Feb. 6, 2022).

20. https://www.intellecap.com/wp-content/uploads/2020/01/GHANA-IMPACT-INVESTMENT-REPORT_jan_2020.pdf. In 2017 Ghana ranked 120 on the Ease of Doing Business Rankings (last visited Feb. 2, 2022).

21. *Id.*

22. Global Steering Group (GSG), *Ghana Impact Investment Landscape*, INTELLECAP (June 2019).

23. https://gsgii.org/nabs/ghana/ (last visited Feb. 6, 2022).

IIGH is a platform that brings together entrepreneurs, intermediaries, suppliers of capital such as foundations, corporate organizations, investors, financial institutions, policy makers, market builders, and other stakeholders such as faith-based organizations and civil society organizations.[24] The objective of IIGH is to facilitate coordination between the different players toward fostering the development of the impact investing market in Ghana. It also seeks to promote impact investing–related news and events, provide tools and resources, and connect various stakeholders to facilitate learning and investment.[25]

Common Funding Products and Vehicles

Act 865 created minimum investment limits for foreign capital investment coming into the country. These minimum investment requirements are $200,000 for developing a joint venture with a Ghanaian partner, $500,000 for 100 percent foreign ownership, and $1 million for trading activity.[26]

The financial markets in Ghana are highly debt driven. Most of the capital flowing into the country is debt, including traditional banking sector and micro-financial institutions.[27] This preference for debt has made the financial industry in Ghana highly crowded, with 33 commercial banks, 77 nonbanking financial institutions, 141 rural and community banks, and 564 microfinance institutions. Total assets of the industry at the end of March 2016 were up 18.8 percent.[28] In 2017–2018 the Bank of Ghana embarked on a banking sector clean-up and reform to promote the financial system's safety, soundness, and stability. The first post-assessment report of the 2017–2018 banking sector described growth in the banking sector, including credit growth and overall banking sector resilience.[29]

24. Global Steering Group (GSG), *supra* note 22.

25. https://www.intellecap.com/wp-content/uploads/2020/01/GHANA-IMPACT-INVESTMENT-REPORT_jan_2020.pdf (last visited Feb. 2, 2022).

26. https://www.state.gov/reports/2020-investment-climate-statements/ (last visited May 9, 2022).

27. https://www.intellecap.com/wp-content/uploads/2020/01/GHANA-IMPACT-INVESTMENT-REPORT_jan_2020.pdf (last visited Feb. 2, 2022).

28. https://www.state.gov/reports/2021-investment-climate-statements/ (last visited May 9, 2022).

29. https://www.bog.gov.gh/wp-content/uploads/2020/03/Banking-Sector-Report-January-2020.pdf (last visited Feb. 6, 2022).

Drivers for Impact Investment in Ghana

Some of the significant drivers for impact investment in Ghana are:

- The need for mechanized farming methods in Ghana's agro-sector. Even though agriculture contributes about 20 percent of Ghana's GDP, the country still relies on subsistence farming methods.[30] The government of Ghana has enacted the *Planting for Food and Jobs*,[31] *Youth in Agriculture*,[32] and *One District One Factory*[33] programs to boost growth and development in the agro-sector. The enactment of these programs has created a ripe environment for impact investments in sustainable farming while addressing food security issues.
- The need for a reliable source of electricity, including renewable sources, to drive industrialization. An abundance of water sources and sunshine opens opportunities to develop hydro and solar energy as alternatives and complementary sources of energy in Ghana.
- Additional areas of need include reliable water supply in cities and portable water supply in rural areas, construction of roads and other infrastructure, enhanced information, and communications technology (ICT) infrastructure to boost economic growth, enhanced growth in social service sectors such as healthcare and education, and microfinance for women and small-scale industries generally.

Growing Sector Opportunities

There are many growing sectors in Ghana for impact investment, as illustrated by the preceding listings of drivers. Currently, renewable energy accounts for about 1 percent of total power generation, but the government aims to increase renewable energy to 10 percent by 2030.[34] With the assistance of international development agencies, Ghana is

30. https://www.trade.gov/knowledge-product/ghana-agricultural-sectors (last visited Feb. 8, 2022).

31. https://intercontinentalgroupghltd.com/2021/06/21/planting-for-food (last visited Feb. 8, 2022).

32. https://mofa.gov.gh/site/programmes/youth-in-agriculture (last visited Feb. 8, 2022).

33. https://1d1f.gov.gh/ (last visited Feb. 8, 2022).

34. https://www.trade.gov/knowledge-product/ghana-market-opportunities (last visited Feb. 6, 2022).

poised to invest significant resources in the design and construction of several thermal power plants. In addition, the country is upgrading its transmission and distribution systems[35] to diversify and industrialize its agro-processing, mining, and manufacturing sectors.[36]

Challenges in Impact Investing

Awareness of financing options beyond commercial banks is severely limited, with very few enterprises knowledgeable about alternative financing options. Impact investors that operate in Ghana, whether local or foreign, are not in tune with the needs of most Ghanaian enterprises. When enterprises approach commercial banks for finance, they struggle to obtain the loan or credit facility they need. Banks in Ghana tend to lend only to clients who can provide large amounts of collateral in assets and savings, which is an obstacle for most social enterprises in Ghana. The most common financing mechanism for impact investors in Ghana is debt. Given the high interest rates, enterprises that can access loans find it hard to sustain debt repayments. Many entrepreneurs lack financial literacy, do not employ consistent bookkeeping practices, and struggle to administer their staff and activities effectively, thus hindering growth and opportunities for social enterprises and entrepreneurship in Ghana.

Opportunities for a Growing Market (Future of the Market)

Social enterprises in Ghana are very young, as more than 50 percent were created in the past five years.[37] The average age of founders and leaders of social enterprises in Ghana is between 25 and 34. Women entrepreneurs run 39 percent of social enterprises in Ghana. Social enterprises create opportunities for impact investors to collaborate and help shape young enterprises. The novelty also provides opportunities for a generous equity share, high risk and high rewards for investors with the right appetite, and a chance to help humanity. Most social enterprises pursue goals that support and promote human rights and dignity.

---

35. https://www.hydroreview.com/world-regions/china-to-increase-development-of-renewables-including-hydro/ (last visited Feb. 2, 2022).

36. https://www.state.gov/reports/2020-investment-climate-statements/ (last visited Feb. 2, 2022).

37. https://pulsenews.co.kr/view.php?year=2019&no=934995 (last visited Feb. 2, 2022).

In Ghana, several new social enterprise ventures deploy innovative business models to address poverty, unemployment, health, educational opportunities, and other social problems for urban and rural poor.[38] The achievements of social innovation and its real-time impact[39] in vulnerable communities have created an opportunity for interested institutions to invest and drive the concept of impact investing in Ghana and the continent of Africa.[40]

The COVID-19 pandemic and the country's lockdown in March 2020 halted Ghana's rapid growth and led to a sharp decline in commodity exports.[41] Ghana's economy is very dependent on international trading and imports. Before COVID-19 and the lockdown, Ghana's economy was projected to grow and register double-digits.[42] In 2020, real per capita GDP declined by 1.7 percent, although it was projected to return to its pre-COVID-19 level in 2021. Growth is expected to average 5.1 percent yearly from 2021 to 2023.[43] To help its recovery, Ghana received $1 billion equivalent in the recent International Monetary Fund's Special Drawing Rights (IMF-SDRs) allocation, which will support economic recovery.[44]

As stated in the 2019 GSG Country Report on Ghana, the country's "strengthening economic environment, stable political environment and growing social enterprise sector render the country well suited to the development of an impact investment industry." It made attracting foreign direct investment a priority to support industrialization plans and overcome an annual infrastructure funding gap.[45]

The possibilities of the African Continental Free Trade Area coupled with the overall robust Industrialization Agenda of the African Union, signal a turning point for countries on the continent to transform their

38. C. Hagin & L.D. Caesar, *The Antecedents of Success among Small- and Medium-Sized Enterprises: Evidence from Ghana*. J Glob Entrepr Res (2021), https://doi.org/10.1007/s40497-021-00285-y (last visited May 9, 2022).

39. https://www.digitaltimes.africa/scaling-the-growth-of-impact-investing-in-african-economies/ (last visited Feb. 8, 2022).

40. *Id.*

41. https://www.worldbank.org/en/country/ghana/overview (last visited Feb. 2, 2022).

42. https://www.borgenmagazine.com/impacts-of-covid-19-in-ghana/ (last visited Feb. 6, 2022).

43. https://www.worldbank.org/en/country/ghana/overview (last visited Feb. 8, 2022).

44. https://www.worldbank.org/en/country/ghana/overview (last visited Feb. 6, 2022).

45. https://2017-2021.state.gov/report/custom/ee034f068f/index.html (last visited Feb. 2, 2022).

economies from commodity and import-dependent to industrialized economies. The continuous emergency of technological advances will continue to propel the efforts of countries like Ghana toward industrialization, while meeting their obligations under the Sustainable Development Goals.

24

Kenya

Linda Gitonga[1]

Market Overview and Impact Investing Growth

Since the COVID-19 (coronavirus) pandemic, there has been a boost in impact investing due to increased awareness of climate change and social challenges such as unequal access to healthcare as well as racial and gender inequality. In 2020, compared to a year earlier, there was an increasing level of maturity in the global impact investing market with more assets being invested with identifiable impact management systems.[2]

According to a 2021 AVCA private equity industry survey, over the next three years, Kenya, Egypt, Nigeria, and Morocco were viewed by the largest number of limited partnerships as attractive destinations for private equity investment in Africa. Among all countries, Kenya was chosen by most partnerships (47 percent).[3]

According to a UN report, impact investment momentum in Kenya is growing fast due to a young, enterprising, and ambitious population.[4] For foreign direct investment (FDI), Kenya is among the top markets in East Africa. The number of recorded FDI projects in the country peaked in 2015 at 96. In 2016, however, there was a 58 percent decline, to 40 projects, following terror attacks by Al-Shabab militants. Since then, the number of FDI projects in Kenya has been rising again, and in 2019 FDI came close to 2015 levels, attracting 95 FDI projects, around 9 percent of

1. Attorney at Williams & Connolly LLP, Washington, D.C.

2. International Finance Corporation (2021), *Investing for Impact: The Global Impact Investing Market 2020*.

3. AVCA Private Equity Industry Survey (2021), https://www.avca-africa.org/research-publications/data-reports/african-private-equity-industry-survey-2021/.

4. United Nations (2019), *Kenya Impact Investment Landscape*, https://kenya.un.org/en/15992-kenya-impact-investment-landscape.

the total in Africa. The value of FDI projects in Kenya in 2019 reached $3.86 billion, an all-time high.

To maintain this drive, in 2019 Kenya launched an investment policy that laid out plans to increase the level of public and private investment to at least 32 percent of gross domestic product (GDP) by 2030. In 2019, the total project value of FDI was worth about 4 percent of Kenya's GDP.[5] Economically, Kenya has seen GDP growth averaging between 4 and 6 percent annually since 2011, and there is little indication of decline: in 2019, the World Bank estimated the annual growth to be 6.1 percent, making it one of the fastest growing economies in sub-Saharan Africa.[6]

Kenya is so dominant that some impact investors express concern that the Kenyan impact investing landscape is already saturated. However, the investing momentum in general is strong. According to Briter Bridgers, Africa Investment Report 2021, Kenya ranked third in total volume of funding in Africa, with Nigeria coming in first, followed by South Africa.[7]

The Kenyan banking sector has been moving aggressively to expand small and medium-sized enterprise (SME) lending, and SMEs are increasingly able to access financing through both impact investors and conventional sources. Nevertheless, many banks remain risk averse and are often unwilling to invest in early-stage ventures. If willing to lend, banks typically require extremely high collateral ratios, occasionally higher than 100 percent of the loan amount. Since many early-stage businesses are unable to meet these requirements, impact investing fills an important gap in the market for early-stage financing. By identifying innovative solutions addressing difficult sectors and circumstances that conventional investors may overlook or dismiss, impact investing provides needed capital to businesses that would otherwise struggle to access financing.[8]

Growing Sector Opportunities

Impact investors are actively looking for deals in Kenya's fast-growing second-tier cities, particularly opportunities in agricultural aggregation, financial services, renewable energy, and mass market consumer goods.

5. Investment Monitor (2021), *An Investor's Guide to East Africa*, https://www.investmentmonitor.ai/analysis/an-investors-guide-to-east-africa.

6. World Bank Kenya country data.

7. Briter Bridges (2021), Africa Investment Report.

8. The Global Impact Investing Network (GIIN) (2015), *The Landscape for Impact Investing in East Africa*.

Most non-Development Financial Institutions (DFI) impact investors have expressed interest in agriculture and financial services as target sectors. In contrast, DFI overwhelmingly favors direct investments in financial services (more than 38 percent of all investments) and energy (roughly 14 percent of all investments).[9] Some of the sectors that investors favor are described in the following subsections.

Education

Access to education remains a substantial challenge in Africa. Of all regions, sub-Saharan Africa has the highest rates of education exclusion. More than one-fifth of children between the ages of 6 and 11 are out of school, followed by one-third of youth between the ages of 12 and 14. According to UNESCO Institute for Statistics (UIS) data, almost 60 percent of youth between the ages of about 15 and 17 are not in school.[10]

Access to quality education remains a huge challenge in Kenya. With the introduction of free primary school education in Kenya, access has improved; however, the quality of education offered in public schools remains low. One example of investments in education in Kenya is Bridge International Academies (BIA), which is working toward providing basic education. BIA started in Kenya in 2009 and is now in four countries in the region. It developed an innovative "academy-in-a-box" franchise model that can be easily replicated and scaled. Leveraging technology and data, BIA creates efficiencies both in terms of costs and quality. BIA received early investment from impact investors including the Bill & Melinda Gates Foundation and UK Department for International Development (DfID), and then secured growth capital from larger financial institutions, such as the International Finance Corporation (IFC).[11] They have more than 300 low-cost private schools and more than 100,000 students in Kenya. It charges an average fee of US$7 per month per child.[12]

Energy

Significant investments have been made in the energy sector by government and private commercial projects. Impact investors followed seeking to improve energy access in the country. Between 2005 and 2015,

9. *Id.*

10. UNESCO, Education in Africa, http://uis.unesco.org/en/topic/education-africa.

11. Bridge Int'l Academies (2013), http://www.bridgeinternationalacademies.com.

12. *Id.*

DFIs made more than US$1.5 billion worth of investments in the renewable and clean energy markets (off-grid energy projects primarily), making energy one of their preferred sectors.[13] Both forms of investments contributed to huge benefits for the community: access to electricity in Kenya jumped considerably, from 32 percent in 2013 to 73 percent by the end of April 2018.[14]

Supported by impact investment, the private sector plays a key role in power generation, particularly in the operation of diesel-fired plants, together with geothermal and wind generation, whereas the state-owned KenGen dominates in hydropower. Impact investing support has been provided by the World Bank Group's Multilateral Investment Guarantee Agency political risk insurance. Kenya has 2,295 megawatts of installed on-grid capacity across 42 plants, plus an additional 11.5 megawatts in 19 off-grid stations in remote parts of the country. Installed capacity consists of 70 percent renewable sources, with potential to produce 10,000 megawatts of geothermal power from the Rift Valley Basin. Kenya is one of the lowest-cost developers of geothermal power in the world.[15]

Financial Services

The link between financial inclusion and development is premised on the assumption that people, particularly the poor and the marginalized need access to formal financial services. Services such as credit, savings, insurance, and money transfers are needed to cope with everyday needs and possibly improve their livelihoods, particularly in countries with limited infrastructure and resources. Financial technology (fintech) projects such as mobile money have been increasingly acclaimed as convenient, secure, and efficient ways of providing access to formal financial services or those excluded from mainstream banking.[16]

Kenya enjoys one of the highest penetrations of digital finance, with 72 percent of adults having used mobile banking in 2017. With about 93 percent of Kenyans conducting everyday transactions online, mobile payments dominate. Indeed, the expansion of the sector's leading company, M-Pesa, is considered an unparalleled case of a company originally set

13. The Global Impact Investing Network, *supra* note 8.

14. The energy progress report, Kenya.

15. IFC (2019), *Creating Markets in Kenya: Country Private Sector Diagnostic*.

16. Serena Natile, *Digital Finance Inclusion and the Mobile Money 'Social' Enterprise: A Socio-Legal Critique of M-Pesa in Kenya*, 45(3) Historical Social Research / Historische Sozialforschung 74–94 (2020).

up to manage microloans through mobile phones that ended up dominating a significant number of transactions.

Progress in expanding financial inclusion in Kenya is attributed to rapid innovation by the private sector in collaboration with the public sector.[17] Nairobi is a well-established center for innovation in financial services in Africa. The rise of mobile phone–based money transfer service M-Pesa has revolutionized how business is conducted in Kenya and broadened financial inclusion across East Africa. The central bank of Kenya played a critical role in its success by creating a supportive regulatory environment at an early phase of development. This adept and efficient regulatory action has encouraged the growth of myriad other fintech innovators and businesses in Nairobi with the goal to be as transformative as M-Pesa.[18]

Policy Framework and Government Initiatives

A major focus of the current political administration in Kenya has been removing key hindrances to Kenya's private sector growth. The administration has rolled out initiatives aimed at attracting and retaining investment, fostering an environment to accelerate industrial development, and growing the private sector. The environment for private sector–led growth in Kenya has been improving, but only slowly in most respects. Kenya fares somewhat better than most of its neighbors, it is only inching closer to better-performing economies in the World Bank's (2019) Doing Business report, moving from 80th in 2018 to 61st (out of 190 countries) and third in sub-Saharan Africa.[19]

The government's long-term development plan, Vision 2030, coupled with adoption of the new Constitution in 2010, aims to transform Kenya into a middle-income country by 2030. Some initiatives are already moving forward. Since 2008, the government has pushed economic growth and social development through political, structural, and economic reforms.

Upon being reelected in 2017, President Uhuru Kenyatta unveiled the Big Four Action Plan, which aims to accelerate economic growth and achieve the targets set out in the Third Medium-Term Plan (MTP-III). It prioritizes food security, affordable housing, manufacturing, and

17. IFC, *supra* note 15.

18. CDC Investment Works, *What's the Role of an Impact Investor Like CDC in Kenya?*, http://www.cdcgroup.com/en/news-insight/insight/articles/whats-the-role-of-an-impact-investor-like-cdc-in-kenya/.

19. IFC, *supra* note 15.

affordable healthcare as the key enablers for job creation, economic growth, and social safety. In the case of manufacturing, the administration expressed a willingness to boost four manufacturing subsectors, namely, the "blue economy,"[20] agri-processing, leather, and textiles. The targets of the Big Four Plan include 500,000 low-cost houses, universal health coverage, a ten-fold increase in exports, irrigation of an additional 1.2 million acres of land, millions of new jobs, establishment of new industrial zones, and improved access to energy.[21] The administration has also undertaken some initiatives to promote the impact investing/social enterprise sector.

Micro and Small Enterprises Authority

The Micro and Small Enterprises Act established the Micro and Small Enterprises Authority (MSEA), housed within the Ministry of Industrialization and Enterprise Development.[22] MSEA was established in 2013 to promote, develop, and regulate the Micro and Small Enterprises (MSE) sector in Kenya. The authority is responsible for developing and reviewing policies and programs; promoting and developing the MSE sector; and monitoring and evaluating the implementation of policies, programs, and activities related to MSE and social enterprise development. In addition, the authority coordinates, harmonizes, and facilitates integration of various public and private policies, programs, and activities related to micro and small enterprises in Kenya. Since inception, MSEA has facilitated more than 1,450 MSEs to participate in various exhibitions countrywide. It has also supported entrepreneurial and skills upgrading programs by training more than 2,000 MSEs across various counties.[23]

Sourcing Opportunities

According to a KPMG survey on deal activity in the East African region, 75 percent of investors investing in Kenya mentioned that their source

20. According to the World Bank, the blue economy is the "sustainable use of ocean resources for economic growth, improved livelihoods, and jobs while preserving the health of ocean ecosystem," https://www.worldbank.org/en/news/infographic/2017/06/06/blue-economy.

21. IFC, *supra* note 15.

22. Micro and Small Enterprises Act, https://www.industrialization.go.ke/index.php/policies/99-micro-and-small-enterprises-act-2012.

23. Data from MSEA website, https://msea.go.ke.

of funding originates from international investors based in Europe and North America.[24]

Sustainability-Aligned Fund Managers

Between 2015 and 2019, US$1.5 billion was deployed into 217 sustainability-themed deals in the East African Community (EAC) region,[25] with 88 percent in Kenya. Energy, financial services, and healthcare are the top three sectors attracting most funding, with the energy sector accounting for 41 of the total SFM portfolio.[26]

Development Financial Institutions

Development Financial Institutions (DFIs) continue to drive the social investing space in the East Africa region through direct investments, programmatic interventions, and funds of funds approaches. Twelve DFIs invested US$6.6 billion in 326 deals between 2015 and 2019; US$981.2 million of the total capital was indirectly deployed through funds of funds. Kenya accounted for 46 percent of the total DFI deal value, although Ethiopia is becoming a preferred destination for DFI investment, ranking second after Kenya. The financial services sector dominates the DFI portfolio (37 percent) followed closely by the energy sector (33 percent).[27] Others include family foundations, corporate social investors, and high net worth individuals.

Challenges in Impact Investing

The significant improvement in impact investing over the last several years has not been without challenges. Some of these challenges are on the part of the investee, such as limited access to formal financing, and lack of access to market information and facilities such as office space. On the part of the investor, there are a limited number of viable deals in Africa, making it more expensive to invest due to fierce competition.

---

24. KPMG & EAVCA: Private equity sector survey for East Africa for the period of 2015 to 2016.

25. An intergovernmental organization composed of six countries in the African Great Lakes region in eastern Africa: Burundi, Kenya, Rwanda, South Sudan, Tanzania, and Uganda.

26. Intellecap (2020), *The Landscape for Social Investments in East Africa*, https://www.intellecap.com/wp-content/uploads/2020/11/The-Landscape-of-Social-Investments_East-Africa.pdf.

27. *Id.*

The investor also faces a problem when exiting an investment since it has limited options due to underdeveloped markets.[28]

Limited Availability of Innovative Fund and Deal Structures

According to a 2020 survey carried out by the Global Impact Investing Network (GIIN), finding high-quality investment opportunities with a track record is a significant challenge for more than a third of investors.[29] Linked to the difficulty in sourcing investment-ready social enterprises is the challenge of finding deals and funds that speak to a range of investor preferences and that are not prohibitively costly. Due to the lack of record of accomplishment of many impact investment funds, investors may incur high transactional costs in deploying capital due to extensive due diligence and deal sourcing processes. Fund structures that reduce risk and cost to the investor (for instance by including first-loss guarantees, etc.) are still uncommon. Local entrepreneurs are often poorly equipped to engage with foreign investors on their terms. The majority of investees are raising investment for the first time and are inexperienced, naïve, and unprepared, resulting in a mismatch between impact investor expectations and the local entrepreneur's hopes and capabilities.

Access to Finance/Credit

In the World Banks' 2019 Doing Business report,[30] Kenya improved by 19 positions to rank 61st globally, with notable improvements on protecting minority investors, getting credit, and resolving insolvency. Kenya's best indicator is "Getting Credit," in which the country ranks eighth globally, an improvement from 29 globally in the 2018 Doing Business report. Kenya improved on access to credit by implementing a functional secured transactions system. The new law regulates functional equivalents to loans secured with movable property, such as financial leases and fiduciary transfer of title.[31]

Significant gaps in access to finance for micro, small, and medium enterprises (MSMEs) still hinder firms' growth and productivity in Kenya. For instance, private credit growth has slowed significantly, falling from its peak of about a 25 percent growth rate in mid-2014 to its lowest level in over a decade of 1.6 percent by mid-2017. However, in the

---

28. E. Mungai, Challenges for Impact Businesses in Africa, in Impact Investing in Africa (2018).

29. Global Impact Investing Network, 2020 Annual Impact Investor Survey.

30. IFC, *supra* note 14.

31. *Id.*

first half of 2018, it improved, going up to 4.3 percent. The latter growth is attributed to a stable political climate and an improving economy, with the country's GDP increasing 5.7 percent in the first quarter of 2018, from 4.9 percent in the first quarter of 2017.[32]

Limited credit availability hinders robust economic expansion, as observed in several economies in Europe and elsewhere after the global financial crisis. In Kenya, the slowdown in credit growth was also explained by the introduction of a lending interest rate cap that proved detrimental to private credit growth. In 2018, the government acknowledged this negative effect and proposed repealing the relevant section in the Banking Amendment Act of 2016 in addition to downgrading the banking sector's rating to "satisfactory" in 2017, from "strong" in 2016. In March 2019, a high court in Kenya ruled that the law capping interest rates was unconstitutional and suspended the ruling for 12 months to allow lawmakers to reexamine the law.[33]

Opportunities for a Growing Market (Future of Market)

Two leading growth markets in Kenya are healthcare/pharmaceutical and agriculture.

Healthcare/Pharmaceutical

Kenya's pharmaceutical subsector has the potential to improve access to essential medicines in the domestic and regional markets, particularly since there is a strong political push to meet growing demand. The key is to have enabling conditions where "brand Kenya" becomes synonymous with high-quality standards for medicines to ensure public health and improve consumers' trust in local products. The combination of a growing middle class, accelerating urbanization, and the increasing burden of noncommunicable diseases within the domestic and regional EAC markets are increasing demand for affordable and accessible high-quality medicines.

Kenya is the fastest-growing pharmaceutical market in the region, with expected annual growth of between 7.6 and 12 percent over the next five years. However, domestic pharmaceutical manufacturers supply only one-quarter of the local market, which means there is heavy reliance on imported medicines. There is potential for Kenya's pharmaceuticals

32. *Id.*
33. *Id.*

subsector to become competitive, as illustrated by its role as the third-largest exporter of pharmaceuticals in Africa, exporting 30 percent of local production, mostly to the EAC. Focusing on quality could increase market access for firms meeting international standards and create consumer demand.[34]

Agriculture

Agribusiness, including agriculture and downstream processing activities, is the largest sector in Kenya's economy. Agricultural production generates 26 percent of GDP, provides 63 percent of employment, and accounts for 57 percent of exports, and downstream agri-processing is estimated to generate an additional, but comparatively low, 3.2 percent of GDP and 2.4 percent of employment. Many aspects of the agribusiness sector in Kenya provide a source for optimism. Kenya has been able to leverage its relatively limited but fertile and high-altitude arable land to develop a wide range of high-value-added crops. Together, growth in the tea, cut flowers, and green beans value chains account for more than 65 percent of agricultural exports, which represents major success stories for Kenya that other countries in the region are eagerly attempting to replicate.[35]

In the medium- and long-term, as ag-tech platforms affect the lives of millions of Kenyans, analysts expect three trends to emerge. First, as income opportunities in agriculture rise because of technological innovations, the outflow of young people from agriculture and rural areas may slow or even reverse. Second, as agri-SMEs benefit from a more competitive supply chain and sector structure, a growing number of domestic firms may make inroads in regional or global export markets. Finally, as digitalization drives business formalization, revenue generation from agriculture is expected to rise and have a significant positive impact on Kenya's finances.[36]

---

34. *Id.*
35. *Id.*
36. AVCA (2021), *Horizon Kenya: Exploring Trends Set to Shape the Future in Kenya*, https://www.avca-africa.org/media/2890/horizon-kenya-exploring-trends-set-to-shape-the-future-in-kenya.pdf.

25

Nigeria

Victoria Banke Olagbegi-Oloba[1]

Market Overview and Impact Investing Growth

Nigeria is a country faced with an avalanche of socio-economic challenges, such as hunger, poverty, unemployment, poor healthcare, poor/inadequate infrastructural facilities, illiteracy, among others, which affect its growth and development.[2] Notwithstanding, in recent times, impact investments have continued to grow in the country. Its impact, however, is not significant amidst the plethora of challenges facing the country. These challenges impede the expansion and maximum realization of its potential to deliver social, economic, and environmental returns on a larger scale. This will require stakeholders to reassess the guiding principles of impact investing and collaborate more to build a stronger socio-economic society in Nigeria.[3]

From a more positive standpoint, with a population of about 216.7 million people,[4] the second largest and fastest growing economic market in Africa, Nigeria is an ideal place for impact investment. The socio-economic and environmental challenges in Nigeria create an opportunity for impact investors.[5]

---

1. Law lecturer, Adekunle Ajasin University, Akungba-Akoko, Ondo State, Nigeria. Email: Victoria.olagbegi-oloba@aaua.edu.ng; banke_dunni@yahoo.com.

2. Chinenye Uwanaka, Nathaniel Ojobo & Sandra Chude, Impact Investing: A Brief General Analysis from the Nigerian Perspective (2021).

3. *Id.*

4. Nigeria: Population between 1950-2022-Statista (last visited May. 9, 2022) https://www.statista.com/statistics/1122838/population-of-nigeria/.

5. Sandra Eke, *Why You Should Consider Impact Investment in Nigeria*, Mondaq (Jan. 07, 2020), https://www.mondaq.com/nigeria/financial-services/880850/why-you-should-consider-impact-investment-in-nigeria.

Nigeria is a natural location for a variety of industrial activities due to the availability of natural resources, affordable labor costs, and large market. Its manufacturing sector is re-emerging due to improving performance of consumer and household goods industries. It produces a considerable proportion of goods and services for the West African subcontinent.[6] The industry sector contributes an annual average of 23 percent of the national gross domestic product (GDP). The major activities include oil and gas (9 percent), manufacturing (7 percent), and construction (5 percent). The sector is strategic to government's objective of diversifying the economy in line with the government's Economic Recovery and Growth Plan.[7]

Nigeria holds enormous promises, prospects, and opportunities, especially in view of her size and her natural resources. Nigeria is a leading economic powerhouse on the African continent. Moreover, the substantial proportion of its citizens underserved by basic goods and services provide a wide variety of opportunities for both financial and social/environmental impact. There are other key reasons why the Nigerian market is good for impact investment. Some of which are:

- Exceptionally large internal market with access to regional and continental markets,
- Blessed with trainable workforce with competitive wage demand,
- Considerable disposable income,
- Predictable macro-economic policy framework, and
- Supportive government policy geared toward industrialization.

Policy Framework and Government Initiatives

There is no single body of laws or regulatory framework in Nigeria that governs or seeks to govern impact investment in the country. However, Nigeria has a plethora of laws affecting impact investment.[8] These laws include Companies and Allied Matters Act,[9] Investments and Securities

6. *Opportunities*, NIGERIAN INVESTMENT PROMOTION COMM'N (last visited Jan. 1, 2022), https://www.nipc.gov.ng/opportunities/industry/.

7. *Id.*

8. UWANAKA, OJOBO & CHUDE, *supra* note 2.

9. *Companies and Allied Matters Act, 2020*, FED. REPUBLIC OF NIGERIA OFF. GAZETTE (2020), https://www.cac.gov.ng/wp-content/uploads/2020/12/CAMA-NOTE-BOOK-FULL-VERSION.pdf?__cf_chl_f_tk=K6Bp9w32wmlLyInnGah1Vj_r1pmYuqOJmZZCCAYWU.E-1642484477-0-gaNycGzNCKU; *see also Companies and Allied Matters Act, 2020 Explanatory Memorandum*, FED. REPUBLIC OF NIGERIA OFF. GAZETTE (2020), https://r6a8n4n6.stackpathcdn.com/wp-content/up

Act,[10] Industrial Inspectorate Act,[11] Industrial Development (Income Tax Relief) Act,[12] National Office for Technology Acquisition and Promotion Act,[13] Nigerian Investment Promotion Act,[14] Finance Act,[15] Consolidated Rules and Regulations of the Securities and Exchange Commission,[16] Foreign Exchange (Monitoring and Miscellaneous Provisions) Act,[17] Rulebook of The Nigerian Stock Exchange,[18] and Immigration Act,[19] among others.

In view of the many government institutions that investors must deal with when obtaining relevant certifications, permits, and/or licenses, the Nigerian government, through the Nigerian Investment Promotion Commission (NIPC), created a One-Stop Investment Center (OSIC) in 2016. The center was established on the principles of convenience, efficiency, simplicity, speed, and transparency.[20] By creating the one-stop approach,

loads/2020/08/Companies-and-Allied-Matters-Act-2020-1-1.pdf (The 2020 Act repealed the Companies and Allied Matters Act, Cap 20, Laws of the Federation of Nigeria, 2004.).

10. *Investments & Securities Act 2007*, SEC NIGERIA (2007), https://sec.gov.ng/investment-and-securities-act/.

11. *Industrial Inspectorate Act Cap. 180 L.F.N. 1990 Act Cap 18 L.F.N. 2004*, https://kwaracails.edu.ng/library/law/nigerian_laws/INDUSTRIAL_INSPECTORATE_ACT_CAP_180_LFN_1990_ACT_CAP_I8_LFN_2004.pdf.

12. *Industrial Development (Income Tax Relief) Act* (1971), https://taxaide.com.ng/files/INDUSTRIAL%20DEVELOPMENT%20(INCOME%20TAX%20RELIEF)%20ACT.pdf.

13. *Cap N62*, LAWS OF THE FEDERATION OF NIGERIA (2004); *see also Revised Guidelines for Registration and Monitoring of Technology Transfer Agreements in Nigeria*, NAT'L OFFICE FOR TECHNOLOGY ACQUISITION & PROMOTION (Apr. 2018), https://notap.gov.ng/new_dev/wp-content/uploads/2022/03/notap_tech_trans_agreement_revised_guidelines.pdf.

14. *Chapter N117*, NIGERIAN INVESTMENT PROMOTION COMM'N ACT (last visited Feb. 6, 2022), https://www.nipc.gov.ng/product/nigerian-investment-promotion-commission-act/?__cf_chl_f_tk=6zzXIXpw8D6FRdAx7.lRwsmOLt7yJJ0f.kN2xhdZrug-1642487564-0-gaNycGzNCSU.

15. *Finance Act 2020: Official Gazette*, FED. REPUBLIC OF NIGERIA (2020), https://ngfrepository.org.ng:8443/handle/123456789/3067.

16. *SEC Nigeria's Consolidated Rules and Regulations at 2013*, SEC NIGERIA (2013), https://sec.gov.ng/regulation/rules-codes/.

17. CAP F34 L.F.N. 2004.

18. *The NSE RuleBook 2015*, NGX (2015), https://ngxgroup.com/ngx-download/the-nse-rulebook-2015/.

19. *Id.*

20. Mos Abaka, *NIPC Launches e-One-Stop Investment Centre*, WORLDSTAGE NEWS (Nov. 2, 2021), https://worldstagenews.com/nipc-launches-e-one-stop-investment-centre/.

NIPC aims to bring together relevant regulatory bodies and institutions for individuals seeking certifications and or licenses to do business in Nigeria.[21] OSIC helps investors (including impact investors) to quickly set up their businesses in Nigeria.[22]

A few years after creating OSIC, NIPC launched its e-One-Stop Investment Center (e-OSIC)[23] to promote efficiency in processing investments. The e-OSIC serves as Single Window Investors' Platform (SWIP) where participating agencies' procedures are streamlined. With the launching of e-OSIC, investors can have remote access to services offered by OSIC, apply for business registration, submit relevant documents, and make appropriate fee payments. The initiative was fashioned in line with the e-government initiative of the Nigerian federal government.[24]

Growing Sector Opportunities

There are investment opportunities in the following key industries in Nigeria.

Oil and Gas

Oil, natural gas, and other oil and gas-related products account for 90 percent of the nation's total export volume and more than 80 percent of government revenues in Nigeria. The country produces a daily average of 2.5 million barrels of crude oil, ranking it as the largest African producer and sixth in the world. In terms of oil export volumes, the country ranks eighth in the world. Nigeria equally has the largest natural gas reserves in Africa and ranks seventh in the world. The country is, therefore, eager to capitalize on this valuable resource after many years of flaring from oil fields.[25]

Manufacturing

Nigeria's manufacturing sector has been growing in recent times in direct response to various interventions/programs implemented by government. The sector's capacity utilization has grown from an average of 35 percent in the 1990s to an average of 54 percent in the last five years. Its

21. Uwanaka, Ojobo & Chude, *supra* note 2.
22. *Id.*
23. Abaka, *supra* note 20.
24. *Id.*
25. *Opportunities*, *supra* note 6.

contribution to national GDP has also grown steadily, to an annual average of 9 percent in the same period.

Lagos and its surroundings are home to about 60 percent of Nigeria's industrial activities. Other key industrial centers are Kano, Aba, Ibadan, and Kaduna. Nigeria's most important manufacturing industries include beverages, cement, food processing, textiles, and detergents.[26]

Cement Industry

The cement industry is an important activity in the economy, with Nigeria becoming home to the world's largest emerging cement companies. The industry is dominated by two firms that control more than 80 percent of the domestic market: Dangote Cement and Lafarge WAPCO Cement Plc. The demand for cement is seasonal in nature and is expected to continue to grow, as there is a huge housing deficit and an increasing demand for cement in road construction.

The industry's prospects for growth have attracted investments from both domestic investors as well as foreign multinational companies. While foreign investors are acquiring existing investments, domestic investors such as Dangote Group and BUA Group have established new plants.[27] Over the past few years, there has been an aggressive drive toward the modernization and expansion of cement plants, which have seen the industry's capacity multiply, currently at over 45 million tons, and efficiency improve. Recently, the industry started exploring the possibility of exporting cement to neighboring West African markets, which means there is room for more investment in the industry.

Textile Industry

The textile garment and footwear industry accounts for about 2 percent of GDP.[28] The textile industry was once ranked as the second largest in Africa, after Egypt's, with more than 250 factories operating above 50 percent capacity. At its peak, the industry averaged an annual growth rate of 67 percent, and employed about 25 percent of the workforce in the manufacturing sector, fed by locally grown cotton. The industry is currently estimated to be able to produce about 1.4 billion different pieces of textile products. With huge demand for clothing by a fast-growing population, the industry has been unable to meet domestic demand for African

26. *Id.*
27. *Id.*
28. *Id.*

prints, shirting, bed sheets, furnishing fabrics, towels, embroidery lace, garments, table and bed linen, guinea brocades, wax prints, java prints, jutes, fishing nets, among many other textile products. Nigeria is noted for its production of cotton, silk, and other fibers, which are primary materials for the textile industries.

On an annual basis, the area under cotton cultivation is about 0.2 to 0.6 million hectares, in the Savannah areas of the country. Annual production is in the range of 300,000 tons of seed cotton or 110,000 tons of lint (about 607,735 bales of cotton lint) and 400,000 tons of seed cotton. Small-scale farmers dominate production, with farm sizes ranging from 3 to 5 hectares all under rainfed ecologies. Seed cotton yield ranges from 0.6 to 1.5 tons per hectare. About 98 percent of the crop is grown to *Gossypium hirsutum*, while the balance is grown with *G. barbadense*. There is, however, a dearth of cotton milling factories in the country resulting in the exportation of the raw cotton. The implication of this is that the textile industry in Nigeria now relies on imported processed raw materials. Although the textile industry might have lost some of its prominence, the potential of being a leader on the continent is still apparent.[29]

Food Processing Industry

The food processing industry is another fast-developing industry in the Nigerian manufacturing sector. The industry has grown at an average of 3 percent over the last five years, contributing an annual average of 4 percent to GDP and employing about 5 percent of the local workforce. Although the industry is composed of small and medium enterprises, there is a consistent upsurge of new entrants by multinational food companies, and an aggressive expansion of existing operations to meet local market demand.

This has been motivated by the expansion of the middle-class with rising incomes and growing awareness of food safety and dietary quality, which in turn has increased demand for low-carbohydrate, low-fat, and even sugar-free food and beverages. Some of the new investments on the horizon include Dangote Group's $800 million investment in dairy production, and the planned investment by a consortium of Vicampro Farm, Black Pace, and Kiremko in a potato processing factory in Plateau and Kaduna. Projected to cost about US$45 million, with a processing capacity of 30,000 to 40,000 tons, the plant will be the largest in West Africa.

Large bakeries, plus biscuit and waffle factories, are increasingly being built. These investments complement existing investments

29. *Id.*

by Cadbury Nigeria, Unilever Nigeria, De-United Foods Industries, Friesland Campina WAMCO Nigeria, and many more. Despite the increasing investments by local processors and continued upsurge of multinational companies into the industry, the bulk of intermediate and processed inputs are still being imported into Nigeria. Demand is, therefore, higher than supply in the industry.[30]

Brewing Industry

Nigeria has the second largest beer industry in Africa, next to South Africa. Despite the global downturn in beer consumption, Nigeria's market continues to thrive.[31] The industry is expected to grow at about 23 percent over the next few years. The landscape of the industry is dotted with major multinational brewing companies jostling for position in the domestic brewing market. The market is regional in nature with local brands holding sway in their respective regions.

At the national level, the industry has moved from being a duopoly market to an oligopoly one with Nigerian Breweries Plc (NB Plc) at 61 percent of the market, Guinness Nigeria at 27 percent, and Consolidated Breweries with 10 percent being the major market holders. South African Breweries Miller (SABM), a more recent entrant to the market, continues to grow. NB Plc, a local subsidiary of the global brand Heineken, has the largest capacity and coverage, with about eight breweries located across the country, with an estimated total annual capacity of 13.5 million hl. Guinness, owned by Diageo, operates four breweries with an estimated total annual of 7.5 million hl. Despite this capacity, coupled with other smaller plants, there is still a gap in demand.[32]

Challenges in Impact Investing

Insecurity, unclear policies, and cumbersome regulatory environment (which NIPC is working assiduously to solve), concentration of actors in particular locations, and limited power supply are major challenges for impact investing in Nigeria.

The government of Nigeria is working to curb all forms of insecurity in the country. It is aware of the major challenges inhibiting the growth and development of manufacturing—especially the problem of power supply. According to a report on the NIPC website, there is a huge

30. *Id.*
31. *Id.*
32. *Id.*

commitment for Nigeria to generate a minimum of 10,000 MW of power and ensure effective distribution of this power before the end of 2023. The government is also committed to removing all non-fiscal barriers to investment and ensuring a competitive business environment that would promote free entry and exit for investors, irrespective of nationality.[33]

Conclusion

There are enormous investment opportunities in Nigeria. Although fast growing, the Nigerian market can still be said to be in its infancy. There is, therefore, an urgent need to accelerate the growth of the market, remove barriers, and build early market infrastructure to foster social and economic development and deliver prosperity for all within the country.

33. *Id.*

26

South Africa

Myriam Mossi[1]

Over the last several years, impact investors globally have developed substantial and particular interest in sub-Saharan Africa. The 2015 impact investor survey from J.P. Morgan and the Global Impact Investing Network (GIIN) showed that more assets have been allocated to sub-Saharan Africa (59 percent) than to any other emerging market, and more plan to increase their portfolio allocation to sub-Saharan Africa than plan to increase allocations to any other geography.[2]

Market Overview and Impact Investing Growth

Historically, South Africa's Apartheid—literally meaning "separateness"—was designed not only to keep the country's non-white majority apart from the white minority but also to decrease Black South Africans' political power. This system of legislation dates to the passage of the country's 1913's Land Act. The act forced Black Africans to live in reserves and barred their working as sharecroppers.

The change away from Apartheid began with pressure on corporations from investors to divest from South Africa. In 1985, Columbia University students in New York organized a sit-in and demanded that the university cease investing in companies doing business with South Africa. The combined efforts of protests and responsible investing resulted in $625 billion in investments being redirected from South Africa by 1993.[3]

1. Attorney licensed in New York.
2. Yasemin Saltuk, Ali El Idrissi, Amit Bouri, Abhilash Mudaliar & Hannah Schiff, *Eyes on the Horizon: The Impact Investor Survey*, Global Impact Investing Network & J.P. Morgan (May 4, 2015), https://thegiin.org/knowledge/publication/eyes-on-the-horizon.
3. https://www.investopedia.com/news/history-impact-investing/.

Nowadays, South Africa is one of the strongest emerging markets globally. As of 2020, South Africa is ranked 114th out of 187 countries in the United Nations Human Development Indicators (HDI) index. While the country's HDI score is above the regional average, it remains below the global average.[4] The country surpasses countries such as Hungary, Italy, Brazil, and Thailand.

The country leads the continent in industrial output (40 percent of Africa's total output) and mineral production (45 percent of total mineral production) and generates most of Africa's electricity (over 50 percent).[5] Today, South Africa is not only self-sufficient in virtually all major agricultural products, but, in a normal year, it is also a net food exporter. Over the past five years, agricultural exports have contributed on average about 8 percent of total South African exports.[6] The combination of a highly developed first-world economic infrastructure and a huge emergent market economy has given rise to a strong entrepreneurial and dynamic investment environment.

However, at around 25 percent, unemployment rates in South Africa are high—twice the regional average and four times the global average. Notably, 70 percent of the country's unemployed population is under the age of 34.[7]

South Africa has a myriad of social and environmental issues that can be addressed through impact investing.[8] Impact investing can be a tool to systemize the process around addressing the country's social challenges, while proving to investors that they don't have to sacrifice financial returns for social good, as opposed to grants and aid, making it more purposeful, rather than simply being a corporate box-ticking exercise.[9]

Elias Masilela, chair of Impact Investing South Africa (IISA), says interest in impact investing in South Africa is being fueled by growing socio-economic imbalances, poor economic growth, high rates of unemployment, deepening poverty, and gaping inequalities. South Africa has also woken up to the devastating impact of climate change, especially on the agricultural sector. In addition, growing uncertainty about policy response and implementation is also a contributing factor. Masilela

4. https://thegiin.org/assets/documents/pub/Southern%20Africa/SouthAfrica_GIIN_southernafrica.pdf.

5. https://www.southafrica-newyork.net/why-invest-in-south-africa/.

6. *Id.*

7. *Supra* note 4.

8. https://www.accountancysa.org.za/impact-investing-matters/.

9. https://www.me.mercer.com/our-thinking/wealth/africas-untapped-potential-for-impact-investing-can-create-brighter-futures.html.

believes impact investing will gain better traction as it is private sector driven and will most likely yield better returns.[10]

A 2017 global investor survey by Schroders found that 81 percent of South African investors reported sustainable investment growing in importance in recent years. Financial returns for impact investing can be in line with traditional investing, differentiating it from philanthropy. It includes a wide spectrum of returns, from more patient to risk-adjusted market-related returns. Instruments include grants, debt, and equity, and everything in between. Investments can be made into businesses ranging from very early to later, more established stages.[11]

Along with many other nations, South Africa has committed to achieving the Sustainable Development Goals (SDG)[12] as part of its National Development Plan (NDP) with specific targets identified for 2030. Impact investing allows the private sector to support the government in achieving these targets. With the COVID-19 pandemic, achieving the SDG has been difficult, particularly with governments required to shift resources and take on new levels of debt to deal with the threats of this pandemic.[13] The pandemic has exposed and amplified existing economic vulnerabilities, placing more pressure on the government to raise funding, and thereby increasing their already heavy debt burden.[14] South Africa's budget deficit is now expected to reach 5.7 percent of GDP in 2021/22, compared with 7.8 percent estimated at the time of the MTBPS (Medium Term Budget Policy Statement).[15]

Furthermore, the National Treasury has revised South Africa's economic growth estimates to -6.4 percent in 2020, 4.8 percent in 2021 (compared with the 5.1 percent projected in the 2021 MTBPS), 2.1 percent in 2022, and 1.6 percent in 2023.[16]

10. https://www.dailymaverick.co.za/article/2021-08-09-impact-investing-businesses-with-an-impact-mindset-are-more-likely-to-be-successful-in-the-long-term/.

11. *Supra* note 8.

12. https://sdgimpact.undp.org/faq.html.

13. https://www.iol.co.za/personal-finance/investments/impact-investing-a-catalyst-for-sas-growth-52f63f97-77ac-4572-b5f0-0e7e8d923100.

14. https://www.iol.co.za/personal-finance/investments/impact-investing-a-catalyst-for-sas-growth-52f63f97-77ac-4572-b5f0-0e7e8d923100.

15. http://www.treasury.gov.za/documents/national%20budget/2022/review/FullBR.pdf.

16. *Id.*

Growing Sector Opportunities

In order to meet the basic service needs of their populations, African governments have historically supplemented public spending with inflows of official development assistance (ODA) from developed and other emerging markets. The 2008 financial crisis and the resultant volatility of ODA inflows left the governments of many African economies vulnerable to unpredictable fluctuations in available public expenditure. Studies have shown that declines in ODA lead to subsequent declines in public spending on development priorities, which could potentially jeopardize poor households' ability to access necessary basic goods and services.[17]

The South African government has introduced wide-ranging legislation to promote training and skills development and fast-track the building of world-class skills and competencies. A strong network of universities and other tertiary education institutions is home to a host of leading international academics and researchers, with the majority of research and development in South Africa undertaken at the country's universities.[18]

South Africa also offers investors sophisticated financial infrastructures and strong investment opportunities. The South African Reserve Bank (SARB) oversees the banking services industry in South Africa. The nonbanking financial services industry is governed by the Financial Service Board (FSB). South Africa has the following principle financial service markets:

- JSE Securities Exchange South Africa (JSE)
- South African Futures Exchange (Safex)
- Bond Exchange of South Africa (BESA)
- Alternative Exchange (Altx)

The JSE is governed and licensed externally by the Stock Exchange Control Act of 1985. The Safex and BESA markets are governed by the Financial Marketers Control Act of 1989. The markets are self-regulated internally.[19]

South Africa has also created a support ecosystem for social enterprises to thrive by creating social investment plans. The country has also created learning hubs for knowledge exchange (e.g., the Bertha Centre for Social Innovation and Entrepreneurship (BCSIE)); formed practitioner

17. *Overview. Towards Human Resilience: Sustaining MDG Progress in an Age of Economic Uncertainty*, UNDP (2015), https://www.undp.org/publications/towards-human-resilience-sustaining-mdg-progress-age-economic-uncertainty

18. https://www.southafrica-newyork.net/why-invest-in-south-africa/.

19. *Id.*

networks (e.g., The African Social Entrepreneurs Network (ASEN)), and impact fund social stock exchange platform (South African Social Investment Exchange platform (SASIX)—a philanthropic initiative with the Johannesburg Stock Exchange).[20]

The profile of Africa's impact investors primarily includes fund managers and asset management funds, development finance institutions and donors, private equity managers, institutional investors, and foundations. Investments have tended to focus on sectors where the government cannot adequately deliver social services, such as healthcare, education, and finance, and where a viable market solution can provide goods and/or services.[21]

In South Africa, non-DFI (development finance institutions) impact investors have shown an overwhelming preference for equity in impact deals. Equity accounts for almost 90 percent of capital disbursed, though three large deals alone account for 60 percent of equity capital disbursed. It should be noted, however, that the research team was unable to determine the instrument used for around 45 percent of deals, accounting for around US$477 million in capital disbursed.[22]

Pension fund managers interested in impact investing can find a wide variety of investment vehicles aimed at themes such as affordable housing, agriculture, microfinance, renewable energy, and water, as well as telecommunications and transportation infrastructure. There are opportunities to invest in improving many of the needs most important to a pension fund's members or communities.

For instance, pension funds managed by Alexander Forbes Investments have made allocations to the Alexander Forbes Investments South Africa Private Markets portfolio, a multi-strategy, multi-managed diversified portfolio that provides exposure to impact sectors including clean energy, infrastructure, microfinance, education, retirement accommodation, and affordable housing.

Futuregrowth Asset Management, which manages assets on behalf of pension fund clients, runs a number of funds focusing on socially responsible or developmental assets, including the Infrastructure & Development Bond Fund, which makes investments that facilitate infrastructural, social, environmental, and economic development in South Africa. The

20. https://futureafricaforum.org/scaling-the-growth-of-impact-investing-in-african-economies/.

21. A. Bugg-Levine & J. Emerson, *Impact Investing: Transforming How We Make Money While Making a Difference* (2011).

22. *Supra* note 4.

fund includes the SA Taxi transaction, which has provided loans to the taxi industry over the past ten years. This has contributed to the creation of 130,000 direct and 220,000 indirect jobs for drivers, managers, and service providers, while also providing transportation options for South Africans.

Sanlam Investments Alternatives, another example, offers pension funds the opportunity to invest in its Affordable Housing Fund created to develop clean, safe, and habitable communities for the disadvantaged.

When pension funds aim to make a difference in the communities they serve, impact investing can help promote country-specific agendas while delivering positive financial returns for institutional investors in pension funds.[23]

Another huge factor is the global mindset of millennials. According to a report by the Economist's Intelligence Unit, 87 percent of millennials believe that business success should be measured by more than just financial performance, and 93 percent believe that social impact is key to their investing decisions. In their entrepreneurial and philanthropic pursuits, they are seeking to marry profit with purpose, and are motivated by the size of their impact and their ability to measure it.[24]

Challenges to Impact Investments

Impact investing is growing globally, with the increasing interest in social entrepreneurship and innovation within African economies.

Despite the growth of impact investment in the South African market, several barriers can be identified. One of these was how new and unknown the idea of impact investment was in the country. Another was the lack of investment-ready deals in South Africa where impact investors could get involved. Another factor is the lack of detailed and clearly formulated social or environmental impact objectives.

The lack of financial and technical support for small and medium-sized social enterprises could also be a barrier. Investors are currently all competing for the same pipeline of bankable social enterprise-based projects. They expressed the need for more support from among others, the development banks, to grow these enterprises so they become mature enough to have a lower risk profile.

Other barriers included the lack of standardized, detailed reporting measures. One of the key elements of an impact investment is the

23. *Supra* note 9.
24. *Supra* note 8.

need to measure and report social and environmental change. In contrast to financial reporting, the guidelines available to entities to report on environmental, social, and corporate governance management are less sophisticated.

Some guidelines do exist. Initiatives like the impact management project[25] are also useful: the project aims to create worldwide consensus in measuring and managing impact.

Much work, however, remains to be done. Measuring changes in human behavior at a beneficiary level is not as easy as measuring data points. One also has to be cognizant of the context in which an impact investment initiative exists because a developed world perspective is often different from that in the developing world. This transparency will be key in growing impact investment based on how to match financial and impact objectives, as well as the techniques used to effectively report the impact.

Despite several barriers, there is a lot of evidence to suggest South Africa has a growing impact investment market. There is an increasing call in contemporary market economies for ethical, socially inclusive capitalism. So now is a good time for South Africa to get ahead of the curve and prioritize this sort of capitalism. Asset owners and asset managers are also becoming more receptive to the notion that they can affect social and environmental change through the financing they extend.[26]

Opportunities for a Growing Market (Future of the Market)

As the world is slowly emerging from the global COVID-19 pandemic, investment strategy in emerging economies should be created to adapt ecosystem for long-term impact investing. Relevant stakeholders should be educated on the concept of impact investment and its potential to support the nation's economic resilience and recovery. This would require targeted outreach and engagement efforts with the relevant potential funders, including domestic institutional investors, retail investors, philanthropic foundations, venture capital funders, and high net worth individuals. With consistent efforts on this, increase in impact capital becomes feasible as their understanding of the investment strategy improves.

25. https://impactmanagementproject.com/.

26. https://theconversation.com/despite-barriers-south-africa-is-a-good-place-for-impact-investments-111456.

Priority sectors that will make the most positive impact to the economy should be identified and special policy interventions should be tailored to suit. This should help in creating investment opportunities. Establishing social capital markets for social stock exchange will be instrumental in developing a vibrant public impact investing market for both retail and institutional investors.

Fiscal frameworks and incentive structures will have to be reviewed such that they encourage private partners in order to mobilize them as pioneer drivers for impact investment.

Impact capital must be recognized as a distinct investment strategy and not a charitable offer, and appropriate corporate legal frameworks should be set up. Impact investors will also need to be assured that their activities are recognized and regulated. This will further ease its access into the investment market.

Governments can establish frameworks and templates for practicing standard principles for impact assessment and reporting, and encourage consistency in practice by social enterprises and listed companies (for capital markets).

Going forward, the most important source of long-term finance should not be foreign aid nor huge debts but impact investments, foreign direct investment in Africa's productivity, trade, increased domestic savings, entrance into international capital markets, and revenue generation from the internal economic activity of empowered citizens.[27]

27. https://futureafricaforum.org/scaling-the-growth-of-impact-investing-in-african-economies/.

Index